Blanche Arral

Opera Biography Series No. 15

Series Editors
Andrew Farkas
William R. Moran

A portrait of Blanche Arral, inscribed: "Monsieur Brooks—bien sympathiquement, Blanche Arral." Courtesy Alexander Turnbull Library, Wellington, New Zealand.

The
EXTRAORDINARY
OPERATIC
ADVENTURES
of
BLANCHE ARRAL

by

Blanche Arral

Translated by Ira Glackens

William R. Moran, Editor

AMADEUS PRESS
Portland · Cambridge

For permission to reproduce photographs from their collection, we are grateful to the Alexander Turnbull Library, National Library of New Zealand, Te Puna Mātauranga o Aotearoa, Wellington, New Zealand.

While every effort has been made to trace copyright holders and obtain permission, this has not been possible in all cases; any omissions brought to our attention will be remedied in future editions.

Published in 2002 by

Amadeus Press
(an imprint of Timber Press, Inc.)
The Haseltine Building
133 S.W. Second Avenue, Suite 450
Portland, Oregon 97204 U.S.A.

Amadeus Press
2 Station Road
Swavesey
Cambridge CB4 5QJ, U.K.

ISBN 1-57467-077-8

Printed through Colorcraft Ltd., Hong Kong

A CIP record for this book is available from the Library of Congress.

Contents

Reminiscences of Madame Blanche Arral: An Introduction

by Ira Glackens

FIRST IT IS NECESSARY to explain a little about myself. I have, since about the age of six, been fascinated by beautiful singing voices. At that time I was given by my grandmother the three duets from *Hänsel und Gretel* sung by Alma Gluck and Louise Homer on old single-sided Red Seal records. I fell in love with the voice of Alma Gluck—a love which now, nearly sixty years later, has not dimmed.

From Alma Gluck I began listening to other singers, particularly sopranos, and so my collection of records began to grow, at first acquired with my allowance.

In those days a ten-inch Red Seal record—for I favored the red ones—cost from one to two dollars, depending on the artist. Twelve-inch records were one dollar fifty cents to three dollars, if a solo, and more for concerted numbers. There was a snobbish and subtle gradation in these matters, and a *Lucia* Sextet sung by top performers like Caruso, Sembrich, and so forth could go as high as seven dollars in prewar currency. This made these items status symbols. How smart the Victor Records people were!

I recall going to Landay's Record Shop on Fifth Avenue when I was about eleven and buying, with a dollar I had been given by my mother, *An die Musik* sung by Margarete Ober. I still have all these records.

In the early 1930s began the boom days for old record collectors. The Depression was upon us, radio was king, and phonographs were hauled to the attic or thrown away. Record dealers went out of business in hordes, and their wares were remaindered for low prices. I filled out my collection with twelve-inch double-sided Red Seal records of things like all the *Faust* items sung by Caruso, Farrar, Journet, and Scotti, for sixty-nine cents apiece. Among these were, of course, an occasional rare and long since deleted item.

But the greatest haul occurred at a five-and-ten-cent store on East Fourteenth Street, New York—I think it was Grant's. There one day a friend and I, out looking for bargains, came upon counters piled with even older and rarer material, single-sided Red Seal records by singers of historical fame, doubtless from some long-forgotten stock in a warehouse. Many had those old, cluttered labels bearing dozens of copyright dates and lists of prizes won at international expositions, at which the collector's heart beats faster.

Among these treasures was a single-sided ten-inch disc of an early vintage (around 1909)—"El bolero grande" sung by Blanche Arral. "Soprano with orchestra, in Spanish," was the explanation in the upper right-hand corner of the label.

I had never heard of this oddly named lady, but she was a Red Seal artist in the great days. I had always been in favor of Spanish songs, and the record was ten cents. I could scarcely go wrong. (Twelve-inch records were, I think, fifteen cents.)

The voice and charm of Blanche Arral were infectious. The tone was even, clear, and round, with a suggestion of the clarinet rather than the flute, the low notes were astonishing, and the verve and obvious pleasure she took in her singing were enchanting. Her style had a lilt.

It was Philip Miller, at the time music librarian at the New York Public Library, who told me the astonishing news that Madame Arral was living in New Jersey and advertising for pupils in the *Musical Courier* or one of the other musical papers. I wrote her a fan letter to Cliffside Park, New Jersey, got an answer, and the result was that I found myself one day on the Hoboken ferry clutching two dozen roses in assorted colors.

The trip to Cliffside Park was a tedious one. Having reached the ferry at the foot of West Forty-second Street (by subway and trolley), one had, at the Hoboken side, to climb a long, steep hill and there wait in the rain, sleet, wind, or whatever for another trolley, which went clanging for miles through the most depressing sections of New Jersey, with names like West New York and Guttenberg—all pool parlors, cheap stores, and places where horrid food was served.

Madame Arral, whose name in private life was Mrs. George B.

Wheeler, lived in a most unassuming house surrounded with a glassed-in porch, on a small lot on a most unassuming street.

A short, rather stout lady answered the bell. She was scarcely five feet high, looked as foreign as could be, and wore perched on her head an enormous nut-brown wig. It was impossible to judge her age, though as a matter of fact she was then about sixty-seven. She spoke with great animation, had a ready smile, snapping black eyes, and burst frequently into gales of the most engaging laughter. In this I heard the tones I was familiar with in her Victor records (of which I had acquired several more).

She led me into her parlor and left me there while she went for a vase for the roses. The small room was chiefly occupied by moth-eaten stuffed dogs and cats, which peered at me with their glass eyes from every nook and corner. On one wall hung a life-sized photograph of the erstwhile prima donna. The head of this full-length picture appeared in the old Victor catalogue and had hung, it was clear, in the theater lobbies where the lady had sung around the world. Another, slightly smaller photograph depicted the soprano as Lakmé. (She was the second ever to sing the role, so she claimed, when she was understudy at the Opéra-Comique for Marie Van Zandt, who had created the role.)

The lady spoke a curious language of her own devising. It was a mixture of French and English, much of the latter tongue being pronounced as if it were French; her English grammar, too, partook largely of French grammar. The words *a quart*, for instance, came out "un car." One had to have a working knowledge of French to understand her English.

Mr. Wheeler was a Vermonter and a principal of the local grammar school. He made his appearance when school let out. He was much younger than his wife, probably in his fifties, and a friendly man.[1] We got on at once. I think he liked me because, having lived a great part of my life in northern New England, I spoke his language.

This was the beginning of a friendship and numerous visits to Cliffside Park, which only ended with the war and the lady's death. It was also the genesis of her memoir, which she called *Bravura Passage*. I was astonished at the adventurous life the little prima donna had led and suggested that we should get it down in black and white. She readily consented. She told me that she had been *buried*, and I had brought her back to life again as we toiled over the book and she lived again her glamorous past.

Blanche Arral and Ira Glackens, Lake Bomoseen, Vermont, 23 July 1937. "The day we finished the singer's autobiography," wrote Glackens. Photo by George B. Wheeler. Courtesy William R. Moran.

She was very industrious, and every time I came to Cliffside Park she had many pages more for me to read in French. I drew her out and asked questions, and finding that with all her industry the book would never be done, I urged her to talk and then went home and wrote down all she said. I found I could remember very well, and this had the advantage of my being able to guide her along, bring her back to the point if she strayed, and have obscure points elucidated.

Sometimes Madame Arral came to New York to see friends or do errands. I met her by appointment once at the flat of her old friend Madame Pilar Morin, the original "Pierrot the Prodigal" and a once famous pantomimist, who kept up some sort of connection with the Belgian colony and the Belgian consul and had a consulting doctor there.[2]

On one occasion my mother gave a small luncheon party for her; there were about eight guests. It struck me how much a woman of the world she was, how finished her manners, how agreeable her personality. After all, she was from an upper-crust family, her father having been Count Jean Gregoire Lardinois of Liège.

Then we often met at the Algonquin, where the lady always wanted "an old fashion," as she called it, before she had to journey back to Cliffside Park. The waiters at the Algonquin, used to theatrical people, all recognized her as being *someone*, though they didn't know who. She wore several small decorations given her by her royal personages, like the khedive of Egypt, the czar of Russia, and her own king of the Belgians. ("I am Belgium," she explained to me on our first meeting, meaning *Belgian.*)

I introduced her to two or three of my record cronies, and she was much delighted with the attentions showered on her. In fact she was an extrovert, still full of vigor, and enjoyed social events. Her life at Cliffside Park must have been dull to extermination for one who had been applauded on five continents and now dwelt among people who neither knew nor cared anything about her achievements.

Madame Arral had one of her pupils sing for me. Anabella White, the daughter of a local cop, had a beautiful lyric voice, and Madame Arral, a pupil of Cabel and Marchesi, had trained it to perfection. But I saw there was no temperament, background, or ambition to go any further there.

As we went on working with the book I was more and more astonished at the things I learned about the lady and her adventures, but it was impossible to get any clear chronology from her. She had no head for dates, and probably had her reasons. Being very short she thought of herself as a child. Massenet had written a small part for her in *Manon*—to hear her talk you would think she was ten at the time. *Manon* was first performed in 1884, a date easy to ascertain, and when, after the singer's death, her dates were made public, it turned out that she was nineteen at the time—young to be sure, but no infant phenomenon.

The book had been going on for a year or two, and in one great attempt to finish it, I journeyed to Lake Bomoseen, Vermont, with my typewriter in the summer (I think) of 1937. Lake Bomoseen is near Rutland, George Wheeler's native town, and he possessed a small cottage on the lake which was his dream home. In about ten days we finished the manuscript—full of faults, never edited, but in existence.

It is not surprising that the few who have read it often question the facts and episodes recounted. For the later years there were the clipping books, of which I made full use. All the Australian and New Zealand days are fully documented and not exaggerated. As to the tales of Rasputin and Mata Hari, I have no reason to disbelieve my old friend, though details must surely have been lost or altered in memory. Of her work with Thomas Edison there is ample proof, and the commercial cylinders she made for him are explained. Among them is "Charmant oiseau" from *The Pearl of Brazil*, which is in the same class with Emma Calvé's version, and "Micaëla's Air" from *Carmen*, which is the best I ever heard on or off record. In this number, incidentally, Madame Arral told me that the recording technician signaled her that the cylinder was coming to an end, and she had to cut short her final note. Or perhaps it was a *Brazil*.

Of the forty-eight cylinders she made for the fabled Gianni Bettini, which are listed in his catalogue for 1899, not one is known to exist.

Some years after she had recorded for Victor, that company approached her with the proposition that she make *fifty* records for them. These were to be largely from French *opéras comiques* and operettas (Offenbach, Audran, and others). The repertory was chosen in several consultations—then came the rub. She was offered fifty dollars flat for each item. Making records is and was very hard work, and she turned the offer down. It was argued that she would be put back in the concert field, that she couldn't expect seven hundred fifty dollars per disc as she had been paid in 1909, now that she had been absent from the scene for some time.[3] But Arral said she had retired and had no wish to concertize anymore. What we have all lost!

At another time Columbia tested her and turned down the test. Columbia, with its faulty equipment of that time, couldn't even record the pure and birdlike voice of Blanche Arral.

The singer was a practical woman and had marked executive ability, which is why she could manage her own tours with such success. Had she been wiser about her career, however, she would not have spent so much of her time in exotic places. The only famous house she seems to have sung in, outside Russia, was the Opéra-Comique, where she was a *pensionnaire* at the beginning of her career.

Her later beauty business, which she developed as a mail-order house with formulas she claimed to have acquired when she was the inmate of a harem in Constantinople ("Madame Blanche Arral's Eau de Jeunesse" was one of the items), came to grief when, during an illness, she gave the running into the hands of a man who proved to be a crook and used the mails to defraud. She lost all her money in the crash of 1929, her last savings going down with a New Jersey bank. Her husband's salary as the principal of a grammar school could not have been great. She made pin money from a few pupils.

George Wheeler had trouble at his school. There developed a feud between the little boys and the little girls—a war between the sexes. When school let out the battle was daily resumed in the schoolyard. The teachers were at their wits' end.

"Why you not let out the girls five minutes before the boys, George?" asked Blanche. This solved the problem.

"Pauvre Georges," she said to me privately. "Il est pédagogue!" And this was followed by a peal of laughter.

She told me how they had come to get married, but I am hazy on the facts. It was, as I recall, when she was living in Orange or East Orange during her work with Edison. They met through friends. "Why not we get married?" she said.

I dare say it was as successful a marriage as most, especially considering the differences in their ages.

"George say," she told me once, "there is too much prima donna around here!" And again the peals of merry laughter, on a rising scale of about two octaves. But Madame Arral was surprisingly lacking in prima donna airs or any pretense, although she remained thoroughly continental.

From the debacle of her fortune the lady had preserved a small summer cottage in a woodland setting in Alpine, New Jersey, a few miles north of Cliffside Park, on the Palisades. Here, one summer afternoon, George Wheeler drove us. Being continental, the hostess had provided an excellent picnic supper and included half a gallon of good red wine (zinfandel). That little party remains in my memory with great pleasure; we all had a splendid time.

One day the singer found in her attic a cylinder recording she had made for Edison, which, being faulty technically, had not been issued. This recording she gave to me. It was the "Cours-la-reine" scene from *Manon*, followed by a bit of the waltz from the gambling scene, "A nous les amours et les roses," which is usually cut from modern performances. The record has been dubbed and issued several times since; the original cylinder is no longer in my possession.

The "Cours-la-reine" scene, a showy number nobody seems able to sing correctly anymore, ends with Manon's lines:

> Et si Manon devait jamais mourir,
> Ce serait, mes amis, dans un éclat de rire!
>
> (And if Manon should ever die,
> It would be, my friends, in a burst of laughter!)

I was away in World War II when Madame Arral died, in 1945. A year or two later George Wheeler was driving through New Hampshire, where my wife and I were living, and he phoned us and came to lunch with his new wife. The agreeable lady had been a teacher in his school. They were happy and congenial, and I was glad that he had a more suitable companion. He told me that the day Blanche Arral died, in a nursing home, she began to laugh her musical, infectious laughter. All day long, peal after hysterical peal echoed through the house, and only ceased at nightfall with the singer's death. A shiver ran through me. Had Blanche Arral been Manon for the last time, fulfilling her boast?

George Wheeler was in a frenzy to get rid of his past. He sold the house and disposed of all his wife's possessions. The pictures, the clipping books, all her scores, her few records: he sold everything for small sums to record collectors who seemed to have descended like vultures. Her old costumes and stuffed animals fed a bonfire, but a few old photographs were saved out for me.

After the visit in New Hampshire there were a few exchanges of cards, and then I never heard from George Wheeler or his wife again. They must long since have died.

Washington, D.C.
21 February 1973

About Ira Glackens

The son of noted painter William James Glackens, Ira Dimock Glackens was born in New York City on 4 July 1907. He was brought up in Europe and New York, and served in the Coast Guard during World War II. After the war he settled in the White Mountains of New Hampshire where he dabbled with farming and became an authority on apple growing, about which he published a number of papers. He maintained a lifelong interest in the lyric theater and was a collector of classical vocal recordings. He wrote several books, the first of which were biographies of his father: *William Glackens and the Ashcan Group: The Emergence of Realism in American Art* (1957) and *William Glackens and the Eight: The Artists Who Freed American Art* (1957). He spent many years collecting background information for his next book, *Yankee Diva: Lillian Nordica and the Golden Days of Opera* (1963), an outstanding work. His last books were a fantasy entitled *Pope Joan: An Unorthodox Interlude* (1965) and the novel *A Measure of Sliding Sand* (1976). He occasionally wrote major articles about historical recordings and those who made them (see "The Mapleson Collection," *Gramophone*, London, November 1938). For many years Ira and his wife Nancy spent their winters in Washington, D.C., later moving to Shepherdstown, West Virginia, where he died 23 November 1990.

Acknowledgments

FIRST THANKS must go to the late Ira Glackens, who persuaded Madame Arral to write the book in the first place and then worked with her on the English translation from the original French. After considerable pleading on my part, he rescued the original manuscript from a barrel stored in an out building on his New Hampshire farm.

I must thank my many friends and associates who read the manuscript and agreed with me that this material was important enough to get into book form. I must admit that on first reading it I found there were places which left in doubt the veracity of the story, so I kept notes on various happenings mentioned which could be verified. Aside from a few slips which could easily be attributed to anyone recalling happenings of many years past, the story has proven to ring true!

I thank all those who took the trouble to write me and offer enthusiastic support for the project. Among these, Jim McPherson offered many good suggestions for editor's notes and provided an afterword which relates some of the singer's activities that fall at the end of the story. He and Bill Fyfe of Toronto are the source for the earliest known Lardinois picture (from *Nos Artistes: Portraits et Biographies*, a French publication of 1895). Alfred de Cock was able to come up with dates of various appearances in France and Belgium and important new information about Clara Lardinois's debut (8 December 1882). Bill Main of Wellington, New Zealand, was able to locate some "new" photos in the government archives. My thanks to Sara S. Hodson, curator of literary manuscripts at Huntington Library in San Marino, California, for searching library files for references to Blanche Arral in the Jack London collection. Kathleen

F. Cohen and Andrew Farkas of the University of North Florida Library in Jacksonville, Florida, have been most helpful. Jack Belsom of New Orleans went to a great deal of trouble trying to verify performances of Arral and Bernard Bégué in his city. Jack Rokahr of Los Angeles provided numerous photocopies of material from his vast collection of French operetta scores.

My thanks to all of them.

WILLIAM R. MORAN

The
EXTRAORDINARY
OPERATIC
ADVENTURES
of
BLANCHE ARRAL

❖⊱═⊙═⊰❖

$$1$$

MANY BREAD CRUMBS have I seen in my day, but if there is one
particular crumb I remember more than any other it is surely
the one I saw in Rasputin's beard. I have in my time received
innumerable roses from friends known and unknown, but the rose I remember most is one that Mata Hari wore in her hair when she danced on
the eve of her flight from Java. I have seen many a luxuriant wig, but the
wig I call to mind is one of the hundred Isabella II of Spain wore in her
banishment in Paris. I have weathered many a storm, but none like the
hurricane in Hanoi when an ornamental lake blew into my salon—many
a calm too, but none quite so calm as the mud flat in the middle of the
Yangtze River.

The more memories one has, the less seriously one must take them.
Since I was the youngest of seventeen children to begin with, my early
days, though pleasant, were seldom calm. Even then the future was destined to be full of change and adventure, for nothing ever quite suited me
as it was.

My eldest sister Sidonie's first child was born about the same time as
myself. Sidonie was very ill, and my mother nursed both daughter and
granddaughter. I came to regard this as a great calamity. I was always a very
tiny person and my brothers, great strapping fellows, teased me unmerci-
fully. From their great height they surveyed me critically from top to toe.
"Clara," they used to say, "you are no bigger than a boot!" Then they
shook their heads and added, "And I'm afraid you never will be, *hélas!*"

After these taunts I wandered about the house bathed in tears of dismay and chagrin. One day my mother asked why I cried so much. In fury

I shouted at her, "I shall never grow any bigger because you gave my milk to my niece, Valentine!"

I was born in Liège, Belgium, the center and spiritual capital of the Walloon country. My father was Count Jean Gregoire Lardinois. My mother was Caroline Frédéric, and her family too was from the province, but not the city, of Liège. Though I used to like to think we had Spanish blood in our veins, due to some gay Castillian adventurer come to fight for his king in the rebellious provinces of the Low Countries, there is no evidence whatever of any such romantic episode in our family history.

When my parents were married they were given, as by custom, a book with spaces to record the births of twelve children, but they had to add an extra page to the book. My brothers were named Firmin, Léon, Charles, Albert, George, and August. My sisters were Sidonie, Mélanie, Clémence, Maria, Marguerite, Blanche, Jeanne, Louisa, Lucie, Angèle, and at last came Claire—myself—but everyone called me Clara.

Of course, there was a great difference in our ages so that I never knew all my brothers and sisters well, some marrying and leaving home before I was born. My brother August, a beautiful and extraordinarily intelligent child according to all accounts, died of meningitis before I appeared on the scene. At the age of three I had meningitis too, and the doctors abandoned hope. In despair, my dear mother and my sister Jeanne vowed to make a pilgrimage to Notre Dame de Chevremont, a shrine near Liège. This consisted in climbing barefoot up a steep hill covered with sharp stones, to the shrine on top. When they reached home the doctor announced great hope for my recovery.

Fortunately for such a large family as ours we lived in an enormous house. We all had rooms of our own and met for meals in a dining room that looked like a banquet hall. Father sat at the head of the table, glancing severely up and down the length of the board. I cannot remember whether it was his piercing steel-blue eyes or his muttonchop whiskers that made us most afraid of him, but we all were, and we knew well that children were to be seen and not heard and to speak only when spoken to. Our meals would have been even more somber affairs had not my brother Charles and sister Angèle, when unobserved, taken delight in making fearful grimaces at me across the table, knowing that sooner or later I would be carried off into gales of laughter at their antics. I laughed easily then—and, I am glad to say, still do—but I fear there were times when poor solemn Father thought he had brought a little imbecile into the world, for of course I would never tell what I was laughing at.

Such minor matters as laughter or tears never disturbed my mother. Her problem at meal times was hot and well-cooked food. After our good old-fashioned custom, every dish as it came from the kitchen was set out in a sort of pantry for her inspection. All our old houses had this special serving room, and the productions of the cook were lined in a row on the broad oak table for the mistress of the house to pass upon before they were admitted into the dining room. Mother had a great deal to do, for, with visiting relatives and the children of my married sisters, we thought nothing of sitting down twenty or more at table.

Over the whole house hung a very ecclesiastical air. Piety was bred in our bones. One of my uncles was an abbé, and Father's only sister was the mother superior of the Convent Hospital de Bavière in Liège. It was no wonder that my eldest brother was studying to become a priest. His fervor was so great that he built a chapel in a neglected summerhouse in the garden, complete with altar and even a small melodeon, so that he might perfect the art of saying Mass. My sister Jeanne played the melodeon, and another sister, Mélanie, who had a lovely soprano voice, sang. I was too young to join them in these holy rites and was left to play in the garden outside, guarded by my old nurse, Françoise. But always I stood transfixed, with tears streaming down my face, when the sound of music floated through the trees.

One day Father learned of the happenings in the summerhouse. Deciding promptly that these amateur masses had better stop, he quietly locked the door. Thereafter Mélanie's voice soared no more through the garden, the organ was silent, and my brother went his own way.

I had, however, a small piano of my own which I loved dearly, and though it was a poor and unexciting thing compared to the magic strains of the melodeon in the summerhouse, I tried my best to reproduce what I had heard. Though I was only five or six at the time, music already enchanted me and was a part of my life.

Mélanie had her lessons in the schoolroom once a week. I was very jealous of her and made it a practice to hide in the schoolroom closet with the door ajar, listening to her with the utmost absorption. Afterward, when the coast was clear, I flew back to my room and on my little piano played over all the same songs by ear. What is more, I sang them note for note. This was of course splendid training.

After a time Jeanne discovered my secret and was very proud of what I had done. It was she who had assumed my particular care from infancy, and I loved her dearly. In fact she was proud of almost everything I did, and now she asked Professor Verken, Mélanie's teacher, to hear me. He consented. I, who was not a shy child, stepped immediately forward and to his astonishment sang Mélanie's most difficult songs, duplicating every phrase and trill. When I had finished, the good professor cried out in delight and even went so far as to invite me to sing for his class at the conservatory, sputtering praise and amazement in his thick Prussian French. This invitation I should certainly have been delighted to accept—even then I loved an audience!—but my father, on being informed of the project, would have none of it. Mélanie laughed good-naturedly but observed that I would do better to confine myself to more suitable songs for one of my years, like "Frère Jacques" and "Sur le pont d'Avignon." But I knew better. I had made a beginning and would not go backward. I felt myself worthy of greater things. Let them wait!

About this time there was a change in our home life. There were a great many conferences behind closed doors, and music and other unnecessary noises were forbidden. Although I did not understand the details, I learned that our beautiful house had been condemned to make way for a bridge across the River Meuse, which ran at the foot of our property. Father had refused many offers of various sites in the vicinity on which to build and finally decided to move his family to Brussels. And now he was often absent in Brussels, attending to business.

Before moving, Mélanie had promised to sing at a concert given by La Legia, the choral society of Liège. This society had won first prize in many European competitions and had a splendid reputation. It was a good deal of an honor to appear as soloist with it. Nevertheless, a cold in the head is no respecter of honors, and when the day came Mélanie was unable to sing a note. The president of the society came in consternation to the house, hoping to persuade her to attempt the program notwithstanding, but he himself soon realized it was an impossibility.

I was a small but interested witness to this interview in the salon. I saw the poor gentleman's disappointment. I realized the predicament he was in. And I did not have the least vestige of a cold. "If you like, I can replace Mélanie," I said in a business-like way. "I can sing her program." And without more ado, I began Mélanie's most florid number.

The president of La Legia accepted my services, and to the fact that Father was absent in Brussels may be attributed my early and unexpected debut in public. I was just ten years old. I sang, for the choral society, Mélanie's program: "The Lost Kiss," "Jennie la meunière," and for the final number the celebrated air "Connais-tu le pays?" from *Mignon*. For the last refrain of this aria, "'Tis there I would love and die—'tis there, yes! 'Tis there!", carried away by my own emotion, I suddenly fell on my knees and clasped my hands as I did when saying my prayers. Perhaps it was the thought of leaving Liège and my own dearly loved home, or perhaps it was merely a feeling of giving the audience their money's worth— I do not know. But the action created a sensation. I had made a hit. Later, when I sang Mignon, I used this effective little bit of business and always brought down the house. Yet curiously enough I have yet to see another Mignon do the same.

Laden with flowers, applause ringing in my ears, I'm sure I went home an insufferable little person. Poor Mélanie! However, when Father returned and heard of my triumph he was far from pleased. Dear Jeanne did her best to smooth things over, and soon enough I returned to my normal place in the household.

Nevertheless I now had an even greater incentive to practice my music. All day long my hands went up and down my little piano keyboard, and I sang until hoarse. In some alarm, Father remonstrated with me, saying I worked too hard. Humbly I replied that I wanted to become a great artist like my grandfather, for my paternal grandfather had been a fine amateur organist. At this, Father would kiss me and let me go.

I was very unhappy at the thought of leaving Liège. My particular delight, to sit and look down at the Meuse (which in summer takes on a peculiar brilliant blue) and watch the little pleasure boats (*bateaux mouches*, they are called) scurry up and down the river, was over. But the time came and with the rest of my family I was bundled into the train. We filled several compartments. Though it was a simple journey, for me it took on gigantic proportions. I had often ridden in the country on horseback with my brothers, but the speed of the train and the rapidly changing landscape enraptured me. Every cottage, stream, and haystack received my complete attention, and I am told that I babbled incoherently about them all to the great amusement of other travelers. When I think now how many times I made this trip in later years without so much as a glance at this beautiful landscape, I understand the old proverb, "Tout nouveau, tout beau." Then, everything was new and beautiful to me.

Well, on to Brussels!

2

OUR NEW HOME was in the Faubourg St. Giles. I thought it a nice house, but nothing was ever quite the same again. Poor Father had left all his friends in Liège and for a long time seemed completely lost in Brussels. But gradually he, as well as the rest of us, grew accustomed to this new life. New diversions—and better still, new friends —presented themselves.

One of these was Prince de Caraman-Chimay, a trustee of the Brussels cathedral and, more important to me, president of the Brussels Conservatory of Music. He came often to our house, first on business connected with the church and then more and more as a delightful friend and counselor in the ways of a new city.

Being concerned intimately with musical life, on many of his visits he had occasion to hear Jeanne and Angèle play the piano and Mélanie sing. He always seemed pleased at these little concerts and said many enthusiastic things about the talent shown by my three sisters, urging them to continue their studies and embrace every opportunity to know more of the world of music.

Sometimes Angèle brought home with her a young student from the conservatory, likewise a native of Liège, and he and she played duets, with Mélanie to lend her voice. I remember this disheveled youth from Liège days—he was even then developing into a superb violinist. His name was Eugène Ysaÿe, and he was the son of a locksmith. So wrapped in his music was he that nothing else mattered at all. On one occasion he came to the house to play with Angèle for some guests of ours. Right in the middle of their performance I glanced down and noticed that Eugène was wearing one red sock and one yellow one. This was a wonderful joke to me, but I did not dare to tell him afterward, nor anyone else, and had to enjoy my observation all by myself. I doubt if he ever discovered it! Music was the only thing that mattered to him—and indeed, from about this time, to me either.[4]

In the stress of moving and the excitement of a new life, my success as a singer, still vivid to me, seemed completely forgotten by everybody else. I observed this with considerable chagrin and after some hesitation decided it was high time I gave myself a little puff, since nobody else seemed disposed to do so.

"I can sing too!" I announced one day, at the close of one of these impromptu concerts. "I can sing anything that Mélanie can sing!"

Mélanie had just sung particularly well, and for a moment I was abashed and rather fearful of my impudence, as a hush fell on the assembly and everyone looked at me.

But Prince de Chimay was a man of the world and did at once the only possible thing under the circumstances: he asked me to sing. Though by now Mélanie looked not very pleased, I felt the sympathy of Jeanne; seating myself at the piano, I had the impudence to sing Mélanie's program right over again.

At its conclusion there was another dreadful hush—then the prince called me to him, took me in his lap, and kissed me. I remember that moment so well! He had the most beautiful almond eyes and long beetling brows—and a black beard parted carefully in the middle, as was the custom in those days. I liked him, all but the beard.

He insisted that I should take lessons at the conservatory, and his enthusiasm at my performance was so genuine that even Father had to believe in it, although the notion did not please him at all. Nevertheless, since he was beholden to the prince for many favors, it was politic to accept the really valuable offer made in my behalf; for, as I have said, the prince was president of the conservatory, and he promised to look after my studies with an especial interest. The matter was arranged then and there.

Shortly afterward, conducted back and forth by my old nurse Françoise, I started my studies at the conservatory.[5]

My sister Angèle, who was already studying piano, was allowed to go to her classes unaccompanied. It occurred to me that there was no reason why I could not do the same. Much as I loved good, simple Françoise, I felt far more important without her at my side.

From our house we walked to the Porte de Hal and there boarded the tram which took us past the conservatory door. I was greatly impressed by this car because just before boarding it an extra pair of horses was attached to pull us up a steep hill. To my childish, egotistical mind it was as though they were added for my special benefit. Our Brussels trams were very good ones; and, being the first in Europe to be lighted by electricity, although horse-drawn, they were called "electric cars."

The open space around the Porte de Hal was lined with benches where nursemaids and governesses sat with their charges and gossiped together. Françoise would be quite content and comfortable among them, I felt sure; and, carrying my small portfolio which I never allowed another to touch, and wearing my rubber cape I thought so beautiful that I never went without it, rain or shine, I would cut a very important and dashing figure alone on the tram with four horses pulling me. This I explained carefully to Françoise, but she seemed unconvinced until, as a last argument, I pointed out that on my return we could take the ten centimes allotted for her fare and purchase two cream puffs on the way home! I hope Françoise enjoyed her morning chitchat as much as I did my intoxicating independence and importance. I know we both enjoyed the cream puffs.

Once a week I went to the prince's house and played piano accompaniments for him. He was an amateur violinist of considerable skill, and we enjoyed our work together. Both the prince and princess took a great interest in my progress and treated me like a daughter.

One day the prince said to me suddenly, "Clara, would you like to go on the stage?"

"Yes," I said, "but of course only in concerts!" I pictured clearly Father's dismay even at that.

One day shortly after this, when I arrived for my visit and practice with the prince, I was introduced to a strange gentleman. This was Alfred Cabel, who had been a celebrated baritone in his day. His real name was Cabu, and his wife, Marie-Josèphe Cabel, then dead, had been a famous star of the Opéra-Comique in Paris where she had created many leading roles, including Meyerbeer's Dinorah and Philine in *Mignon*.[6] Alfred Cabel was at this time in poor health, teaching singing in Brussels. The prince had brought him to the house, unwilling to depend entirely on his own judgment about me.

Cabel proceeded to try my voice carefully and pronounced it excellent, with the result that I took lessons from him for a year. These lessons were paid for by the prince out of his own pocket and took place at his house. Only Jeanne was told the great secret. As Cabel's health grew poorer he gave up all his pupils except me. A few years later he would die.

Fortunately, Cabel was a wonderful teacher. He excelled in placement of the voice and in fact was a true voice doctor. What he taught me has remained the groundwork of my singing method. He did not teach "pieces" but actually the technique of singing, though later I did study one or two arias with which to display my ability when the time arrived. The chief of these was the beautiful air "Quelle serenité" from Massé's *Paul et Virginie*. This lay perfectly in my voice and displayed it to best advantage. Beginning in my low register, which even then was strong, the recitative was in splendid contrast to the bravura of the air itself with its leaps and runs and trills. Another piece I worked hard at was the air from Gounod's *Philémon et Baucis*, "O riante nature."

At the end of three years I received first prize at the conservatory for solfeggio and harmony. Angèle won first prize for piano.

My days at the Brussels Conservatory, my long studies there, were over. Everyone was pleased at my successful graduation, but to my chagrin I discovered that Father thought this was the end of my musical career. I had won first prize in both my courses, and this ought to be enough to satisfy anyone. But it did not satisfy me. I knew this was only a beginning but wondered if Father was not right. The obstacles to further progress seemed insurmountable, and I grew very despondent. The moment had come, as it does to anyone studying, when a greater, more final step yet remains to be taken.

About this time Sidonie's husband, my godfather, was planning a short trip to New York to represent a family firm, a big manufacturer of silk goods near Lille. This was to be his last trip, as he had finished his law studies and was now planning to settle down and practice at home. He promised to take Sidonie along, a belated wedding trip; and I, already anxious to see more of the world, begged my godfather to take me too, as a recompense for having finished my courses at the conservatory with honors. I was a happy girl when my plea was granted!

For all French-speaking people visiting New York, Martin's in University Place was the only hotel. It was later the Lafayette. I was rather disillusioned, for I had pictured all the hotels of New York as grandiose establishments magically illuminated with gas and overrun with page boys glittering with gold buttons, the lobbies crowded with magnificent ladies in bustles, and gentlemen in tall hats speaking hundreds of languages. Instead of all this, we arrived at a small, comfortable family hotel with a café, just as any in Brussels—and everyone spoke French. It was a rather bitter moment. Instead of the large orchestra of my dreams, the restaurant had only a pianist and three violinists.

Many gentlemen called to see my godfather on business, while their wives paid their respects to Sidonie. Few of them spoke French, and this was some comfort. Even today I am surprised at foreigners who surround themselves with everything which reminds them of home when traveling. I want to have everything as different as possible.

One day Sidonie told me to put on my best dress, as a number of people were coming to dinner. Martin's at that time had only one private dining room, far too small for all our guests, so we had to take a long table in the main dining room, occupying the center of the floor. Our guests, I learned, were the heads of A. T. Stewart (now Wanamaker's), Lord and Taylor, and other large department stores with whom my brother-in-law was doing business. There were likewise the two brothers Givernoud and their wives, who happily were French, and the brothers Emanuel and Paul Gerli, rich Italians who had come to study business in America. I mention them because we became very close friends a few years after, when they heard me sing at the Opéra-Comique in Paris, and later still in New York. I was placed between the Mesdames Givernoud, and when they learned I was already a young singer they asked me to sing. After many objections from Sidonie, I decided to do so, if the little orchestra would accompany me—of course, I had already made friends with the musicians. I left my place quietly and went up to the director. As he was French, he knew all the French operas and songs, and together we decided that I should sing "Connais-tu le pays?" from *Mignon* and, if I received an encore, Gounod's "Sérénade." I mounted the little platform and the director announced my song. I remember it as if it happened last night! I was much offended that everyone in the restaurant did not at once cease all conversation and gave a sweeping and indignant look at every table in the room. There was an immediate silence. I sang the two songs and the response was tremendous. Turning to the maestro, I whispered something and then made a sign and cried, "Tout le monde debout!"

The orchestra gave one chord and I sang "La Marseillaise." Everyone finished the song with me, after which the orchestra played the American anthem and I was overwhelmed with flowers. People snatched the bouquets off the tables and presented them to me, and I received them with gracious dignity. I have never forgotten the great emotion of that night and consider it my real debut in America. Sidonie was proud, of course, but afraid of the emotional reaction.

That night in my dreams I was alone on the stage of an enormous opera house. A huge symphony orchestra began "Connais-tu le pays?"—and my voice would not come out of my throat. I rent the air with screams, and poor Sidonie had much trouble in quieting me. It was many years before I sang in America again.

One day shortly after this, Sidonie told me she and her husband were obliged to go to a luncheon at Delmonico's given by the people who were present at our dinner, and that I must stay home as it was to be a business affair. But I knew it was because she was afraid I would sing again!

She put me in the hands of Madame Martin, who was the cashier in the café. I must say that I was not displeased, as I had a little plan in my head. Sidonie had taken me walking and shopping, but I wanted to go alone and inspect the toy shops on Fourteenth Street. I had my lunch with Madame Martin and then announced my plan. She did not seem to approve and spoke of the imprudence of it, since I did not speak English. I removed my leather belt and asked her to write "Hotel Martin, University Place" on it, which she did, seeing my determination; but she admonished me to speak to no one, man or woman, and if I found myself lost to go to the corner of the street to show my belt to a policeman. I thanked her with a hasty kiss and soon was on Fourteenth Street looking at the wonderful shops with which at that time it abounded, giving special attention to dolls and puppet theaters. And after I finished one side of the street I began on the other.

For a long time I paused, entranced by a street organ and the clever monkey which soon had taken all the change out of my pocket. Little girls and their mothers were crowding around, and one spoke to me in English. However, I remembered Madame Martin's warning and remained dumb.

By now it was late and time to return, but in a moment or two it was clear that I was lost and it would be necessary for me to speak at last.

There was a man in front of a shop whose mission it was to hand ladies in and out of their carriages. Going up to him, I took off my belt and pointed to the writing. To my great surprise, he asked me in French if I was lost, and I said yes. As he was very busy with arriving and departing shoppers, he took a whistle from his pocket and blew a blast. A moment later, a huge policeman appeared, with fierce mustachios, a club, and all the trimmings of a constable of the period. My terror was great and I burst into tears. My friend reassured me that I would be escorted home. The man took me by the wrist and started briskly off. I could hardly keep up with him, and everyone turned and stared—wondering, no doubt, what the little girl had done to be whisked off in such a manner by a policeman.

A few days later we sailed for home, and a big smiling Negro carried our luggage up the gangplank. As my brother-in-law tipped him, he bowed ceremoniously, but at the same time I said to Sidonie with horror, "Oh, look at the big black man!" He turned to me, saying in French, "We have a black skin, Mademoiselle, but our hearts are the same as yours." And bowing again, he disappeared.

Father was in bad health at this time and also depressed by family sorrows. He had never fully recovered from the move from Liège, and now his only sister died. Added to this, my brother, once so ardent a student of divinity, lost his vocation. Instead of joining the priesthood he enrolled at the university. To Father this was a great blow. In the midst of these catastrophes my sister Clémence married a young Romanian lawyer and went to Romania. Before she left, Father extracted a promise from her to return every year to see him. And, although she had fourteen children, she kept her promise.

Father's spirit really seemed broken now. He relaxed his severity and even gave in to some of the ideas and wishes of others.

Cabel had abstracted from his friend Léon Carvalho, director of the Opéra-Comique, a promise to give me an audition. Yet on the ever burning subject of a trip to sing for him in Paris, Father remained adamant in his refusal. He could see no reason why I should want to sing for others, nor could he see anything but willful waywardness in my desire to venture abroad, since I was so well appreciated at home.

One day, from the window, I saw the prince coming to the house. I guessed his mission at once. He had not given up hope of bringing Father around to our way of thinking, and this day, somehow, I sensed a certain finality in his determined walk. I decided to do a little eavesdropping.

In my father's study hung some heavy velvet curtains, placed there to deaden the sound of our singing and piano playing. Stealthily, I took my place behind these curtains. As suspected, the prince had come with further arguments in my behalf. He said it would be a crime to prevent my progress toward a career, with my voice, musical and histrionic abilities, and, in short, every other attribute it was possible to invest me with. Nevertheless, Father had not lost his decisive character on this one topic. He declined flatly to listen to the prince's eloquence; to every argument put forth he returned a more outspoken refusal. At last, goaded past patience, he slammed his hand on his desk and cried in a loud voice, "No daughter of mine shall ever be found on the stage!"

This was my death knell. There was no mistaking the tone of his voice. Stifling my sobs, I slipped away and rushed upstairs to the medicine chest. I was frantic with despair. I knew there was a bottle of iodine in the medicine chest—fortunately a weak solution, which Mother kept to rub on our chests for a cold, because I attempted to swallow the whole bottle and did indeed manage to get some of it down. The burning was terrific. My mouth felt like a furnace, and my shrieks of agony brought the whole family running. If I could not sing, I wanted only to die.

Several years later (for this story has a sequel), the house doctor at the Opéra-Comique examined my throat through a laryngoscope. He remarked upon the peculiar black color of my vocal cords, as though burned or dyed with iodine. Some singers used to gargle with a few drops of iodine in water before singing, as this was supposed to clear the voice, and the doctor knew of the effect of this drug. My vocal cords had been burned and toughened by the severe dousing I gave them, and in the doctor's opinion this accounted for my unusually strong and rich low notes. But I do not advise this treatment for those desiring to strengthen their low register.

The result of my frantic act was Father's consent to my trip to Paris. Perhaps he had come to the conclusion that a daughter on the stage was preferable to a dead one after all.

The great day came. I had a new pleated plaid skirt for the occasion and a blue silk blouse with gold buttons. My hair was done in two pigtails, and on my head perched a little black patent-leather *cannotier*, the very latest model.

The prince had gone to Paris by an early train, instructing Mother to take me to a certain small hotel in the rue des Petits-Champs, the Hôtel de la Michaudière, where he was to meet us. He called us shortly after our arrival with exciting news. He was an acquaintance of Marie Van Zandt, at this time the reigning favorite of the Opéra-Comique, and had made an engagement for me to sing for her the next day. He wanted me to sing for various people qualified to judge, not being content with the opinion of any one person.

So the next day he conducted Mother and me to Marie Van Zandt's apartment in the American quarter, in the avenue du Bois de Boulogne, for Van Zandt was an American, from Texas.[7]

She was unlike anyone I had ever met: tall and thin with long arms, a long neck, and a small, round, sympathetic face full of gaiety and charm. She received us very kindly and spoke to me encouragingly in her strong American accent, for her knowledge of French was somewhat limited in spite of her high position in Paris and the fact that she later created the role of Lakmé. Léo Delibes wrote this opera especially to suit her high, light voice.

In the salon were several other people, among them a stout, pleasant lady, Van Zandt's mother. Madame Jennie Van Zandt had been a singer of renown in her own day in America, at one time even heading her own opera company, and had done much to further an interest in opera in the United States.[8]

We were offered tea and gâteaux. However, being a serious though small prima donna (as I felt already), I said, "No thank you. I never eat before I sing."

And then I sang my showpiece from *Paul et Virginie*. Everyone was delighted at my performance, and Miss Van Zandt declared that on no account must I be allowed to give up my studies. She praised both my voice and my interpretation of the air, which she said was full of feeling, and added that she would introduce me to Carvalho herself at once. The appointment was made for the following day.

Then I had my tea and gâteaux.

We did not use the letter from Cabel, with which we were armed, to remind Carvalho of his promise of sometime before; and I fear this wounded Cabel. In the musical world, one is treading continually on egg shells, and it is well to bear this in mind.

It was my first sight of the Opéra-Comique. Never had I imagined any place so beautiful. Everything was different from real life: the pieces of scenery—castle doors, stretches of enchanted forest—lying here and there, the peculiar smell of painted canvas, and the high dark auditorium with empty seats and boxes stretching up into the shadows impressed me particularly. It was my own toy theater come to magic life. I was, for a moment, overawed by it.[9]

In the first row sat solemnly a few important-looking people. I was conducted onto the stage and from there I could see Monsieur Carvalho, Miss Van Zandt, and her mother.

Jules Danbé, a noted conductor, was present to accompany me. He enjoyed great fame in Paris at the time and conducted the premieres of many operas, including those of *Mignon* and *Lakmé*.[10]

Before I began to sing, Miss Van Zandt suddenly rose from her seat and, coming up to the footlights at one side of the proscenium, whispered to me, "Don't be afraid of all these people. Sing the way you did at my house yesterday. Imagine that you are there, not here."

So I recovered myself and did not really feel afraid. Thanks to my long studies with Alfred Cabel, I had confidence in my ability to render my air from *Paul et Virginie*.

When I had reached the end, everyone began to talk and whisper. I thought I had finished, but the prince de Chimay detached himself from the others, came up, and asked me to sing "Connais-tu le pays?"

At the end of the aria I did my usual business of falling to my knees, and I am very glad I did it. In concerts one is supposed to stand like a stick, creating every illusion with the voice alone—that is the style. But creating a mood is the great purpose, and who can make an arbitrary rule in art? Besides this, my action showed that I had inspirations of my own, in acting as well as in singing, and for this reason might expect to be of more interest to the impresario of an opera company.

Everyone was greatly impressed by the unexpected ending I had given to my song. Miss Van Zandt asked who had taught me this, and I replied, "Nobody!" She was much pleased and amused, for one of her roles was Mignon (and a charming Mignon she made). She said, "I am too tall to do anything like that gracefully. You have the advantage over me. But tomorrow night I am singing Mignon here, and you must come as my guest to see how I do it."

To attend the opera as guest of the prima donna—nothing could have impressed me more. Our time was up, however, and Mother had to take me back to Brussels the next day. Carvalho was interested in me and wanted me to begin at once to prepare some roles while continuing my studies. Poor Mother told me afterward that when she heard me sing she wept, because she knew that from that moment I was lost to her forever.

Marie Van Zandt! I shall always remember her with gratitude. She took a real interest in me and showed me the warm and spontaneous nature which had made her stage presence so delightful and fresh a novelty to the Parisians. Her clear, light, flexible voice, her bright, intelligent face, and her easy, friendly manner had endeared her to the public, and she was the first of a long line of American singers who made their earliest successes in Paris. Emma Nevada, Sibyl Sanderson, Emma Eames, Mary Garden, and many others followed in her footsteps.

But the end of her Parisian career was tragic. In spite of being a great favorite with her colleagues, to whom she was always generous, there were some who were jealous of her and managed to bring about her downfall.

One evening she was billed to appear in her creator's role of Lakmé, but at the last moment she sent word to the management that she was ill and unable to sing. It was too late to change the bill, and she was notified that she must appear, ill or well. She made the effort. Her doctor gave her a powerful drug to help her through the performance and waited in the wings. I was at home that night. My friend Arthur Cobalet, who sang

Nilakantha, a role he had created, came to tell us of the incident after the performance.

Though Van Zandt managed to get through the first act, in the second she reached the limit of her strength. The second act of *Lakmé* is set in the Indian marketplace. Nilakantha, the priest whose temple has been desecrated by foreign feet, brings his daughter, disguised as a pariah girl, and forces her much against her will to sing, thinking the sound of her voice will make the guilty Englishman betray his identity. It is a tense moment. "Chante, Lakmé! Chante, Lakmé!" Nilakantha sternly demands in his sonorous bass. To her father's inexorable command, she sings the famous air, the Bell Song. But that night Lakmé failed to obey. Poor Marie Van Zandt, at that dramatic moment, could no longer continue. She swayed on her feet and clutched for support. The audience at first, as frequently happens when untoward events occur on the stage, took this for an effective piece of business, but Cobalet perceived that something was amiss. Thinking Van Zandt had missed her cue, Danbé, the conductor, began again the opening bars of the Bell Song. It was of no use. Van Zandt fainted on the stage, and the curtain was rung down in confusion.

This was the signal for attacks upon her in the press, one paper saying that she had appeared so drunk that the curtain had to be lowered. Her adherents declared she had been drugged through the machinations of a rival prima donna—anything but the obvious truth. The fact that the American colony always appeared at her performances and gave her enormous applause and encouragement had not a little to do with this unhappy catastrophe. Many felt that native singers were unduly put in the shade; it was a tactless and mistaken policy to overdo a foreigner's ovations.

Riots were staged outside the opera house; all Paris was seething with the scandal. One explanation that was offered later concerned the French government, which, to draw public attention from some event that had to be kept as quiet as possible, organized the riots and made the unfortunate little American the scapegoat. Nevertheless, though Van Zandt sang again—once while a riot was actually going on outside in the street, amid great excitement, the audience standing on their seats and waving and shouting—her career in Paris had come to a close.

However, I am glad to say that Van Zandt continued singing in other countries, making a great success in America where *Lakmé* was brought out for her at the Metropolitan in 1892, and she only retired upon her marriage some years later. She died at Cannes in 1919.

I am happy to tell this, the true story of Van Zandt's troubles in Paris; because, although this was forgotten years ago, it created much talk at the time and did great injustice to a fine artist and a generous woman.[11]

3

THE FIRST REAL SORROW of my childhood was quitting Liège, especially as this meant leaving my nephews and niece (the same Valentine whom I had once considered the cause of my diminutive stature), the only friends of my age. But a deep, wracking feeling of tragedy took hold of me on my return from Paris. In spite of the success of my audition and the flattering kindness and interest displayed by Carvalho and Marie Van Zandt, on seeing my home again I burst into uncontrollable tears and flung myself into the arms of my dear Jeanne. She at first supposed me to be shedding tears of joy, but I sobbed unrestrainedly; and almost hysterically, rushing upstairs to my room, I continued my paroxysm of despair. Then Jeanne discovered that I was wailing through my tears: "I don't want to go to Paris! I don't want to leave you! I don't want ever to sing again!"

Luckily Father was absent in Liège, for if he had seen and heard me then he would certainly have found ample arguments to keep me at home for the rest of my life.

Mother had recommended to her a widow named Madame Leroy who accompanied me to Paris two weeks later when I really embarked upon the preparations for a career. Madame Leroy pleased me at once, chiefly I think because she made the conquest of Toto, my Brussels spitz. Toto was to accompany us to Paris, as indeed was the puppet theater, my most prized toy, made for me by my brother Charles—for to leave this behind was unthinkable. Scenery and puppets for productions of *Cinderella* and *The Sleeping Beauty* were carefully packed along with my clothes. I wanted to take my little piano, likewise, and almost everything else I owned. But I was reconciled to the trip when Jeanne pointed out that it would be foolish to transport all my belongings to Paris, as I did not yet know if I were going to stay there. The thought that the parting was not to be permanent having been borne in on me by this sensible reasoning, I gradually became reconciled to going and even anticipated the trip as another adventure; and finally we were off—a day early, to be gone before Father returned from Liège and thus to avoid further arguments and a possible injunction to stay in Brussels.

How to transport Toto to Paris had been the problem. At this time dogs were not allowed in the compartments of trains in Europe, as they

The young Clara Lardinois. Courtesy William R. Moran.

still are not in many places, and a trip in the baggage car would have terrified poor Toto to death. Good Madame Leroy saved the situation. For days before we left, she had been busily training Toto to crawl into a rolled-up traveling rug by giving him a lump of sugar after he was called out. He had soon learned the trick and even begged to get inside the rug.

The day of departure came. How it rained—as it turned out, fortunately! Between my tears and the rain I nearly forgot the traveling rug, but Madame Leroy had it well rolled and firmly grasped by its leather handle. She had taken possession of an empty compartment and put the rug and our luggage in the rack opposite our seat, warning me not to talk too loudly for fear of waking Toto, who was sleeping peacefully.

We had hoped to be alone, but just before the train pulled out the door was flung open and three enormous ladies and a venerable gentleman entered, taking their places opposite us and just under our luggage.

Madame Leroy looked innocently out the window and observed that it was a pity it was raining so hard. Our traveling companions, we learned with relief, were bound only for Mons, an hour's distance from Brussels. All went well until, shortly before reaching Mons, the fattest of the three ladies began mopping herself with her handkerchief.

"This," she complained, "is the worst compartment I have ever traveled in. It is raining inside as well as out!"

In Paris we went directly to the pension in the rue Michaudière. It was whispered that Madame Mendez, the proprietress, was the widow of a Spanish general who had lost his life either in one of the Carlist Wars or the Revolution of 1868, which deposed Queen Isabella II. Whether he was loyal to his queen or to the revolutionists, however, I do not know. Madame Mendez, who was French, invariably wore a black silk dress and had magnificent jewels, all of which she put on to rustle down to dinner. She was very agreeable and obliging to those who passed her severe tests and were deemed sufficiently genteel to be admitted to her exclusive hotel.

We were given a pleasant room with an alcove remote from the other guests so that my singing would disturb as little as possible (Madame Leroy, who was a capable pianist, accompanied me). Classes at the conservatory began in two weeks, and during this time we "did" Paris. The Louvre, the Cluny, Notre Dame, Napoleon's tomb—all were visited, and by the time the conservatory opened I felt I knew Paris well.

After a preliminary examination I was put in the second of the three classes for singing, and at the same time attended a class in the art of acting, for many of the pupils at the conservatory were studying for an operatic career.

I worked hard for six months with only one or two visits home. At the end of this time Léon Carvalho wanted me to sing for him again in order to observe my progress. I was the type he was searching for, for a new production of *Le Pré aux Clercs*. Though there were many capable singers, they were all robust and mature ladies, while in this as well as in many other operas the roles to be filled were those of young girls. Therefore, my youth, as well as my small size (which had caused me such bitter pangs in days gone by), were now my chief assets.

I sang for Carvalho accordingly, in the presence of my patron and benefactor, to whom I owe everything—the prince de Chimay. Carvalho decided that I now needed intensive coaching for opera, and the one teacher for this was obviously the great Madame Marchesi. She asked for an audition, and I was taken to her studio by the prince and Madame Leroy.[12]

I shall never forget my first sight of this great woman. She came into the room dressed as always in severe black, her eyes looking intensely right through me, but her manner was friendly and kind. She asked me many questions, as she always did her prospective pupils, and laughed a good deal at my answers. I felt at my ease at once. Only after I had spoken with her for some time did she ask me to sing. I inquired what she would like me to sing, and she said "Anything"—her pianist would have any music I chose.

The prince suggested the air from *Paul et Virginie*, and I accordingly launched into my *cheval de bataille*.

Marchesi's dictum was that I had a pure coloratura voice and that I was singing too low. She had no place at the time, as she gave her attention to only a limited number of pupils, but expected soon to be able to take me on.

In the meantime I continued my studies at the conservatory. A month or two later I received a letter from Marchesi giving me another appointment. Upon seeing me again, her first question was whether I was seriously seeking a career. I assured her I was. Marchesi was unwilling to waste her time on dilettantes and would not accept pupils who held no promise of fame for themselves—as well as for her. She inquired whether I had an engagement with the Opéra-Comique. I said, "I understand Monsieur Carvalho is anxious to have me as soon as I have completed my studies with you." She looked doubtful at this, and I added, "Why don't you ask him?" Then she laughed again and told me I was to come to her twice a week.

I studied with Marchesi for nearly a year. After a while I left the conservatory, not only to give all my time to Marchesi but also because my lessons there conflicted with Marchesi's own teaching. With her I studied particularly the music of *Mignon* and *Faust*, and Carvalho asked me to come as often as possible to attend rehearsals at the Opéra-Comique to learn the ways of the stage. In my opinion these rehearsals were more of a help to me than anything else. Seeing the singers at work was of enormous benefit. I profited by their good work, as well as by their errors; likewise, as Carvalho's prodigy, I came to meet a number of important people. Among them were Jules Massenet and Léo Delibes.

I think it was after my debut, when I returned to study certain roles with Marchesi, that I first had what should have been the pleasure of meeting Nellie Melba. She had but lately made her enormously successful debut in Brussels, and her name was on every tongue.

It is quite possible to feel antipathy for an artist while admiring her talent, and this was my sentiment about Melba. I must say that though I never knew her well I had opportunities to learn the traits of her character, and I did not like them. In the first place, I knew that Melba caused Madame Marchesi a good amount of suffering. As Marchesi had done so much for Melba, this was an inexcusable thing, though it was always Melba's opinion that she had made the reputation of Marchesi and not the other way around.

When Melba called on Marchesi it was not her wont to wait two minutes in an anteroom, even if a lesson was going on in the studio.

One day when I was there and in the middle of an aria, the door burst open without a knock or the least warning, and a tall, large-boned lady walked into the room. I made a sign to the accompanist and continued without interruption to sing. I can see the lady yet! Great was her astonishment at my not having stopped singing, and she walked completely around me staring at me with truly terrifying eyes.

"Je suis la Melba," she said.

I continued my song to the end.

"Yes," I then said. "I heard you in Brussels, in *Hamlet* and *Faust*. And I prefer Madame Calvé in *Faust*."

"Probably because she has black hair," Melba said, looking at my own dark hair.

"No," I answered calmly. "It was because she was so sweet."

I had of course said too much. Madame Marchesi, who was standing behind Melba, made me a sign with her eyes to say nothing more. But I was not yet ready to be silent. I thought that if Miss Van Zandt and Monsieur Carvalho had been so kind to me, Madame Melba had no cause to look at me in such a manner or to treat me so rudely.

In a whisper to the accompanist, I added, "Melba was quite good as Ophelia, however."

To change the conversation, Madame Marchesi asked Melba if I did not have a lovely voice. "You must excuse her," she added in an undertone. "She is still only a child."

Melba said aloud, "Perhaps she will arrive with a great deal of hard work, but I counsel her to be less impertinent and to eat a lot of good soup, to grow taller." And she walked out of the room without looking at me—luckily, for she would have seen the tears dropping down my cheeks. I heard her talking loudly in the corridor to Madame Marchesi, who had followed her out of the room. A few moments later Madame Marchesi came back alone.

She kissed me without saying a word.

My lesson was finished for that day and I went home having gained a great enemy in Melba. However, through no action of my own, I would have an amusing revenge on her some years later when we were both singing in Melbourne. What, I wonder, would Melba have thought if she had then known that the *petite impertinente* would have her revenge in Melba's own native city![13]

Speaking of Melbourne has led my mind back to some talk I heard years ago about how just an appellation this was. To suggest that Melba did not come from Melbourne, or indeed originally from Australia at all, seems fantastic; the story of Melbourne being her birthplace (from which she derived her name) has been often related, and I do not refute it. But there was a story at one time current in Paris that Melba had Swiss blood in her veins, that her mother came from a small village in German Switzerland. The celebrated Lucienne Bréval, who created a number of Wagner's heroines in Paris, likewise came from this same town, though she was a naturalized Frenchwoman. Be that as it may, it is indeed a fact that of all the singers Melba sang with Bréval was the only one she never attempted in any way to molest; and when Bréval sang Chimène in *Le Cid* in New York, Melba appeared in the secondary role of the Infanta. What the connection between Bréval and Melba was I do not know, though certainly it used to be said they were half-sisters. Imagine the consternation it would have caused if it had come to be known that Melba, fêted so many years as the most distinguished daughter of Australia, had been born in a mountain village near Zürich! And no wonder, if this was so, that Melba always remained on good terms with Lucienne Bréval.

Bréval was six or eight years younger than Melba. Her voice was bigger and more robust than Melba's exquisite string of crystal beads, though it was always a lyric voice, and she gained her effects by her broad dramatic style and the intensity of her passion—in striking contrast to Melba's cold and possessed personality. At the time Bréval created Strauss's Salome in Paris, she had grown somewhat portly. When it came to the Dance of the Seven Veils, she danced the dance of the first veil, consisting chiefly of postures and movements of the arms. Then she slipped for a moment behind a column, and when she emerged she had miraculously lost a good fifty or sixty pounds! The dancer in all other respects looked exactly like Bréval, which made the effect truly startling.[14]

Melba's voice was so delicate that she had always to preserve it and mete it out in careful parcels. She was very clever as a whistler, and when she wanted to run through her music before a performance she would whistle it, thereby saving her voice for the public. But even the public got as small a slice of it as was possible for Melba to give. A friend of mine in Melbourne once said to me, "I asked Melba how she was able to go on her long tours of one-night stands through Australia, and she answered, 'Oh, I don't give them all I have!' Then I thought of you and how in one evening you sing practically all the soprano's music from an opera on these same tours!"

It was so. And I confess I do not see how it is possible for an artist to hold anything back when standing before the public. He or she has to give everything—the presence of an audience demands it. One cannot restrain oneself when inspired. But Melba learned how, and she sold her singing by the yard.

After I had been studying with Marchesi for nearly a year, Carvalho wanted to put on, as part of a double bill, a two-act opera called *Le portrait*, written by Théodore de Lajarte, the librarian of the Paris Opéra. The role was that of a young girl, and Carvalho decided this would be a good opportunity to try me out, as it were, to see what I could do and what the reaction of the public would be. So he offered me a contract for three years, and after more arguments at home Father was finally prevailed upon to sign it, for, of course, I was still a minor. For the first year I was to receive the munificent sum of three hundred francs a month; for the second year, four hundred; and for the third, five. In other words, sixty, eighty, and one hundred dollars. I was to supply all my own clothes and so forth, except *costumes d'epoch*.

It was Carvalho's plan to put me on without any previous fanfare or advertising of any sort; then, if I proved a success, I was to receive an official debut.

What excitement my first bulletin of rehearsals caused me! On my arrival at the Opéra-Comique I told all and sundry that this time I had come to work; I was no longer an onlooker. The composer had come to my hotel to coach me in the part; and at the rehearsal, though the others still read from manuscript, I consequently knew my music inside and out.

When the day of the dress rehearsal came I was astonished at the fearful and grotesque appearance presented by my fellow actors, all heavily made up with grease paint. I had no idea how to make up, but the wardrobe mistress and the coiffeur promised to do it for me. However, the great black eyes they produced, shaded heavily with purple, struck my heart cold. I stared at myself in the mirror in astonishment and dismay. Never would I go onstage like that! I looked like Jezebel and Lady Macbeth rolled into one!

They explained that from the front of the house my appearance would be normal, but it was no such thing. Carvalho and Lajarte burst into laughter upon seeing me, and both rushed backstage demanding to know who had made up *la petite* in such a manner. It was a joke played upon me by my good friends.

Before the premiere two days later, I had taken lessons in makeup and painted my own face. I was in a daze. In the wings, as nervous as the proverbial author on his first night, Lajarte frantically gave me last-minute instructions. "Leave me alone! I know what to do!" I hissed back. My cue came. I stepped forth and sang my entrance song without any catastrophe. Danbé, who had played the accompaniment at my first audition, conducted. Being very short, I was able to look out at the audience and yet see the conductor without appearing to be observing him at all. But Danbé, who did not realize this, kept waving his arms to attract my attention. I remember him rushing back at the end of the act to ask why I did not keep looking at him like the other singers, despite my indignant assurances that I saw him very well. In the excitement and bustle it is small wonder that I remember very little of my first opening night.[15]

4

THE POSITION OF *pensionnaire* at the Opéra-Comique is no sinecure. I had come with a repertory of some ten or twelve roles, learned at the conservatory and under the guidance of Madame Marchesi; but if I had worked hard to learn them, I soon discovered what real work was. I knew the chief roles in such operas of the older repertory (besides *Mignon* and *Faust*) as *Le Pré aux Clercs, Les diamants de la couronne, La dame blanche, Le domino noir*, and *Fra diavolo* (I was delighted with Zerlina): now I found myself called upon to sing them all.

Those who sang at the Opéra-Comique and the Grand Opéra of Paris were divided into two sorts—guest artists, called *sociétaires*, who sang from time to time and were paid per performance, and the large brotherhood of *pensionnaires*. The *pensionnaires* had to be ready to go on in any role of their repertory at very short notice. If you had never sung the role before you were given six hours notice in order to have time to make any arrangements or run through the business with other members of the cast; if you had sung the role, no matter how long ago, four hours were deemed sufficient notice.

Imagine what this meant! One had less freedom, indeed, than a girl in boarding school. If one left the house, even for a stroll in the street, exact word of one's destination had to be left behind with someone in the house in case of an unexpected call from the opera house—and the regular repertory was enormous.

At least two people knew every role in every opera in case of an emergency. I alternated my roles with a Mademoiselle Merguillier, and instead of being jealous, I had an unbounded admiration for her. We shared

Clara Lardinois as Salomé in Massenet's *Hérodiade*. Courtesy William R. Moran.

a dressing room, and she was always a most kind and helpful friend to me. Whenever she sang, I attended the performance in the *pensionnaires'* box, to watch her action and business and learn more of the possibilities of the role. She had a beautiful voice, and her vocalization was charmingly light and deft. She sang the Queen of the Night in *The Magic Flute* splendidly, and in this opera we appeared together, for I was cast as Pamina, her daughter.[16]

I was supposed to sing three times a week or twelve times a month. If we sang more often than our contracts called for, we received extra pay. This was a great treat for me as I always sang more than my stipulated number of performances, and Madame Leroy, who held the purse strings, decided that this bonus might be mine for pin money. To me it seemed a fortune.

During my days at the Opéra-Comique, the principal guest artists that we *pensionnaires* supported were Marie Heilbronn, Marie Van Zandt, and Emma Nevada.

Carvalho's wife, the great Madame Marie Miolan-Carvalho, an echo from an earlier day, was in her decline and seldom sang. This is easily understood when one considers that she was the original Marguerite in *Faust* when it was produced at the Théâtre-Lyrique in 1859. I heard her but twice; the first time was as the countess in *The Marriage of Figaro*, at which performance I sang Cherubino. In spite of advancing years she was not stout, but her voice, rather than diminishing, had grown lower in pitch. She was from the south of France and a great favorite of the public, who always crowded the house at her appearances.[17]

Marie Heilbronn created the role of Manon. In private life she was the marquise de la Panouse. She was said to be a Jewess. At this time she was no longer in her youth, and if the truth must be told, she had become a trifle *forte*, though her carriage was good and she had a well-proportioned figure. She did not appear young enough to depict with success the innocent convent-bound Manon of the first act. Nevertheless, I have never since seen the entrance of Manon in the gambling scene of the fourth act done so gloriously. She was no longer Heilbronn but the marquise de la Panouse! That entrance was breathtaking and magnificent. Her voice too, which exerted a powerful charm on me, was extremely brilliant.[18]

It is unfortunate that the great *Manon* gambling scene is very much cut almost everywhere the opera is now performed, including the Metropolitan in New York.

Massenet was nothing if not a good showman, and a good businessman as well. He knew much of the music of *Manon* to be beyond the powers of any but first-rate singers, and he knew some of the rapidly changed and elaborate sets to be beyond the scope of provincial opera houses. As this would mean a great pecuniary loss to him, he made a second version of *Manon* for the provinces, eliminating the necessity for too complicated scenery and replacing some of the music. A trio was dispensed with, as was the showy air of Manon, "Je marche sur tous les chemins." This latter was replaced with the now popular Gavotte, "Obéissons quand leur voix appelle." Even so, the simplified version of *Manon* has become better known now and is usually performed in place of the original one.

I attended all the first rehearsals of *Manon*, sitting in an obscure corner behind a bit of scenery. Little by little, however, I emerged from this hiding place, in order to have a better view of what was going on, and when Massenet noticed me he made me come and sit beside him. I recall attempting to make myself as small and invisible as possible, for I entertained a sort of fear of Léon Carvalho.

I still see Carvalho as he used to come on the stage during rehearsals of *Manon*. Although not particularly large, he always managed to take up an immense amount of room with his sweeping gesticulations, aided and made more telling by the use of his cane, which he brandished about like a battle axe. More than once I have ducked an imminent clip on the side of the head as that cane flew in a circle about him. He wore trousers that were much too big for him and a very roomy jacket, beneath which his body seemed lost. He was inordinately proud of his neck and throat, which were indeed very fine, and he wore his collar wide open to display these objects of beauty, with a large bow tie flowing over his chest. I did not know his age, but he was not gray and had preserved a very youthful appearance. He looked exactly as if he were about to burst into an air from *La bohème*.[19]

I used often to wander into his office, and he made quite a pet of me, calling me Clara. Whenever I said anything that amused him he burst out laughing and gave me a kiss. In fact I never lacked kisses at the Opéra-

Comique. Léo Delibes, Albert Carré, Jules Danbé—all of whom I referred to as Les Gros Bonnets (The Big Hats)—treated me like a little girl.
I was exuberant by temperament, and they never seemed to have any desire to restrain me. If anyone did anything that pleased me I spontaneously gave him a kiss, and when Massenet presented me with a box of
bonbons, a kiss was his thanks. Later I lost this little habit and likewise
overcame using too well what my friends referred to as *mes beaux yeux.*

This reminds me of the first time I was presented to Sarah Bernhardt.
It was in her dressing room at the Théâtre de la Porte St. Martin.

"Ah, tu es la petite Lardinois!" she exclaimed. With a gesture of her
hand she made me back away from her, and looking me over from top to
toe, said, "My child, you have eyes so large they almost make the circuit
of your head!" Then she added, dramatically, "And they will be the perdi-
tion of your soul!"

Sarah Bernhardt remained the great heroine of my life. In later years,
whenever I was in Paris, I went to see her, and she always found time to
receive me, if only for a moment.

On one of these later occasions I waited in the boudoir of her dressing
room. Behind the door, which was slightly ajar, Sarah was making up
for her performance. A long mirror reflected the brilliantly lighted little
room and Sarah, seated at her dressing table while her maid worked over
her face. I dared not breathe for fear the maid might close the door. Her
transformation was amazing! When she finally put on her wig, the Divine
Sarah was twenty years younger.

"Come, little Lardinois, I can see you now," she called in her golden
voice. I was ashamed. I had no right to learn her secret, but I could not
ignore this revelation. We spoke a few moments, and when I left I kissed
her hand so as not to disturb her makeup. I was returning to New York,
and she made me promise to call on her there, as she was expected to
follow soon. Several years later she did appear at the Palace in New York
and in several other cities of the Orpheum circuit. Alas, Sarah's need of
money forced her into vaudeville and hastened her death.

At her final farewell in New York I had the privilege and honor of
singing "La Marseillaise." A number of her friends were present on the
stage. When I came toward her with a bouquet of roses, she took me in
her arms and, tears pouring down her cheeks, was only able to say,

"Thank you, ma chère petite." She was surrounded with adorers and I made my escape, overcome with emotion. I never again saw the greatest artist of the age.[20]

From the day I left Brussels for Paris, Madame Leroy had been at my side. Only on the stage itself could I feel alone and independent, and the good days on the Brussels tram, riding alone to my lessons with old Françoise left behind with the nursemaids, seemed wild liberty by comparison.

Massenet would say, "My child, it is hot and stuffy in here. What you need is fresh air and sunlight. We shall go for a walk." It would be a rest between rehearsals—we rehearsed every day. The first time, Madame Leroy prepared to follow us. But Massenet had a way with her.

"We intend to return, my good Madame Leroy," he said. "Reposez-vous!"

Poor woman! She had no understanding of theatrical life. And poor me! When home again, what things I had to hear! A young lady *comme il faut* does not go promenading on the boulevard with a monsieur. I was no longer a child. Young ladies do not kiss gentlemen who give them a box of chocolates. And so on. One night, when I had sung Zerlina in *Fra diavolo* without a rehearsal and Carvalho was particularly pleased with my achievement, he gave me a kiss. This was more than Madame Leroy could bear. She declared that she was going to write at once to my mother that she wanted to return to Belgium. She could no longer take the responsibility of my chaperoning. I felt myself lost and promised to be more circumspect in future and was obliged to tell my friends that they must no longer give me an occasional kiss. Still, I welcomed her statements that I was no longer a child. That was good news and made me feel both independent and important.

The rehearsals of *Manon* went on with growing excitement. Everyone looked forward to the new opera, which promised to be a great success. Often, during rehearsals, Massenet took me into a small study put aside for him which contained a piano. It amused him to play the music over and make me sing it by ear. To his delight I sang not only the music of Manon herself but the tenor and baritone parts as well. However, I was sorry that I had no role in the production and one day expressed this regret to the composer.

"I should like to be in the cast," I said. "And since I cannot sing Manon

THÉÂTRE NATIONAL DE L'OPÉRA-COMIQUE

DIRECTION *LÉON CARVALHO*

MANON

OPÉRA-COMIQUE EN CINQ ACTES ET SIX TABLEAUX

de MM. HENRI MEILHAC et PHILIPPE GILLE

Musique de

J. MASSENET

Représenté pour la première fois le 19 Janvier 1884

PERSONNAGES

Manon Lescaut... Mmes MARIE HEILBRONN	Le Chevalier **Des Grieux** ... Mrs TALAZAC
Poussette.......... _ MOLÉ-TRUFFIER	Lescaut...................... _ TASKIN
Javotte.............. _ CHEVALIER	Le Comte **Des Grieux**..... _ COBALET
Rosette............. _ RÉMY	Guillot de Morfontaine... _ GRIVOT
La Servante....... _ LARDINOIS	De Brétigny................. _ COLLIN

L' Hôtelier........................... Mrs LABIS

Deux Gardes { .... _ TESTE
{ .... _ REYNAL

Le Portier du Séminaire........ _ LEGRAND

Un Sergent........................... _ TROY

Un Archer............................ _ DAVOUST

Un Joueur........................... _ BERNARD

CHŒURS

ÉLÉGANTES, SEIGNEURS, BOURGEOIS D'AMIENS, BOURGEOIS DE PARIS, VOYAGEURS ET VOYAGEUSES,

PORTEURS ET POSTILLONS, MARCHANDS ET MARCHANDES, DÉVOTES, JOUEURS, AIGREFINS

Au 3me Acte _ BALLET réglé par Melle MARQUET

Chef d'Orchestre:_ M! J. DANBÉ

Chef du Chant:_ M! ÉMILE BOURGEOIS ____ Chef des Chœurs:_ M! H. CARRÉ

Directeur de la Scène:_ M! CHARLES PONCHARD

Pour traiter des représentations et pour la partition et les parties d'orchestre,
s'adresser à HEUGEL et Cie, Editeurs-Propriétaires pour tous pays.

Droits de reproduction, de traduction et de représentation expressément réservés pour tous pays.

H. et Cie 7067   Baudon graveur

The program from the premiere of *Manon*, as reproduced in the piano score.
Clara Lardinois is listed in the role of La Servante. Courtesy William R. Moran.

yet, make a little part for me!" As an inducement I added, "Perhaps it will bring you luck."

This evidently made an impression on Massenet. Several days later he said, "Do you still want to be in *Manon*?" I assured him that I did. There was a small scene in the second act in which a valet entered carrying a tray and spoke a line or two. For my benefit Massenet turned the valet into a maid. And thus, though I did not expect it (and only played the bit a few nights), my name appears on the score with the original cast. I think per- haps I did bring Massenet luck, for of all his many operas *Manon* is the one most often heard today.[21]

At the same time, I was incessantly singing—one night it would be *Le Pré aux Clercs*, another *Philémon et Baucis*. But my main role was Mi- gnon, the part I loved best and in which I came best to be known. For this opera the house was always sold out and the audience particularly bril- liant and high-spirited. *Mignon* in those days had the reputation of being a "matrimonial agency," for on *Mignon* nights the young people were most in evidence. Young girls, upon making their debut in society, were taken to *Mignon* as their introduction to opera. During the *entr'actes*, which were very long, there was much visiting from box to box and, of course, flirtations, which often led in inevitable stages to engagements and marriages, since these young people were all highly eligible in their parents' eyes.

Another reason that I enjoyed singing Mignon was because the role of Lothario, Mignon's father, was sung by a young *bass chantant* named Arthur Cobalet, who had a beautiful voice and who I found extremely handsome, especially in his last-act costume, that of the gentleman of high degree. Cobalet was from Bordeaux and had joined the company at the same time I had. He was a shy and modest young man, not more than twenty-five, and had made a complete conquest of Madame Leroy. To her he had recounted his entire life, up to joining the Opéra-Comique, and she thought him a most exemplary and sympathetic person.

His story was a romantic one.

He was a foundling and had been adopted and brought up by a kind couple who were childless. They were modest people with little money and when Cobalet was still a young boy he became clerk in a business of- fice in Bordeaux, living with his adopted family in the suburbs. As he

Clara Lardinois as Mignon. Courtesy William R. Moran.

was very fond of the outdoors, however, he used to enjoy house painting in his free time. This occupation, besides furnishing him with a welcome change from the atmosphere of the office, enabled him to earn a little extra money; and being gay and cheerful, as he worked, he sang.

One day Jean-Alexandre Talazac, the great tenor, was taking a walk in the country and heard a magnificent voice singing an old French song. As the singer was invisible, Talazac inquired his name of a peasant. "It's that fool of Cobalet," the man answered, indicating the house where he was employed. Talazac approached the young workman and said, "What are you doing here? With a voice such as yours you belong in the conservatory and in a year at the Paris Opéra."

Two years later, indeed, Arthur Cobalet made his debut at the Opéra-Comique, singing principal baritone roles at the side of his close friend Talazac. While at the Opéra-Comique he created the role of Nilakantha, Lakmé's father, a part which suited him better indeed than did more romantic parts.[22]

Lucien Fugère is one of my most outstanding and happy memories of the Opéra-Comique. We sang together most often in *Le Pré aux Clercs*. I alternated between the roles of the princess and Nicette, the young girl of the inn, and Fugère sang the father. I preferred the role of Nicette, for we sang together many times, and Fugère, who was a fine comrade, helped me a great deal. One of our duets in particular was always encored. Fugère was a very gay and lively soul and could not sing dramatic roles—his *retroussé* nose and laughing eyes did not suit tragedy. But he sang a great deal, even at times tenor roles such as the prince in *Le Pré aux Clercs*.[23] As I did, he sang all the repertoire, particularly shining in Auber's *Le domino noir* and *Fra diavolo*. I believe Geraldine Farrar, the delicious Cherubino of Mozart, also sang Angèle in *Le domino noir*, one of my best parts. In fact the list Fugère and I sang together was enormous, for the position of *pensionnaires* is far different from that of *sociétaires*, those artists who are engaged for one or more star roles. Though paid less, as I have already mentioned, our work was far more arduous, as we had to be ready to sing some twenty-four parts at the drop of a hat.

Fugère was very particular in his relations with the company and had few intimate friends among us. He lived in complete retirement with a younger brother who sang in operettas. They were devoted to each other.

I remember Lucien assuring me that if I wanted to keep my voice in good condition over a long period of time I must live a quiet life. The advice was reasonable but I wondered how Fugère was certain, being only in his late twenties or early thirties. "No after-theater suppers or late hours" was his rule. And he was right, for he appeared in opera when he was over eighty—one of the most amazing examples, perhaps *the* most amazing example, of longevity on record. There is a street named after him in Paris now. Neither at rehearsals nor performances did I ever observe him force his voice. Above all he had an extraordinary clarity in his diction, and he could produce superb tones without hardly moving a muscle. His was great art, and by associating with him I learned a great deal.[24]

He received a heavy disappointment in not being chosen to create the role of Lescaut in *Manon* and so refused to understudy the part. Alexandre Taskin, who did create it, was a very handsome man and an excellent comedian. The role of Lescaut demands more acting than voice, and my good friend Fugère, though tall enough, did not possess the presence necessary for this type of role. Lescaut has an effective song, "A quoi bon l'economie," which is about his only important moment; but this too is removed from American presentations of *Manon*. I wonder there is anything left!

Fugère enjoyed teasing me in a friendly way. Frequently, catching me unaware, he crept up behind me and sang, in mezza voce, an amusing little tune he invented:

> La petite Clara, la petite Clara
> La petite Clara Lar-
> > di-
> > > NOIS!

Emma Nevada was another of our guest stars. She was not pretty but made up for this with her charming little figure, expressive eyes, and gentle, sweet disposition. The first time I went into her dressing room I was much taken aback by the smallness of her nose. In making up, she drew a white line down its ridge. Her voice was very light and high and exquisitely trained—by Madame Marchesi—a sheer joy to listen to. She made her debut in David's *The Pearl of Brazil,* scoring instantaneous success.

Her real name was Wixom. She was a native of California and was accompanied everywhere by her father, a kindly and friendly gentleman with a beard. He was always in her dressing room and was, in fact, Nevada's Madame Leroy. I used to sit on his lap (I seem ever to have been sitting on the laps of bearded gentlemen) and he often attempted to speak French to me, of which he knew not a word. His daughter did little better, and on the days she sang she did not speak a word in any language— a habit I found of much help myself, as I believe the speaking voice, which is below the singing one, tires and brings the latter down if used before performing.[25]

Sibyl Sanderson made her debut about the time I left the Opéra-Comique; the number of Americans who attained the highest position there in those days was surprising. Sanderson, like her compatriots, had a beautiful figure. Massenet became infatuated with her and for her wrote his opera *Esclarmonde*, in which I heard her perform. Her voice was very small but she possessed high notes that were true and pure as a flute. Later, when she married a Cuban named Antonio Terry, Massenet was very much stricken.[26]

Antonio Terry was an extraordinary-looking person and immensely rich. He was accompanied everywhere by a charming young girl who was said to be his niece. His fame rested securely on the magnificently matched pair of American trotting horses which he had imported, and on the first American four-wheeled buggy ever seen in France. Terry was tall, very dark, and from a distance most strikingly handsome. But when observed close at hand the picture was less lovely. He had a face to inspire terror. His flashing eyes had a hard, cruel glitter. He was feared rather than admired. All Sanderson's friends begged her not to marry him, but she persisted. Not long after, at the height of her career, she died.

One of Terry's greatest friends was a Spaniard named Mario Costa, composer of the popular "Chanson de Barberine." Mario Costa was supported by Terry, for he never seemed able to make a penny. He composed an opera for me. The music was light but the libretto so poor that it was doomed to failure. I cannot even remember its name.[27]

Life at the Opéra-Comique was strenuous and absorbed all of my time. I sang not only my own announced performances but also had to substitute frequently for indisposed singers. In this way I first sang Lakmé, in place of Van Zandt, with Cobalet and Talazac. Another time,

Mademoiselle Merguillier was scheduled to sing Mignon. The exigencies of the moment were such that I went on as Philine to another Mignon. Mademoiselle Merguillier's costumes, however, caused a good deal of trouble. She was much larger than I and no amount of hasty refitting could prevent my looking rather odd that night. Nevertheless, the audience was particularly kind.

Those costumes had caused trouble previously. In the scene in which Mignon, in a fit of jealousy, pulls the lace off Philine's dress, other singers were in the habit of simulating a little pale jealousy by pulling off a piece of lace lightly basted for the purpose. But when I first sang Mignon, I was carried away by my role, and when it came time to snatch the lace I *did* snatch it off—to Philine's *un*simulated rage. This was my only unpleasantness with Mademoiselle Merguillier.

On the whole, things ran far more smoothly than generally believed of opera houses, where intrigue, backbiting, and jealous rages supposedly exist. Perhaps it was because we were so busy singing that there was little time to indulge in temperament offstage.

Massenet had great charm of manner and was helpful and considerate of those rehearsing his operas, giving many suggestions for interpreting certain passages, and he was generous with praise when anything really fine was accomplished. Léo Delibes, on the other hand, was a bundle of sore nerves when he heard his music performed. He seemed to suffer rather than enjoy our work and was never prodigal of praise. Once, when I was singing in his new *Lakmé*, I heard Arthur Cobalet ask the master what he thought of "la petite Lardinois." Arthur was proud of my success and wanted others to admire me also. Nevertheless, Delibes merely hissed through his teeth, "Oh, she is extraordinaire—extraordinaire," and abruptly walked away.

In my second year at the Opéra-Comique, as my contract promised, my salary was raised. Even this was no great stipend, although it looked bigger and was of some aid in balancing the budget Madame Leroy had painstakingly devised. I was still more or less a prisoner to the opera house, but my interest was in my work. I did, however, go about a little and meet more people, and I continued to work with Madame Marchesi.

After singing at one of Madame Marchesi's musical afternoons, I was presented to one of the great figures of the epoch—Victor Hugo. Upon hearing that I was Belgian, he took me by the hand and said, "You will bring great honor to your country. I have always loved Belgium and the Belgian people." It was in Brussels that Hugo had found asylum in 1851, when, at the coup d'état of Napoleon III, he was forced to flee France because of his republican proclivities. It was said that he made good his escape dressed as a workman and for luggage carried nothing but part of the manuscript of what was to be his immortal book, *Les misérables*. The wonderful old man had ever since cherished an affection for the country in which he had first found refuge. He died in 1885 and I shall never forget the extraordinary solemnity of the public funeral accorded him. The city was draped in black for the man who had wished to be given a pauper's funeral.

5

MADAME LEROY had made a budget, but *hélas*! As is so often the case with budgets, ours frequently left us with a deficit at the end of the month, and we had to have recourse to my dear mother, whom the cares of a household kept at home in Brussels. However, the prince de Chimay frequently paid us a visit. He never failed to call when in Paris and always demanded every detail of my experiences, transmitting them later to the family—and they in turn charged him with a cascade of small bundles and packages for me. We often took long carriage drives, a treat seldom enjoyed except with him. Altogether he made me feel less alienated from home.

One day he asked Madame Leroy if she did not think we should be better off in a small apartment than in a hotel. To my surprise she evidently did not think so, and the reason was that with the cares of a house she would no longer be able to accompany me to daily rehearsals. The prince observed that I knew my way to the theater by this time well enough at least to come and go by day alone, and that an apartment would be better for us in every way—for although the Hôtel de la Michaudière set a good, plain table, still . . .

I was overjoyed at the prospect of a true *chez-moi*, if Madame Leroy was not. She consented to look about, however, and at the prince's suggestion inquired of the concierge of the Opéra-Comique, who usually knew of apartments for rent in the vicinity of the theater. The good soul, who had been a fixture there for years, directed us to a house in the rue Lafitte only five minutes distant. After rehearsal we went to see it, and took it. There were three small rooms comfortably furnished, kitchen and bath, and its nearness to the theater won Madame Leroy. My delight was high on seeing a piano in the little salon which also served as a dining room.

The day of removal to our new nest arrived. That night I sang Mignon. Cobalet, in his role of Lothario, appeared gayer than usual. Madame Leroy had brought me to the theater, but that evening she left me in the hands of the theater dresser to return to the apartment and surprise me later with a good little hot supper. At the hotel I had to be content with a plate of cold meat and salad in our room. I must have surpassed myself that night, for I received more recalls than usual. At last it was over, and I ran toward my dressing room. I had to pass Carvalho's office. He was standing in the doorway and stopped me, saying, "Brava my little Lardinois!" and before I realized it he caught me in his large embrace and kissed me. At this very moment, in turning my head, I saw Cobalet standing at his dressing room door nearby, on the men's corridor. He looked at me so strangely that even now as I write I see that look in his eyes. It expressed more than sorrow. Still, I was happy in my success and above all with the idea that I was about to go to my own little home for the first time. A large and comfortable bed and the thought of being able to talk at the top of my voice (for since everyone was asleep at the hotel on my return from the opera, we had always to whisper) were intoxicating to contemplate.

Madame Leroy came to fetch me, and in my eagerness to see my new home I felt as if I had wings. Home! It was my home, except for my little child's room in Brussels. Now I was no longer a child, and my good friend the prince had said I was old enough to come and go from the theater alone.

In a moment we had climbed the stairs. Madame Leroy opened the door into the little entry and said, "Clara, go to your room but don't look in the salon." Though full of curiosity, I obeyed, and in so doing thought I heard the front door open and words being whispered. Soon Madame Leroy came back and opened my door, which gave onto the salon. To my great surprise I saw a little table with a beautiful bouquet of roses in its center. The table was set with three covers. She made a sign of silence, fingers to lips, said "We have a guest tonight," and laughed. I thought at once that the prince de Chimay had come. I was more amazed than ever when, opening the door, she admitted Monsieur Cobalet. For a moment I was speechless. I looked from one to the other, not knowing what to say. Then it occurred to me that Monsieur Cobalet would tell Madame Leroy that Monsieur Carvalho had given me a kiss. In a flash I clearly beheld her packing her trunk and leaving me forsaken in Paris. But I collected myself and joyously greeted my guest, hoping at the same time that he would forget that little incident at the opera house—and he did. I told him how happy I was to see him, as though we had not been singing duets an hour before.

Madame Leroy then told me she had learned that Monsieur Cobalet lived in the same house and that he had asked permission to send us some roses to welcome us to the house. Madame Leroy had invited him to our little housewarming—and for the first time, I saw Madame Leroy wink.

I was happy now and Cobalet seemed happy too, gayer than I had ever seen him. I was amazed at how good a cook Madame Leroy turned out to be, for she produced my favorite dish, *bouchée à la reine* with truffles. I learned later that she had bought them all prepared at Bouchards, at the corner of the Opéra-Comique, where I often ate ices with Massenet.

That evening marked a banner day in my life. The music and excitement of the performance over, the joy of my new home, the presence of a comrade of the theater under my own roof (he seemed to have forgotten that I had been with him all evening and acted as though it was a rare treat to see me)—everything combined to put me in the gayest of moods. During that simple little midnight supper, Paris was a wonderful place and I the happiest of young girls.

Cobalet and I lived in the same house and sang in the same operas; when not rehearsing at the theater, we practiced our roles together in my little salon; and when Madame Leroy did not come to take me home at night, we walked home together. Cobalet was a handsome young man and very much beloved by everyone for his upright character and amiable manners; his voice was gorgeous, with wonderfully warm timbre, and he deserved all his successes at the Opéra-Comique.

But one day Madame Leroy suddenly announced that I could no longer receive Monsieur Cobalet in our apartment, nor speak to him in the street—that at the theater they were saying we were engaged to be married! Poor Madame Leroy was in a terrible state. She said that it was all her fault, that she should never have received Monsieur Cobalet into the house, and that if my family heard of the affair she would never be forgiven.

"But Madame Leroy," I objected, "there must be two to every engagement, n'est-ce pas? To begin with, poor Tutur [as I called him] has never spoken to me of engagement—and more than that, he has never even kissed me."

She looked at me wide-eyed.

I continued: "To be engaged one must be kissed at least, n'est-ce pas? And if kissing makes an engagement, then it must be that I am engaged to be married to Monsieur Carvalho, Monsieur Massenet, and Monsieur Danbé, the chef d'orchestre."

Madame Leroy really was scandalized. When I had time to think the matter over I realized very well that this rumor must stop. What would the prince de Chimay think? And above all, Father?

Next morning I arose earlier than usual, resolved to see Arthur Cobalet before he left for the theater. Madame Leroy had gone to market, as she did each morning. I left the front door ajar in order to hear Cobalet when he came downstairs. I was very nervous and upset but determined on the course I should pursue. Soon I heard his footsteps, and when he passed my door he paused. I went out to him and began, "You mustn't come by to see us anymore, you mustn't bring me home anymore, you—" And before I could say anything further, I burst into tears.

Gently he urged me back in the apartment and inquired what was the matter, and I told him what they were saying of us in the theater, vainly trying to stifle my sobs. At this moment Madame Leroy returned and sensed the situation.

Poor Arthur! I made him suffer, most involuntarily, for I know now that he loved me sincerely. Unfortunately, or rather fortunately for me, I understood nothing of all the fervent declarations of love listened to nightly in my roles. In that respect I was indeed still a child. Arthur Cobalet had a great and stoical character. He never spoke of his unhappiness, but I know he suffered, for one day Talazac gripped me by the arm and told me that I had no heart, that I was only a coquette. It was difficult to believe that I really was so innocent and inexperienced after such a length of time in the theater.

The season closed, and though the first year I had stayed in Paris to pursue my studies with Madame Marchesi, this year (my second) we gave up the apartment and returned at once to Brussels.

I made Madame Leroy promise she would tell no one at home of this unhappy state of affairs, and the incident seemed closed. Later I learned that Cobalet had written to her in secret, though she never told me.

During my absence at home Talazac secured Cobalet a fine contract which took him to Marseilles, and when I returned to Paris he was no longer a member of the company. I missed his friendship terribly. Madame Leroy came to install me in a little apartment further from the theater, and as the rent was less and my salary more, I now kept a carriage.

At this time I began to be in demand from authors and composers attached to other Paris theaters, and even received flattering offers from theaters in other cities—offers that would have turned the head of a more sedate young person than myself. Before the end of my third year, Carvalho let me out of my contract to accept one of these new engagements.

I would much prefer to forget the subsequent history of Arthur Cobalet. It was with great sorrow that I learned he had undergone serious mental illness. Several years later he recovered and married a relation of his adopted family.

But we were destined to meet again. It was in Bucharest that we finally came face to face. We were both singing in opera but in different theaters. Our meeting was very friendly and I became acquainted with his wife, who, I learned, knew her husband's story. I heard with deep regret of his death not long after.

Production of an *opéra comique* by Léon Vasseur was planned at the Théâtre de la Gaîté. The role of ingenue had been found impossible to fill, as the part required a very young girl who was able to sing a good deal of difficult music. Carvalho lent me to the Gaîté before the expiration of my contract with the Opéra-Comique. This he was gracious enough to do, and he arranged matters so that I was not required to pay the Opéra-Comique what I earned three nights in the week. *Pensionnaires* of the state theaters are regarded as the property of the state, and my services for those three nights of my contract belonged (so to speak) to the government.

I was glad enough to leave the Opéra-Comique. Had I remained there I should never have risen above the position of *pensionnaire*, and though at first this had seemed a most desirable state, I had grown ambitious and felt I could better myself. The story of Cobalet had come to be known, and I was generally blamed by the company for my hard heart.

How unjust this was may be imagined when I say that the plot of the new opera, *Le droit du seigneur* (hinging, of course, around the feudal custom of the rights of seigniory), recounted the story of a young girl who roused the cupidity of an old lord, who commanded the captain of his guard to marry her in order that he himself might enjoy his seigniorial rights over the wife of his vassal—and after singing the role more than one hundred nights (a long run for those days), and though now grown up, I still had no clear understanding of what the rights of seigniory signified! Incredible as it seems, and perfectly impossible today, this serves as a good illustration of how a child could emerge unscathed from three years of work in the Paris theaters.[28]

6

L*e droit du seigneur* was a big change. Singing nightly in a popular hit,
a role which required a great deal of singing, necessitated rearrang-
ing my mode of life and left me less time than ever for outside interests. The increase in my salary was another thing I was unused to. One
paper said that the management of the Gaîté had built a bridge of gold
for me from the Opéra-Comique.

The roles of the seigneur and his wife were played by Monsieur and
Madame Montrouge, the most famous comedians of Paris. Though in
public one was struck by their thoughtful and loving demeanor toward
each other, it was a well-known fact that they were termagants in the pri-
vacy of the home, and their neighbors were often regaled by the battles
and war cries that issued from the Montrouge windows.

The handsome captain of the guard, whom I was supposed to marry,
was Alfred Numese. He too was famous then, particularly in demand at
private soirées for his amusing character monologues interspersed with
songs. Through him I accepted an engagement to be on the program at a
reception at the Spanish embassy. We went to the embassy directly from
the theater, in our costumes, and gave some scenes from the operetta. On
the same program I discovered my friend Marie Van Zandt, though she
had sung before our arrival. I was complimented warmly by her for my
success and the sense I had shown in leaving the Opéra-Comique. I was inexperienced in the ways of the great world and watched her carefully when
she was presented to the ambassador, emulating to the best of my ability
her low curtsy—which, without practice, I just managed to perform.

That evening stands out in my memory because after the performance

I was introduced to a young attaché of the Peruvian legation, Juan de Iturigui. We became fast friends and he attended the theater night after night, sending me flowers and in various ways acting in the approved manner of a rich young man toward an actress. He asked me to marry him but stipulated that I should enter a convent for a year to purify myself, as it were, from the contamination of the stage. He must have thought that I stood in great need of purification, for later he presented me a magnificent little prayer book, bound and illuminated in gold, on the flyleaf of which he wrote, "Before you think of doing an evil, read these pages!" He was an orphan, but his father had owned much land in Peru, and he united the sophistication and fashionable address of a young cosmopolitan to the gloomy and bigoted cast of mind of the Spaniards of medieval days.

He had a friend, a young Spanish composer of genius living in Paris in poverty, whom I knew he aided financially. Iturigui brought him to my little flat near the Porte Maillot, and we often spent long afternoons listening to his strange and beautiful compositions—new, different, and full of the color and magic of Moorish Spain. His name was Enrique Granados.[29] We became very good friends in spite of the fact that he did not speak a word of French nor I of Spanish. Granados told me he had fallen in love with my voice, and he wrote for me a gay bolero which I introduced into a number of my roles. At first this music, so different from anything I had ever heard, puzzled and bewildered me, but Granados taught me the song and the pronunciation of the Spanish words, syllable by syllable, and this song became very popular with my audiences.

I owned the only manuscript of it, and to my great sorrow it was lost in a trunk which disappeared with all my most prized possessions when I was traveling once from San Francisco to New York. That trunk was sought for years but no trace of it was ever found.

Clara Lardinois, from Jules Martin's *Nos Artistes: Portraits et Biographies*, a directory of artists published in Paris in 1895. Courtesy Jim McPherson.

I was in New York when Granados came over to supervise the production of his opera *Goyescas* at the Metropolitan in 1916. I had not seen him for years but failed to get in touch with him before he sailed for Europe. His ship was sunk by a German torpedo.

Iturigui also took me to call on Elena Sanz.

She was living at this time in a sumptuous apartment near the Etoile. She had grown very stout, but her face was still remarkable for its dark Spanish beauty and her eyes were bewitching. It was she who had the courage to sing Carmen in Spain, and likewise to sing Dalila when produced in Rouen in 1890. *Samson et Dalila* had been performed thirteen years before in Weimar under the auspices of Franz Liszt but had never been heard in France.

Sanz was very cordial. Taking me by the arm, she led me into a small salon where two beautiful little boys in sailor suits were playing by the open fire. "These are my princes," she said proudly. I looked up and saw, over the mantle, a large portrait of Alfonso XII of Spain. The two little boys were as like the picture as two drops of water. "You may kiss the lady," their mother said, and the obedient children graciously did so.

This was the beginning of my great friendship with Elena Sanz.

She had been exiled from Spain on the marriage of Alfonso (father of Alfonso XIII) but enjoyed a pension from the Spanish government. In Paris, however, she was treated like a veritable queen at this time, and her salons were frequented by the greatest people of Spain. Yet in spite of this she lived in constant fear that her children would be kidnapped or murdered, and kept her two princes guarded night and day. Her brother lived with her and always stood between her and the world as a bodyguard, even answering the door.

She said she had heard me sing Carmen at the Opéra-Comique and that in her opinion I had done very well—within the dictates of my own temperament. Shortly, she was giving me lessons, teaching me a new interpretation for the Habanera and the traditional dance for the Gypsy Song in the second act. I also learned from her how to play the castanets, a very difficult art and one which took much practice. She gave me her own castanets, the ones used by her as Carmen, and her tambourine, which I still cherish. I became a more provocative Carmen, profiting by her guidance when I later sang the role all over the world.

To me Carmen was never the coarse and vulgar street wench of some interpreters, any more than she was the elegantly dressed grande dame of

Clara Lardinois as Carmen. Photo later signed "Blanche Arral." Photo by
Lafayette, Melbourne. Courtesy William R. Moran.

others. Of Calvé it is superfluous to speak. Carmen was ignorant and superstitious, fickle and fatalistic, falling in love with an officer in his fine uniform or with a glamorous bullfighter—taking life as it came. While she loved she *did* love, and not for gain. And Carmen was brave! "Devant la mort même, je répèterais. . . . Non! je ne t'aime plus" (Even in the face of death, I would repeat it. . . . No! I do not love you anymore). Within her limitations Carmen was not without nobility, and I tried to bring out these characteristics in her and make her the amorous and impetuous Gypsy, ruled by her heart even if that heart was of flint.

I had the great experience of hearing the original Carmen in the role. Célestine Galli-Marié was a powerful actress and her interpretation remains one of the world's greatest. Her voice was short and of no particular beauty, but her manner of using it was invariably fascinating. She dressed the part in the style of the early nineteenth century and did not make the mistake of covering herself with a queen's ransom in jewels and satins. She sang the Habanera very slowly, almost like a menace, and this was in fine contrast to the Séguidilla, which comes not long after and is all that exists of seductive gaiety.

In the fortune-telling scene she was tremendous, clearly carrying the audience along to her own conviction of death. This may have been due to the fact that Galli-Marié herself believed in the cards, or was said to believe in them. One night while singing the Card Song she suddenly read in the cards that Georges Bizet was dead, and refused to finish the performance until a messenger was sent to Bizet's house to see if this was so. It was. At least, that is the story; I suspect that, as in the case of many interesting tales, it is only a legend. However, it illustrates the character of that great artist.[30]

Elena Sanz told me that, in her opinion, one reason *Carmen* did not have much success when first put on was due to the fact that Galli-Marié took all the music much too slowly. I was in the habit of singing the first verse of the Habanera deliberately and then speeding up for the second verse.

Elena also taught me a Spanish song, "El bolero grande," which remained for the rest of my career one of my most popular encores. The way she sang it was a revelation in the art of interpreting that gay Spanish music—her gestures, her use of the tambourine, and her wonderful voice, big, rich, and deep. Luckily I was able to sing it in the original key of D, just as she did, going down to A.[31]

The former queen of Spain, Isabella II, the cause of the Carlist Wars which brought so much suffering to Spain, had been living in exile in Paris, almost exclusively, since her dethronement in 1868. She had a magnificent palace in the avenue Clabber which she named Palais de Castille and in which she set up a miniature court.

Her character was well known in Paris. She was democratic, friendly, and in her youth a great lover of dancing (she had been called "the queen who danced away her throne"). Whatever her political and private shortcomings, the Spaniards always condoned them, saying proudly, "She is my *española*!"[32] She liked to be surrounded by good-looking young men, was very catholic in her choice of friends, and was said to be generous beyond reason, with no conception of the value of money. When her pension was in arrears, her majordomo was instructed to take her family portraits off the walls and pawn them in order to keep up her lavish style of living and her various charities. Indigent artists, writers, and musicians of all nationalities profited by her bounty. She was said to have a hundred wigs, and she wore so many jewels that one priceless piece was half concealed beneath another.

I was taken to a reception in the Palais de Castille by Iturigui and Elena Sanz. As we went through the anterooms, encountering a stream of people coming and going, I wondered what sort of reception I was about to witness. Her Majesty was seated at the end of a long room, surrounded by groups consisting mostly of young men, and we all went up and kissed her hand as she chattered on, always in French, with here and there a Spanish word interpolated. She addressed her remarks to everyone at once and I was not surprised to notice that Iturigui seemed very much at home.

"Ah, Iturigui," she said, "this is the young lady you speak so much about. And all you say of her is true." She told me she had heard me sing at the Opéra-Comique.

Queen Isabella was very broad in her views, and she looked upon Elena Sanz as her daughter-in-law. I believe she found her son's wife, Maria Cristina of Austria, straitlaced, and the two royal ladies did not get on well, which may account for her kindly feelings toward Elena Sanz, so much closer to her in temperament. She often had her two little grand-sons about her.

After this reception, on various occasions we three used to call on Her Majesty in private. With only one or two ladies-in-waiting in attendance, tea was served and I sang to Elena's accompaniments. The queen liked best the popular airs of the day, songs from the various operettas I had appeared in.

"Very good . . . that is very good . . . here, Iturigui, give the young lady that bunch of flowers over there on the table. And here is a box of chocolates that Marquise de ——— brought me yesterday. Give her those. Young people like chocolates. Now sing the Bolero from *Le coeur et la main.*" Isabella was a personality, and I considered her a royal old lady even if she had been so poor a queen that the Spaniards were forced to ask her to leave.

Her death in 1904 was hastened by an action which I think characteristic. She had received a call from former empress Eugènie, who, of course, was a Spaniard, and who before her marriage had been a lady-in-waiting at Isabella's court. As the empress took her leave, Isabella stood some time in the draught of a doorway to see her out. When one of her attendants remonstrated with her for this needless exposure, she answered, "If you had the misfortune to lose a crown, you would not talk, good soul that you are, like that. Discrowned monarchs are sensitive to a want of attention. If I had omitted any ceremony, the empress might have thought that I considered her a former subject. It is bad enough to fall from a throne which one has achieved, and such a throne as hers was too. Poor soul!"

Elena Sanz was forced to move from her large apartment into an obscure little house in the Bois de Boulogne. Returning to Paris after an absence of years, I called upon her there. Events had occurred in Spain: Alfonso XII was dead, Elena's pension had stopped, and she was living in poverty.

As I looked about the bare little room and realized what had happened to this great artist, once the mistress of a king and the sought-after friend of the great, my heart contracted. Elena made an effort to smile but a moment later was crying in my arms. She gave me one of her magnificent Spanish shawls, originally a gift from Queen Isabella, as a further testimony to our friendship.

The life of Elena Sanz would make an interesting book for she had many vicissitudes. She was an orphan and was educated in a convent in Madrid, the Colegio de las Niñas de Leganes, which was founded exclusively for the education of exceptionally beautiful girls, the worthy nuns reasoning that these girls were particularly in danger from the wickedness of the world. Elena's rich contralto voice attracted attention, and people often attended the services in the convent chapel to hear her sing. Her teacher was one Don Baltasar Saldoni, and his fame grew with that of his pupil. To the aristocratic salons of Madrid, Elena was often invited to sing while still a little girl. Finally her fame reached the ears of the queen, who expressed a wish to meet the prodigy and hear her herself. Isabella was much interested in singing. The queen was so pleased by the diminutive contralto that she paid for her musical education, even sending her to Italy.

Elena was in Paris at the time of the Commune (1870) and the fall of the Second Empire, and she devoted herself to the care of the wounded so assiduously that she was afterward honored by the municipality of Paris for her work. The following year she was in Paris again, on her way to Vienna to fulfill a contract. Isabella, who was now living in Paris, received her at her palace, where she became the spoiled darling of all the people who crowded to partake of the generous queen's bounty. Elena sang at the receptions. One day among the guests was the celebrated soprano Anna de La Grange, once so popular in America, and she encouraged Elena to work hard for the great career that lay ahead of her. When Elena left for Vienna, Queen Isabella made her promise to call upon her son, the prince of Asturias, who was being educated at the Theresine College there, and entrusted her with all sorts of messages for him. Elena was some five years older than the young prince. What the authorities thought of the beautiful young lady, actually sent to call upon their youthful charge by his exiled royal mother in Paris, one can but wonder!

Elena came to America and appeared at the Academy of Music in the days of Pauline Lucca and Clara Louise Kellogg, singing all the great contralto parts. And not long after, when the House of Bourbon was restored to the throne of Spain in the person of the young prince, Elena made her debut in Madrid (in 1877) in *La favorita* with the great Spanish tenor Julian Gayarre. She was only twenty-five. La Favorita remained her role not only on the stage, but off it.

Alfonso had married a young cousin who died within a few months, sincerely mourned by all, and it was Elena Sanz alone who could comfort him. When Alfonso broke his arm, his chamberlain begged Elena to use her power with the king so that Alfonso would consent to keep on the splint; she was an influence for the good. Queen Isabella called her "my daughter-in-law before God," wrote her affectionate letters, and sent her presents. When Elena's first son was born, Isabella rejoiced as over the birth of a grandson.

Samson et Dalila created such a stir in Rouen in 1890 that the management brought it to Paris, where it was performed at the Théâtre d'Éden, a small theater in the boulevards. All Paris hurried there to hear the new work, and naturally everyone was amazed at the failure of l'Opéra to secure so unusual a score. When they did secure it, they brought it out with Blanche Deschamps-Jehin as Dalila. She is usually credited with having created the role, but Elena Sanz deserves that distinction, the lady who sang the German version at Weimar in 1877 hardly counting.[33] And Elena Sanz was the first to give utterance to the now too familiar words:

> Mon coeur s'ouvre à ta voix
> Comme s'ouvrent les fleurs
> Aux baisers de l'aurore!
>
> (My heart opens to your voice
> Like the flowers open
> To the kisses of dawn!)

Deschamps-Jehin, a prima donna contralto of l'Opéra, started her career in an unusual manner. First she was a dancer attached to La Monnaie in Brussels. She had a cast in one eye which gave her a curious, even interesting, appearance. One night consternation reigned behind the scenes at La Monnaie, for the contralto of the evening was ill and there was no one to take her place. Mademoiselle Deschamps-Jehin solved the problem. "That's nothing," she said. "I shall sing the role."

Nobody knew she had a voice or could sing a note, but she saved the performance and was so brilliant a success that her dancing days were over. She married one of the conductors and later joined the Paris Opéra. When she achieved the role of Dalila it was the triumph of a career that had an impromptu beginning. As the Paris Opéra is the house most closely associated with Camille Saint-Saëns's biblical opera, it is interesting to realize that the first of all the Dalilas there was a little dancer from Brussels.[34]

For a while Madame Leroy and I inhabited a small apartment in the avenue de la Grande Armée, far out near the Porte Maillot and just over a popular restaurant run by two brothers, Chez François. Here I received my few friends, Granados, Iturigui, and Iturigui's old foster mother, Asunción, a dreary lady well filling the role of duenna. I learned not to appear to find Asunción a curious name, for Iturigui was very sensitive on this subject, and I was told that in Spain this was a popular name for girls, like Dolores, Carmen, or Pilar. I was busy appearing in *Le droit du seigneur* but was most anxious to move, for though I enjoyed the cuisine of the François brothers (who well deserved their renown), the persistent whiffs of the good things being prepared below, night and day, pleased me less. We were driven to every expedient to disguise those celebrated dishes, even burning incense of various odors, though at times the perfumes from the kitchens underneath blended with our incense disastrously. In short, life above Chez François became insupportable.

At last I made arrangements with the concierge of an apartment house in the Champs Elysées to rent me a room. The top floor of the building was given over to rooms for the domestics who worked in the apartments below, and one such room was vacant. I seized upon this and moved in as soon as possible. I had long wanted to live near the Bois de Boulogne, but apartments here were excessively expensive and I had had enough of boarding houses. Now I was able to take Toto walking every day among the trees.

It was about this time that Léon Couturat engaged me to sing one evening at the silk merchant's club. Monsieur Couturat was one of the richest silk merchants in France, a man in his forties possessing great savoir-faire and with very cordial manners; I was glad to go to his office in the rue de Rivoli to arrange the program, the date, and my fee.

I kept the appointment promptly, but Madame Leroy and I had difficulty in convincing Monsieur Couturat that I, with my hair down my back, *canotier*, and cape, was the same Clara Lardinois he had seen in the operetta. When I laughed at this, however, he declared he needed no further proof: he said no one could counterfeit that laugh. After this there was no further confusion and we made all arrangements for my appearance, a month off. In the meantime I moved into my little attic room.

Madame Leroy thoroughly disapproved of my unconventional choice of lodgings, but I was determined to be near the Bois at last. She was not well at this time, and realizing that there was no necessity for her to stay close to me, begged me to let her go to her home in Mons for a rest and vacation.

Before she left she installed me in my new home. She made blue and white curtains for my windows (which overlooked the courtyard of the house), hired a carpenter to make me a bed narrow enough to fit into a small alcove, secured me a small upright piano, which was carried upstairs with enormous difficulty, and, I found, even made arrangements with the maid who occupied the room next to mine to take care of me. This maid, Melanie by name, and her husband, Alexis, were Belgians like myself. They became devoted to me and I to them, and when I left my attic they followed me and became my servants in my new home.

On the day I moved, Madame Leroy left for Belgium, promising to return when she felt able and to not let my family know that I was alone in Paris. It would have upset my mother, who was forced to remain with my father, as his health was failing rapidly. I never knew whether Madame Leroy was more fond of me or of Toto, but now, embracing us both, she charged Toto to watch over me and see that I was a *bonne fille*; and with many tears and promises on both sides, I saw her off at the Gare du Nord.

My new home delighted me, though I had to explain to Iturigui that the rules of the house forbade visitors. He took comfort in the thought that if he could not call upon me neither could anyone else; but he often accompanied me on my walks with Toto in the Bois, to the Pavillon Chinois for a cup of tea.

When people did try to call at my address I was always out, and so the fiction that I lived in a sumptuous apartment was maintained. The concierge put himself under all the oaths of heaven not to divulge my secret. I used to receive a great many flowers; and when the concierge had carried up to me all my room would hold, he arranged the rest around the courtyard, to the mystification of the other tenants. I doubt if they ever connected those flowers with the soprano they heard singing in the attic, who they inquired about to no avail.

After the theater, if I were accompanied home, my companion was obliged to leave me at my door. Taking the lamp left for me at the foot of the stairs, I then climbed four or five flights to my solitary aerie. At first I did not enjoy this climb, for on the service stairs I encountered pails of garbage left at the back doors of the apartments and, not infrequently, mice, rats, and other midnight visitors who scurried away at my approach. But I grew accustomed to vanishing rats and came to regard them as friends rather than enemies. We all lived up the service stairs.

I sang in due course for the silk merchants, and Monsieur Couturat invited me to stay for supper. However, I could not accept his invitation. I was forced to go to bed to be prepared for the work of the next day and, like Cinderella, had to leave just when the fun began. He offered to take me home and hailed his carriage. Leaving me at my door, he murmured something about my fee, which he said he would deliver within a few days.

He called and he called, but of course Mademoiselle Lardinois never seemed to be at home. Finally he sensed a situation. One afternoon, while I was practicing, there came a knock on my door. Thinking it the concierge with my mail, I opened quickly and saw Monsieur Couturat. I burst into tears.

"My dear child!" he said.

In obedience to his counsels, I finally left my secret room and took a little chalet, which I could afford, at St. James in the Bois. All inflamed with good intentions, he and his wife, whom I grew to know and look upon as the kindest of friends, represented to me the dreadful consequences of my abode becoming known. The newspapers, the talk, the jokes. I could not afford to indulge this whim.

Nevertheless, I felt rather bitter about the gold louis which had evidently extracted my secret from the concierge.

On my last visit to Paris I made a little pilgrimage, revisiting these scenes of my youth, and fared no better than others who do likewise. The *pavillons* in the Bois de Boulogne, which had been the rendezvous of the *jeunesse d'orée*, where Iturigui and I had so often gone together, were sadly different. The beautiful horses and carriages driving by were no more, and gone too was the lighthearted feeling of those times, the gaiety of the young people who met there to walk among the trees or drink a cup of chocolate. The strollers now stared coldly at each other or bowed with ceremonious indifference. I was ill at ease and cold at heart. My pilgrimage had turned out a *chemin de la croix*. I walked through the Bois toward the Arc de Triomphe and there saw a cluster of chairs. My heart brightened. Still, as in my day, there was a concession here to a company who rented its chairs for five sous the hour—La Potinière—where all the old wives of the neighborhood gathered in the sun to gossip and criticize the passersby. Just as in other days, those shrill and gossiping voices fell on my ear. I was glad La Potinière still flourished!

⊷⇒ 7 ⇐⊷

For about six years I appeared continually in light operas in Paris. I had more engagements than could be filled and, among other pieces, played in *Mam'zelle Nitouche, Giroflé-Girofla, Les cloches de Corneville, Le coeur et la main,* and *The Beggar Student.* But this was an unhappy time, for word came from home that Father's illness was becoming worse. I had not seen him since I first sang at the Opéra-Comique. My visits home were always arranged to take place when he was absent. Nevertheless, I think he had begun to relent toward me, for I sent him a King Charles spaniel and a pair of rare American cardinal birds, and to these he grew very attached.

Finally, I received a telegram from Jeanne saying that he was rapidly failing, and I determined to see him. I had great difficulty in getting leave of absence from the management, but after threatening to leave for Brussels without it, if necessary, I was finally permitted to go on Saturday and to return for the Sunday evening performance.

Father consented to see me, forgave me, and bestowed his blessing. Feeling that I had done nothing that required forgiveness, it made me happy nevertheless to see that he had relaxed his severity, though he looked very weak. He lay for hours watching the birds in their cage at the foot of his bed.

The doctors assured me there was no immediate danger but promised to telegraph if a change for the worse took place. I returned to Paris on Sunday. With what feelings I played that night! I appeared again Monday and Tuesday, and after this last performance I was given a telegram which had arrived early in the day: Father had died that morning.

My grief and the nervous strain resulted in a collapse which kept me in bed for two weeks. Jeanne came to care for me, and when I was able I resumed my engagements at the various theaters.

In the summer of 1885 I visited my sister Angèle in Antwerp, partly to see my mother, who was staying with her at the time. This was the year of the first International Exposition at Antwerp, and the city was crowded with visitors from all over the world. The first night, as we went into the drawing room after dinner, Angèle, who had seemed strangely excited during the meal, could finally contain herself no longer. "Clara," she cried, "I have wonderful news to tell you! You know I followed your advice and have been practicing—and in two days I am going to play at the concert in the great hall of the Exposition!" Angèle owned a magnificent piano which she had won as first prize at the Exposition, a Belgian piano of the house of Or. Not only did this piano possess a superb tone and movement, but the rosewood marketry case was magnificent enough for a museum. The great Franz Liszt, who was visiting the Exposition, chose this piano for the concert he intended to give for the benefit of the poor of Antwerp. Angèle was presented to him, and after hearing her play he invited her to perform his *Rapsodie* with him at the concert. This was the greatest honor of Angèle's life—and a great day for her piano too, as Liszt autographed it.

That same evening it became known that I was in Antwerp, and my brother Charles, likewise at my sister's home, met the reporters that came to the house and told them I was too tired to see anyone that night. But he could not thus send away the president of the fêtes, who arrived at about ten o'clock to call upon both Angèle and me. Having made the last arrangements with Angèle for her appearance, he turned and said that it must have been God Himself who had brought me to the city, and added, "You cannot refuse to give your services at the Great Charity Concert the day after tomorrow!"

It did not take long for me to consent.

"Tomorrow morning," he said, "we shall put streamers over the posters: 'Clara Lardinois will sing.'" The concert was to take place in the evening; Liszt was playing in the afternoon. I was overjoyed at being included in that concert, for the other artists were all of tremendous reputation: Eugène Ysaÿe, with whom I was again to be associated; Joseph

Hollmann, the Dutch cellist; Monsieur Pancelet, the flutist; Pol Plançon, the great French bass; La Legia, the choral society with whom I had made my debut so unexpectedly at the age of ten; and for a crowning sensation, Loïe Fuller in her famous skirt dance, "La Serpentine." I had never had the opportunity to see her in Paris and was delighted at the chance now, though Fuller herself was less pleased when she observed the added attraction of Clara Lardinois. She did not withdraw, however, for Leopold II of Belgium was announced to attend the concert and it was not every day that one had the distinction of performing before a king. I had already enjoyed the honor of singing in Brussels in the presence of my sovereign.

Loïe Fuller was American. Her celebrated dance depended in reality upon a trick of lighting which played upon the long white silk folds of her skirt. By means of sticks held in her hands and attached to her garments, she was able to make the skirt, which was very full, rise and flutter in the air like a butterfly's wings. Hers was not a true dance but rather a display of rhythmic motions of the arms. Lights of every rainbow color played over her. The stage was left completely dark and the projectors, hidden in the wings, were managed by her brother. Her act always came at the end of the program, and no one else was allowed on the stage before, during, or after it. Immediately after her act she entered her carriage, heavily veiled, and drove away. This was useful in preventing anyone's making too close an inspection of the system of lights, which were worked by a secret method known only to her own entourage. This entourage consisted of four people. Besides her brother, there was a tall Englishman whom she called her fiancé, and two maids. No one ever saw her clearly. Even on the stage one caught only a glimpse of her figure, and it was impossible to see whether she was pretty or even very young. For many years, however, she enjoyed a great international reputation.

My appearance having been announced, a number of flowers were sent to me from Brussels as well as Antwerp. A large star of red roses was sent by a friend of my brothers, Ali Raiff Bey, military attaché to the Turkish embassy in Brussels. A card with my name was attached to the piece of ribbon, as is usually done; and after my first appearance on the program, when I had sung the air from *The Pearl of Brazil*, the flowers were presented. My next appearance was with Pol Plançon, at this time a member of the Paris Opéra. We sang the Love Duet from *Hamlet,* which Plançon had come to the house to rehearse, having no time to prepare anything less familiar. Then I returned to sing the waltz from *Roméo et Juliette* as an encore, but being unable to carry all the flowers, I was obliged to leave a great many of them on the stage. A number of my bouquets had disappeared, and at the end of Loïe Fuller's dance, Ali Bey, who could not understand why his star of roses had not been presented to me, was surprised to see it being handed to Fuller; and a number of my other bouquets had taken the same road.

I never saw Loïe Fuller again, though I know she continued her Serpentine for a number of years; but it was not the last time I heard of her.

I was walking along Broadway some thirty years later, and at Forty-eighth Street, on a corner, a small specialty shop with some very pretty French novelties attracted my attention. I entered and bought a hat—or was it two hats? At any rate, a charming woman waited upon me, having offered her services in excellent French (no one has ever taken me for an American, even before I have spoken). I returned to the shop a number of times, and each time the same agreeable woman served me.

One day she asked if I had ever known Loïe Fuller. I replied that indeed I had, and looked at her attentively. She burst out laughing and said, "I am she."

"No," I replied stoutly, "she was smaller than you, and you are pretty. She was not."

She laughed again and said, "Well, at any rate, I am her double."

She was, it appeared, Loïe Fuller's sister, and her story was most entertaining. She and her husband were in financial straits, and Loïe hit upon the plan of teaching her the Serpentine so that when she herself was ill, or for any other reason did not want to fill an engagement, she could send her sister on the road, hither and yon, to take her place. She then divided the large earnings. But at last the manager of a small provincial theater discovered the deceit, and Loïe Fuller's sister had to flee in her costume from the rage of the townspeople. The little arrangement came to an end, and after some vicissitudes the "double" settled in New York and opened a shop.

I inquired about the real Loïe Fuller and learned that, having many imitators, and with the public growing weary of her Serpentine, she finally gave it up and was for a time in poor circumstances. Later I heard she was a confidante of the late Queen Marie of Romania. As for her sister, her business failed; she promised to write me her new address, but I never heard from her again. Sometime later I heard that Loïe Fuller was dead. Though her Serpentine was seen everywhere, including the United States, I cannot say whether it was danced by Loïe or her sister.[35]

And here I feel that I must add mine to the tributes of everyone who ever heard or sang with Pol Plançon. "Le beau Plançon" he was called—and both physically and vocally he deserved the epithet. His voice was equal throughout its range, an incredibly rich, musical bass-baritone of exquisite timbre. His vocalization had great finish and style, and he could sing coloratura to the envy of any soprano.

But to return to the concert.

Leopold II and his court occupied a special box, and to honor the king a number of Congolians took part in the program. It was at this Exposition that natives from the Congo were first seen in Europe, and here they performed on native instruments. It had been very difficult to encourage Belgians to go to the Congo because of the lack of comforts and the terrible climate, and the Belgian government was offering prizes and trying in every way to stir up interest. After the natives had performed they took seats at the back of the stage; but they were removed before Loïe Fuller's dance, and the king himself did not stay to see it, departing after Plançon and I, with La Legia, had sung "La Brabançonne."

I must not neglect Liszt's concert. It is impossible to describe the great beauty of his playing; he made the piano sing. And it was true joy to see Angèle, for she was inspired by Liszt's presence. Seated beside the great master, it was as though a beatitude had descended upon her. Her playing was magnificent. It was a great day for the Lardinois family. Liszt himself was so pleased with Angèle that he invited her to give a concert in Budapest, where he was head of the conservatory. However, he grew ill soon after this and the project was abandoned. The next year he went to Bayreuth to visit his daughter, Cosima Wagner—but the heartrending story of that visit, and his lonely death there, has been told.

⊷⟿⊙⟾⊶

For the most part my relations with my colleagues were pleasant, but it was during the run of Audran's *Le puits qui parle* (The Talking Well) that the little affair of the flags occurred and convulsed the company.[36]

In this operetta Mademoiselle Debriège assumed the role of Truth, appearing out of the well, clad in tights (for this was in the eighties). It proved to be one of the high spots of the performance. We had little in common, and she took a great dislike to me. I learned that it was because her cavalier had ungallantly praised the charms of the prima donna. (I had never met her refractory admirer.) She sought every opportunity to pick a quarrel, but I was wary and eluded all pitfalls. Unfortunately, Mademoiselle Debriège at this time was not very popular with her fellow actors. One night, on mounting the stairs to her dressing room after her big scene, her associates laughed. She angrily demanded the reason and then discovered a small French flag pinned onto each of her calves—such toy flags as are worn in the lapel during patriotic functions. Though she represented Truth it was clear that Nature had nothing to do with the contour of those magnificent calves. Nobody knew whether she had appeared on the stage thus adorned or whether the flags had been affixed afterward; but she decided that I was the instigator of the indignity and determined to have her revenge.

One night as we were all snatching a final look at ourselves in the wide mirror in the actor's foyer, Mademoiselle Debriège looked over her shoulder at me and said with a sneer, "After all, when one has a figure like mine, one need not fear comparisons."

The devil was in me, I am afraid.

As I continued to adjust my wig, I said, "That depends—there are some who prefer quality to quantity." With a leap she had me in her clutches; I had to be rescued by those who stood near. After that she was removed by the management and I felt genuinely sorry for my little answer. It was not often that I could be goaded into retaliating, as I felt that a calm disregard of an opportunity for battle usually proved a more effective armor. Mademoiselle Debriège was finally taken back into the company and given her part. There was no more trouble between us.

I think it was in this production that Cécile Sorel and Yvette Guilbert appeared in the chorus, both of whom later achieved fame. Cécile Sorel's long career at the Comédie Française is a matter of theatrical history, and Yvette Guilbert has long been famous for what she was: the greatest *diseuse* France ever produced. In those days she was incredibly thin. Later, while I was appearing in another production, she called on me in my dressing room and told me that she had been studying hard and was soon to make her debut in a concert, and she assured me that I would hear from her again. Indeed, I soon did, for she quickly rose to fame. In her own genre there was never anyone like her.

When I recall that I sang a three-act role night after night, I often wonder what the delicate songbirds of today would do, who consider it a hardship to sing twice a week. Not content with the music set down for me, it became my invariable habit to introduce one or two operatic airs into the performance to lend a little more importance to my role. One night it was the Jewel Song from *Faust* and the Polonaise from *Mignon*; another, the Bell Song from *Lakmé* and the Mad Scene from *Hamlet*. And my selections for that evening were printed in the daily papers with the announcement of the performance. For this reason, when I appeared in other cities my engagement came at the end of the season, before the theaters were closed for the summer, for other operetta singers refused to appear after me. In Marseilles I sang Irma in *Le grand mogol,* one of my most popular roles, and here experienced the excitement of being pulled home in my carriage by enthusiastic students. This custom has gone out with the horse, unfortunately, for it was a colorful and gay one—and splendid advertisement for the driver!

In my little chalet at St. James, I began to entertain a growing list of friends. Alexis and Melanie took good care of me and my increasing family of dogs. Besides Toto, I now had several others which caused me much trouble, more than a whole orphanage of children could have done. Toto bore as best he could the advent of two black French poodles, but when I came home one day with a large white one, the poor little creature gave it one baleful look and was taken with a fit. The veterinary said this was brought on by jealousy, and Toto succumbed. The white poodle brought more trouble. The number of unpleasant things he could do was legion, and when he was given away, I regret to say he bit his new owner's leg.

One of his occupations was to climb over the wall in order to eat chickens belonging to my neighbors, Countess de Dion and her son. Finally, old Madame de Dion sent word that the next offense would cost my poodle his life. I could not blame her.

I did not know the Dions but was often mystified by the curious noises that came from their garden. I finally learned the cause of those strange sounds when the count appeared one day, leading my pony who had escaped through the gate. He was working on a curious contraption called a "horseless carriage." He took me for a ride in it around his garden. To the accompaniment of the *put-put-put*, like a small motorboat, we jiggled up one path and slowly down the next. I was very polite but happy enough to descend to earth. Undismayed by difficulties, the count continued his experiments, and that outlandish vehicle developed into the De Dion-Bouton, the first automobile to be manufactured in France.

I moved once more, to an apartment in the boulevard Haussmann, less inconveniently remote from the theaters. It was here, in 1889, that I witnessed from my windows the riots which took place outside the bank when the Panama Canal Company, organized by Ferdinand de Lesseps, was liquidated by the Tribunal Civil de la Seine after the scandalous corruption and extravagance which had exhausted its assets in Panama. The money for the company had been raised by the sale of stocks, mostly to the poor classes of France, and even by lotteries organized by the French government. Those who had lost all their savings rioted all night, completely disrupting that section of the city. The sight of those poor frantic women, hatless and hysterical, crying out for their property and for justice, of the men battering against the doors of the bank, of the mounted police riding into the crowd, impressed me profoundly—another chapter of horrors in the strange international history of the Panama Canal.

About this time an immense skating rink in the rue Blanche was remodeled into a theater to be called Le Casino—now known to every visitor to Paris as the Casino de Paris. For the opening production it was decided to put on the most spectacular musical production ever seen in Paris; it was backed by Vickers Brothers, the London bankers. The name chosen was a good one, merely *Cocher, au Casino!* There was a ballet as big as that at the Opéra, a huge orchestra, a band on the stage, horses, and three stars. The stars were Madame Montbazon, who created Audran's *La mascotte*, Mademoiselle Méaly, celebrated for her beauty, and myself. Each of us had been promised headline billing and had signed our contracts ignorant of the other two, and the management finally solved the problem by constructing a large horseshoe with our names in a circle.

Original advertisement for Hervé's *Cocher, au Casino!*, in which Clara Lardinois costarred. À l'Imagerie, Paris.

When this was put up it was discovered that my name occupied the top of the horseshoe, while my colleagues decorated either end. Nobody was satisfied, but it was the best that could be done.[37]

In *Cocher, au Casino!* I enjoyed perhaps the most sensational entrance ever accorded an actress. I descended onto the stage in a large balloon, floating down to the strains of an operatic medley, into the middle of the crowd, for I was the representative of the Opéra-Comique. Stepping out of the gondola of the balloon in dazzling raiment, I burst into song, and my song was an extraordinary potpourri to say the least: it began with the Polonaise from *Mignon* and ended with the waltz from *Roméo et Juliette*! *Cocher, au Casino!* was on a grandiose scale. One night the ropes broke and I descended into the crowd too precipitately for comfort, but no damage was done and the performance continued.

While playing in Brussels in 1891 an old Paris friend of mine, the comte de Chambrun, called at my dressing room one evening and asked me as a special favor to sup with him at a friend's house that night. I could not refuse such a request, particularly as I felt it my duty and pleasure to extend hospitality to French friends in Belgium as they had entertained me in France. As we drove through the dark streets I wondered who my hosts were to be, but this I could not learn at first. The comte de Chambrun seemed reluctant to tell me: "When we arrive at the house, say nothing, but follow me. We are going to cheer two lonely people, one of whom is very ill." Strange and mysterious hosts indeed, but before reaching the house, a palatial one in a quiet section of the city, I learned that they were General Georges Ernest Boulanger and Madame Marguerite de Bonnemain.

I had never paid much attention to politics in my busy life, but who that witnessed them could forget the manifestations in Paris in 1889 when General Boulanger had won the elections by an overwhelming majority and had nearly succeeded in overthrowing the Third Republic to set up a dictatorship, a monarchy, an empire—anything he had desired? The crowds were frantic, flooding the streets in the drizzly January weather. It was said that Sadi Carnot, president of the Republic, was ready to flee the country. But General Boulanger lingered instead of riding to the Elysée Palace in triumph. A day or two later he was a political refugee in Belgium.

Madame de Bonnemain was the cause of his overthrow. Her power over him was absolute, and for her he had given up everything. As our carriage stopped we were surrounded by the secret police, but after a word from the comte de Chambrun, we were respectfully admitted into the house. All was quiet. On a couch in the salon lay Madame de Bonnemain, pale and glassy-eyed. Consumption was to claim her very soon. For a while she and the general had lived in style in London but were again in Brussels, seeking medical aid for her. Boulanger, a tall man with mustachios and goatee, had a high forehead and a flat head. His manners were flowery and he appeared to be more of an actor than a politician. His adoration for Madame de Bonnemain seemed the finest trait in his character.

We supped *à quatre* and I did my best to bring a little brightness into the unusual occasion. This man would have ruled France but for the beautiful woman opposite him, who wanted him for herself alone. Her egotism saved France as surely as did Jeanne d'Arc's heroism. She died soon after, and ten weeks later Boulanger drove to the cemetery at Ixelles, apparently in the highest and gayest of spirits, stood over her grave, and shot himself in the temple. On his tombstone he ordered carved, "How could I live two months and a half without you?" His great enemy, Georges Clemenceau, was said to have commented, with much irony, on being told the news, "He died as he lived, like a second lieutenant."

But truly General Boulanger was a romantic episode in the history of France that began like a great new epoch and then fizzled into nothing. All for love of a woman, people said at the time, though that was not the entire truth. Boulanger was not the stuff of which great men are made. Fate played into his hands, but that capricious lady woke up in time to knock the cards to the floor.[38]

8

IT WAS DURING the run of *The Beggar Student* that Raoul Gunsbourg first approached me with an offer to go to St. Petersburg for the summer to sing at the Arcadia, where he was directing a French company. He returned to my apartment many times to renew his offer and his arguments. Certainly I did not want to go: there were too many difficulties. Though advice was asked of the Xaus and the Couturats—in fact, of all my friends, whomever I turned to for strength to refuse—I was met with further arguments and encouraged to accept the offer.

Then I looked for my own excuses. My costumes belonged to the theaters in which I sang, and I refused to wear hired ones. Gunsbourg promised to supply a new wardrobe. Having no companion, such a long trip was out of the question. Gunsbourg urged me to write my family and ask one of my sisters to accompany me; he offered to pay two return fares to Petersburg. But I still lacked a maid and dresser. He undertook to supply one in Russia. I could think of no further excuses.

My sister Sidonie agreed to accompany me. I had always been more afraid of her husband, my godfather, than of my own father, but after sternly extracting from me a promise that I would do nothing to bring disgrace on the family, he consented to give me Sidonie for the summer. I fear most of my family still entertained misgivings about having a professional singer for a relation. I gave my solemn promise to be the soul of circumspection, and we left for Petersburg on the Orient Express.

How long that journey took I do not remember. Except for the voyage to New York, Sidonie had traveled little and was as excited as myself. As we traversed Germany and Poland, our uneasiness about Russia increased. Tales of that fabulous land were not all reassuring; reports of the severity of immigration authorities alarmed us as we approached the frontier. But we passed customs without undue difficulty, and in the afternoon we suddenly glimpsed the Admiralty spire. After passing some neat little villages, the train rolled into the station of St. Petersburg. I was chilled by the dreary sight of the station and the first unprepossessing view I caught of the great city. Everywhere, soldiers—soldiers and the ubiquitous *moujiks*, sad-eyed and silent.

We descended from the train and there, in the large crowd, caught sight of Gunsbourg hurrying toward us, all smiles and carrying large bunches of roses. One had an impression of a great many people, all chattering loudly in French, the men in silk hats and many of them likewise carrying flowers. We were surrounded and, before realizing it, shaking hands and being introduced to everyone in sight. The truth at last dawned upon me: Gunsbourg had corralled over a hundred people, as many as he could collect, and here they were at the station, advertising his new theatrical venture and his imported star.

As we drove off in a legion of victorias, my wonderment grew. Wherever I turned for a glimpse of the new city, I encountered pictures of myself, five feet high, placarded in every imaginable place—pictures of myself in *Le grand mogol*, in which I learned we were to open. Pictures with snakes twined around my neck!

This made me realize that Gunsbourg was an impresario par excellence. When it came to drawing attention to his projects, he had few equals. Incidentally, those pictures were the cause of our first little quarrel. It was gratifying to find oneself peopling a city but horrifying to be represented enveloped in snakes. I declared that my appearance was that of a circus performer.

"Ah, but that is what the people want!" Gunsbourg said. "Sensations, extravagance—you will make an immense impression!"

Those snakes caused me a good deal of amusement. Constructed of pieces of wood in hinged sections, and covered with cloth, they were painted so cleverly that both the color and the shiny look of a snake's skin were perfectly reproduced. Even their heavy weight was about that of a real snake of corresponding size, so that when I picked one out of its basket and twined it about my neck and arms, walking about and charming my pet to the strains of the "Valse des serpents," it acted in the slow, heavy manner of a real snake. In preparing to sing *Le grand mogol* in Paris, I went to the Jardin d'Acclimatation to study the movements of snakes. After some practice I found a way to make my false snake move, by a vibration of the wrist, unperceived by the audience, causing its body to undulate. Dr. Ditmars would have pronounced my serpent counterfeit at a glance, but the audience gasped and many asked how I dared pick up a live serpent and sing to it so lovingly.[39]

We drove directly from the station to the restaurant of Monsieur Cubat, where Gunsbourg had arranged a reception to which were invited newspapermen, critics, theatrical personages, and various members of the French colony. Cubat, a Frenchman, was the proprietor of the most exclusive establishment in Petersburg. His private rooms concealed orchestras, champagne, and caviar which were enjoyed by the most important people in the land. Bills were presented annually to his aristocratic patrons. The amounts of the bills were always paid immediately, until one day the secretary of one of Cubat's debtors (doubtless a prince or duke who had to make a more careful reckoning of his bills than most of his companions), examining the bill closely, found that Cubat's bookkeeper had added the figures designating day, month, and year to the legitimate items. How long the date had been paid for with the entertainment nobody knows, but that ingenuous little mistake was henceforth abandoned.

Gunsbourg had prepared a little villa for us on the island of Arcadia, complete with maid and cook. In truth he was everything to be desired in a manager. One of his great virtues was that he always kept his word. He had promised me fantastic things in Russia, painting the most extravagant pictures of what was to be experienced there, and everything turned out exactly as he foretold.

He had begun life as a sceneshifter, property boy, and general factotum in a small variety theater in Petersburg. One night the actors that were announced on the bill did not appear. The ignorant and disappointed audience, fiery and unrestrained, began to stampede. Missiles flew, voices cried out, people mounted the stage. Gunsbourg appeared on the scene and began to perform the absent actors' parts. He danced, sang, made love, and by sheer aplomb sent the audience back to their seats. That is the kind of man who succeeds in the theater, or in any field.

A week after my arrival we opened with *Le grand mogol*, and my snakes and I made a great success, as Gunsbourg had promised we would. The house was crowded for the run and this continued in every production we put on.

The Arcadia was a summer theater on the Novaya Derevnia, outside the city, in the center of a charming park laid out in the French style with walks, gardens, gazebos, and summerhouses of the inhabitants of the city. The little cottage Gunsbourg hired for us was not far from the theater, but even if it had been, a carriage was at our command.

A carriage and coachman were even greater necessities in Petersburg than a cottage. No one ventured out, not an inch from home, without his carriage. If by chance you walked from shop to shop, it moved along at your side, lest it be thought, dreadful suggestion, that you had no carriage; and the amount of your wealth, your social importance, all was gauged by the *width* of your coachman. Gunsbourg did things handsomely by acquiring a very wide coachman for us.

Every late afternoon in the summer the haut monde of Petersburg drove out en masse in its carriages and made a circuit of the islands about the city proper, ostensibly to congregate at the end of Yelagin Island (known as the Point) to watch the sun sink into the Gulf of Finland, beyond the Neva, but in truth to be seen in its splendid turnouts. It was politic for Sidonie and me to drive in these futile processions, crossing the bridges, passing along the beautiful Prospects to watch the sunset. It was a splendid sight, never to be forgotten. The red sun dipped into the water, leaving the land in a light dusk throughout the summer night. As we turned back I observed a young man in a white uniform drive swiftly past us, attended by one servant. He bowed, waving to friends, and was gone. It was the czarevitch, soon to become Nicholas II.

Everything existed for show. Money in Petersburg flowed effortlessly, passing from hand to hand like jugglers' balls. The number of beautiful women was prodigious, and upon them all the money was lavished. Nowhere in the world, at least since the days of Rome, could a society have continued like this; everything was *bluff.*

Shortly thereafter I learned the real reason Gunsbourg had been importunate in coaxing me to Petersburg, and I was forced to admit that he was truly a genius for theatrical enterprise. It was the summer of 1891. For some time Alexander III had been attempting to improve Russian relations with France. He had become apprehensive of the Triple Alliance of Germany, Austria, and Italy and was convinced that in case of a European war Russia would find herself fighting on the side of France. As the Triple Alliance was aimed at France, the czar saw clearly that its existence weakened Russia. But he did not dare make a public alliance with France lest this strengthen her, making her openly aggressive to Germany; the stage was set for an *entente* between the two countries.

How astute was Raoul Gunsbourg! He sensed all this. Everything French suddenly became very much à la mode in Russia. A first-class French company performing in Petersburg was sure to be well received. Patriotic fervor would help it to financial success. Gunsbourg laid his plans well: it immediately became the fashion to patronize the French company at the Arcadia, and we were to profit by an almost hysterical welcome.

I had hoped to make my debut in *Mignon* or *Lakmé*, but Gunsbourg had arranged my debut in *Le grand mogol*. The real reason became apparent several days later when Madame d'Alba was billed to make her debut in *Mignon*. Madame d'Alba was Madame Gunsbourg, and she insisted in appearing first in an operatic role. She had an agreeable voice, but I believe she had never studied singing seriously. Having the advantage of being the wife of the director, throughout the season she sang on the nights I did not appear. This was more economical for the management than engaging another singer.

Nevertheless, Madame d'Alba was a pleasant and agreeable woman, rather mature for certain roles of her repertory, but withal pretty. She had two small sons to whom she was devoted.[40]

I have never witnessed such delirium as greeted us at the Arcadia. The enthusiasm of the audience, the excitement, the irrepressible gaiety of the Russians: it is simply indescribable. A festive *air de gala* reigned night after night.

Florists paid enormous prices for small displays in corners outside and inside the theater and yet made fortunes. The public, not satisfied with the expensive set pieces sent out from the most important florists of Petersburg, paid absurd prices for ordinary flowers, no matter what they were, to throw onto the stage during the performance.

These performances began very late, seldom before half past nine, allowing the spectators to dine at ease and arrive at the theater, without undue haste, in time for the curtain. The distance from the city to Arcadia, even with the best trotting horses, consumed twenty to thirty minutes. A late curtain benefited the city restaurants and the theater too, for all important restaurants sold seats for the performance. City restaurants lost the after-theater business, however, because it was customary for the gayer elements in the audience to sup at San Markan, a night restaurant about ten minutes drive from Arcadia. If the walls of San Markan could speak, one would hear interesting tales—of love, intrigue, and revenge! Like Cubat's in the city, there were a number of private salons at San Markan, and the service was equally luxurious, with an ostentation the world no longer knows.

The Russian Gypsy singers attached to San Markan were an outstanding element at the establishment. Their beautifully blending voices echoing from room to room, to the accompaniment of strange instruments, lent a bizarre and oriental atmosphere to the place. These singers were artists of the first class and received high salaries. There were always a male and female soloist, and it was customary to engage them to come to your private dining room to entertain your guests; they then went on to the next room and repeated their songs and dances, the custom known in French as *faire la navette*. They belonged strictly to the establishment and never performed elsewhere.

One hears of champagne flowing like water, and this was true of San Markan. The waiters opened three or four bottles at a time, making a circuit of the table in concert. After one round, anything left in the bottle was seen no more: it was not *comme il faut* to pour a second time from the same bottle, even if it remained three quarters full. A new bottle was opened instead. Everything at San Markan was on the same grandiose and wasteful scale.

I became acquainted with a young Italian tenor who had married a Gypsy singer and been received into their own strict sect, accepting baptism and all their customs. His wife was one of the most appreciated soloists, and they raised a large family. He had come to Russia with a troupe of singers, one of which was the great baritone Mattia Battistini. Emma Calvé was also included, I think, but I must truthfully say that I had only heard of the achievement of Battistini.

Assuming the name of Trohysi, the tenor seemed content with his new nationality, if Gypsies can be said to have any. He told me a great deal about Russian Gypsies, assuring me they were of staid and upright character and lived solely for their art. They accepted outsiders into their sect and treated them as one of themselves, unless they did not fulfill their duties or otherwise proved unworthy, in which case their lives were of short duration!

Trohysi's mother and father lived in Newark, New Jersey, of all places. Years later I ran across him there when he was on a visit to his family. He gave a concert in Newark which I attended, and I have never heard anyone, not even Caruso, sing "Celeste Aida" so gloriously as he did that night. I presented him to Thomas Edison, who was looking for voices with which to conduct experiments in recording, but whether or not recordings were made of his voice I am unable to say.

Sidonie was still very pretty and entered wholeheartedly into the festivities and gaieties of that summer. My success was as much a delight to her as it was to myself. She had become a second Madame Leroy, never quitting me for an instant, but so happy and amusing that she was as welcome at the fêtes and dinners we attended as a great personage.

Raoul Gunsbourg's rise in importance from his humble start in the variety theater Nemeti to impresario of a first-class company was a perfect illustration of what to expect from such a man. He was well liked and, just as important, well understood. Success, as is natural, had made him a little showy. "I said to my friend, the grand duke Vladimir . . ." he was wont to say, with a tap on the shoulder. If he had mentioned the czar himself it would have been under the guise of a bosom friend. But people knew his *façon de parler* and merely laughed.

In July a squadron of the French fleet under Admiral Gervais arrived at Kronstadt, the port of St. Petersburg, on a visit of amity. The day of the arrival Gunsbourg announced a grand gala performance of *The Daughter of the Regiment*, to be attended by the admiral and his officers. The auditorium was transformed, the boxes hung with French and Russian flags, and flowers decorated every conceivable spot. The so-called imperial box was occupied by as many grand dukes as could crowd into it. (The imperial family never attended any except the imperial theaters Alexander and Michel.) The opposite box was occupied by the French ambassador, the marquis de Montebello, and Admiral Gervais; French and Russian officers filled the other boxes, and the officers of the Corps des Pages filled the orchestra section. The auditorium of the Arcadia seated twenty-five hundred, and Gunsbourg announced three gala performances, a day apart. The second was in honor of the wives of the French officers who had arrived by special train from Paris, and the third for the French and Russian sailors.

At the end of each act I had to sing "La Marseillaise" and the Russian National Hymn, which I made haste to learn in Russian—no inconsiderable feat. The demonstrations on those nights were fantastic. The Russians worked themselves up to a pitch of excitement that would make the demonstrations of other nations pale into nothing by comparison. When the performance terminated, the audience crowded down to the footlights and flung flowers to the stage until I was nearly suffocated, a literal battle of blossoms. My fellow singers finally attempted to rescue me into the wings, but then Gunsbourg, as the grand climax, appeared on the stage leading Admiral Gervais. I feared the building would collapse under the cries and stamping which rent the air. Everyone rose and sang "La Marseillaise." Admiral Gervais stood at attention, saluting throughout the singing, a tall, thin, and impressive figure, and then advanced and kissed my hand. Finally the curtain was lowered. I was exhausted almost to the point of collapse.

Gunsbourg arranged my escape through a small door at the rear of the theater, and even then we had to enter the villa through the cellar. Outside, a great crowd collected, and we tiptoed upstairs in the dark, not daring to show our presence by lighting even a candle. As the crowd continued to grow, Gunsbourg, whose villa was next to ours, finally came out and announced that I had gone to Petersburg, and then the people dispersed. These ovations occurred at every performance.

Before the departure of the French fleet, a large banquet was organized at which I had the honor of being seated at the ambassador's right. At his request I sang "La Marseillaise" again, both before and after the dinner. On the eve of the sailing of the French fleet, Admiral Gervais entertained at luncheon on board his flagship, at which I found myself this time at the right of the marquis de Montebello. Admiral Gervais honored me with his portrait, warmly inscribed.

For his work in furthering the fêtes and the Franco-Russian Alliance, Gunsbourg was decorated by the French government with the red ribbon of the Legion of Honor, and I was decorated with the Order of Officier de l'Académie. I cannot imagine how many times during this gala season I was called upon to sing the French national anthem, but the occasion that stands out in my memory was that of my presentation to Alexander III and the czarina.

I was commanded to appear at a performance at the imperial theater Michel. The regular company attached to the theater was playing a French comedy, and at the end of the performance, after the Russian hymn had been played by the orchestra, I appeared with a large French flag. Monsieur Michel, the artistic director of the theater, had advised me to wear a white dress in the event of being sent for by the imperial box, so I had donned my last-act costume from *Mignon*, which besides being new was, I thought, becoming. True enough, following my last song, I was summoned to the imperial box.

Although unused to court etiquette, I bowed low at the entrance of the box and so remained without saying a word. The czarina then said kindly in French, "Come forward, my dear child, that we may see your *beaux yeux* closer," and all smiled. I was overwhelmed and did not know what to answer, but the czar filled the silence, saying, "We wish to hear more of your lovely voice at our own theater at Tsarskoe Selo, n'est-ce pas?" and I stammered, "I am at the command of Your Majesty."

The grand duke Vladimir, who was standing nearby, took me by the hand and led me to the czarina, who presented her hand to kiss; and then, moving toward the czar, I made a deep curtsey while he, with a humorous smile, gave a military salute. Bowing my head to all the people in the box, I backed slowly out, not daring to breathe lest my train should bring me to grief. But I escaped with no such calamity, and the duke assured me afterward that I had pleased Their Majesties. However, the members of the company were not pleased, as I soon learned, for they felt they should have been sent for instead of an outsider not even attached to the theater.

$\xrightarrow{\hspace{0.5cm}} 9 \xleftarrow{\hspace{0.5cm}}$

FTER THE DEPARTURE of the French fleet we resumed our regular performances at the Arcadia, and I sang again three times a week, on each occasion a different role. On alternate days new operettas were given. As we played in French and therefore drew our audiences from the upper classes, we had to change the bill often.

Gunsbourg explained that it was customary for the habitués of the theater to invite the star to supper after the performance. These invitations were extended by a group of four, six, or eight, but he warned me that one had to be very prudent in the choice of an invitation, for the grades of society in Petersburg were marked with iron rigor and one descent to a lower stratum branded one an outcast forever. First there were the great nobles, severe and unapproachable; then the younger element, the *jeunesse d'orée*; then the rich merchant class. The nobles did not frequent the houses of the merchants, and even the merchants were of a first and second guild with a strict line of demarcation. It was for this reason that invitations were extended by groups consisting of friends on the identical rung of the social ladder.

Thus we received an invitation from a group of four, consisting of Prince Orlov, Prince Lobanov, Prince Peshkov, and Count Kamarovski. Prince Lobanov, being the eldest, called for Sidonie and me in his magnificent carriage, and for the first time, I passed the portals of the famous establishment of San Markan. It was close by, and I had only to hurry home after the theater to put on an evening dress. My wardrobe was not elaborate, but on account of the heat, light dresses were fashionable, and my favorite was white, the proper color. The invitation, by strict Russian etiquette, was made eight days in advance, and all week I had been nervous with anticipation and ignorant of the correct attitude I should assume. I was therefore most delighted and surprised at the cordiality and kindliness of our hosts, and the dreaded supper turned out an enchantment from beginning to end. Sidonie, I noted with some envy, was perfectly at ease among these gallant foreign gentlemen, and observing her I realized how well the sobriquet she had long borne at home of "the princess" suited her.

My memory of that night is something vague, glittering, and sumptuous. The supper was a work of art in preparation and in serving. Soft music playing from behind an immense screen of every conceivable blossoming plant gave the last touch, which proclaimed the entertainment lifted beyond the usual luxury into an exotic and Eastern repast. With four Prince Charmings in attendance, I felt this was truly one of the *Thousand and One Nights*.

At dessert I was asked to sing a little song, and as there was a piano in the room, I rose and was ceremoniously conducted to it by Prince Peshkov. At that time a song by Denza, "Si tu m'aimais," was much in vogue, and as it was simple and I had sung all evening, I chose that, followed by my Bird Waltz, which had already become my inseparable "Tui-tui-tui" showpiece.[41] Our hosts produced little autograph books encrusted with jewels and begged us to write in each some small inscription, promising not to compare sentiments. I don't remember what was inscribed in the other books, but in Prince Peshkov's I was unable to write anything but what was in my mind: "Vous êtes très sympathique!" That night in truth I felt I was face to face with my destiny, and perhaps, in proof, Prince Peshkov had acquired the right to conduct us home. But when one has supped at San Markan and it is daylight on coming forth, one cannot go home without taking a little drive to the Point. Sidonie observed faintly the lateness of the hour, but already we were on the road and going at a good clip. Finally, however, I was glad enough to find myself home and in bed. I was sleepy and tired out, but it did not prevent my thinking of all that had occurred that wonderful night, and in my mind I beheld one tall, fair-haired Russian gentleman with blue eyes and charming manners —Sergei Peshkov.

Sidonie never allowed my sleep to be disturbed, but that day I was

Clara Lardinois. Courtesy Alexander Turnbull Library, Wellington, New Zealand.

awakened by voices outside on the balcony: Prince Peshkov's carriage had driven up, with his valet carrying a large bouquet of red roses and a rolled-up sheet of paper. My maid brought them to me in bed, and to my surprise the roll turned out to be the music of a song by Tito Mattei, "Ce n'est pas vrai," which I suspected was in answer to the song of Denza, the refrain of which was "Non, tu ne m'aime pas."[42]

After that, every evening found Prince Peshkov in his box at the Arcadia. Gunsbourg, on observing this attention paid me, was in despair, but happily he had neglected to put any clause against such a contingency in my contract. When he became convinced of the seriousness of Prince Peshkov's attention, he came and spoke to me severely, saying that I *could not* thus discourage the attentions of other admirers, as I had to think of him and his business. Though my friendship with Sergei Peshkov was a most quiet and discreet one, I had on one pretext or another refused several invitations to supper with other people. Moreover I was not used to such late hours, and as we rehearsed mornings it was out of the question for me to sing in the evening and then sup till the next day. My arguments on this score with Gunsbourg developed into a quarrel in which I offered my resignation, for his ideas on the subject of Prince Peshkov were utterly opposed to mine. I pointed out to him that my private life was no concern of his. Poor man! How he paced to and fro, his arms to the skies, declaring with all his Russian eloquence that I would shortly bring ruin upon him. He wept over the impending catastrophe (our receipts had been record-breaking).

Sidonie supported me in my stand. I learned later that Prince Peshkov had told her it was, after all, in better taste not to accept these invitations. But as I accepted the invitations of others no more or less frequently than I had those of Sergei Peshkov and his friends, it happened that instead of having a bad effect on our receipts, the attendance grew. It became known that Clara Lardinois, the great success at the Arcadia, unlike other singers and actresses, did not accept invitations with all and sundry to wine and dine at San Markan. Soon the most aristocratic families of the city began to occupy the boxes heretofore frequented only by the gayest of the younger set. Gunsbourg was petrified by this extraordinary state of affairs, something quite outside his comprehension or experience. Society women sent me flowers and presents, and we were even invited to numerous afternoon receptions, a most uncommon occurrence for theatrical people. Gunsbourg was totally unable to understand these sudden favors showered upon us. He called me "the little devil," for never before in the history of the Arcadia had ladies attached to the imperial court been seen in its boxes. This convinced him at last that everything was for the best, and once more he was at my feet.

One day, however, he arrived at the villa like a madman.

"My little Lardinois, you must save me this time: I am lost!" He began his frantic exercise up and down my salon, waving a paper before me and crying pitifully, "If you do not sign this contract I am utterly ruined! Destroyed! There will be nothing left for me but to jump into the sea!"

By now I was used to his explosive style, so I waited with great composure for his explanations. He had learned of the contemplated erection of a theater on the Kamenniy Ostrov Prospect, nearer the city, on the road leading to Arcadia. It was to be called the Aquarium, and the prospectus promised the best singers and comedians of Paris, a superb ballet, and other attractions.

"My dear Monsieur Gunsbourg," I said, "what can I do about this?"

"You can do everything!" he cried. "If you will sign a new engagement with me for next summer, I am saved; because the society women will not go to the Aquarium if you are singing at the Arcadia."

In the consideration of this sad affair I could not help a feeling of satisfaction, even amusement. I was now regarded as a savior by Gunsbourg, who so short a time before had declared with impassioned oratory that I would ruin him. Out of compassion for his present despair I forbore pointing out this interesting paradox. But I would not sign the proffered contract, which was for two years. On my return to Paris I would need to see what engagements were open for the winter and what conditions prevailed in the spring. Moreover, I indicated that the Parisians looked with great disfavor upon their favorites who sold their success abroad. They felt that foreigners who wanted to see their performers should come to Paris.

Gunsbourg scoffed at this suggestion and I said, "Do you know Sarah Bernhardt was hooted on her reappearance after a foreign tour? And Réjane? And Yvette Guilbert?" Not one of them had regained her former popularity in Paris after playing in other countries. This was an unfortunate little idiosyncrasy of French theatergoers at that time, though they may be more tolerant now. Actors who performed abroad excused themselves by saying they earned more, much more, out of France than in it; but there was never any discussion. If Paris made the reputation of an actor, she wished to keep him. If he proved unfaithful, it was a final divorce, with all the rigors and responsibilities involved. It is strange that in Paris they were so *exigeant*, for in all the countries of the world, in the smallest places, I encountered Italian touring companies who anticipated no hisses on their return to Italy (true the Italians are very prolific in singers); and this was true of Spaniards as well. In fact I attribute in part my success in various remote places to the paucity of French operatic singers outside of France: so few dared leave.

Gunsbourg continued his role as the despairing and hopeless theater director. What could he do with his contract for the Arcadia yet two years to run? And his poor wife? And his hapless little ones? To hear his laments was heartrending. I was made of stone for leaving him in so terrible a predicament.

At last I quieted him by promising to think the matter over, saying I would write to Paris that day and give him a final answer in two weeks. He had to make the best of this, and departed in great gloom.

The time for our return to Paris drew near. While I was absent at rehearsals, Prince Peshkov came often to the villa to talk to Sidonie. Sidonie, whom it was impossible to deceive, knew I was becoming more and more attached to Sergei Peshkov and was not taken unaware when he spoke to her of our marriage. In attempts to discuss the matter with me she had never elicited more than a laugh, but now she assumed a very solemn tone and declared that at last I must really examine my conscience and take thought of the future. I confess I looked upon Prince Peshkov as a good, kind friend. He was fifteen years my senior. It was difficult to imagine myself married to a tall, handsome, courtly Russian gentleman who seemed so very much more worldly than myself.

Sidonie, however, pointed out the good side of the proposal. It would be impossible to picture anyone more kind and generous than Sergei Peshkov; and above all, nothing would please my good mother more than to see me safely married. I had promised Gunsbourg an answer in two weeks, and now I made the same promise to Sidonie.

Sergei discussed his family often, and I met one brother and his sister.

As his father was dead, he, the eldest son, was head of the family. His mother, an invalid, was in a sanatorium at some distance from Petersburg. Because of this, and because of the absence of his married brother, Feodor, who was in Constantinople as military attaché to the Russian legation, our marriage had to be a quiet one. Sergei belonged to the Corps des Pages, and the wedding would have to take place in the court chapel.

Several days later I was surprised to receive a visit from the director of the imperial theater Michel. He came to say that he had heard much of my success in Petersburg, and though the repertoire of the theater Michel consisted of French comedies, he proposed to include *opéras comiques* if I would sign an engagement with him for that very winter. He added mysteriously that the suggestion for my engagement came from "a very high source," leaving the asterisks for me to fill in.

Overcome on hearing this—a command so desired by many performers much older than myself—I said nothing of other plans, but promised an answer in a week. Sidonie was not as delighted as myself. She saw her own plans for my future upset, since the prince (she assumed) would not want me to continue a professional life after our marriage. I determined to hear his own opinion.

Paris faded from my thoughts. That which is close at hand has a strong hold upon us, and I pictured a bright future in Russia.

Yet even then Russia had begun to frighten me. It was a country of such dramatic contrasts. I was still inexperienced and ignorant of many things, but I felt (rather than actually observed) a curious, strained atmosphere drawn over everything—festivity, solemnity, work, and play alike. Opportunities to see the contrasts of Russia continually presented themselves.

One of the first receptions to which I was invited took place at the home of the duchess of Leuchtenberg. At these functions very few men were present, and those who were there were officers of the Corps des Pages. *Zakuski* were served on a long table in the northern manner. One was presented with a small plate by a footman and served oneself. Above all, the food was delicious. The caviar was eaten with Krosen Vino, a *red* wine, oddly enough, and vodka as colorless as water. I learned too late that the latter was not water but a most treacherous drink!

Russian women of the aristocracy who were rigid and lifeless when appearing in public, at the theater or elsewhere, unbent only among themselves, at which times they were astonishingly animated. They smoked cigarettes when no women did elsewhere and drank a great deal. I remember being the center of interest at the duchess's home, my novelty being the fact that I was the seventeenth child of my parents. This they thought incredible, and I had to repeat the fact to every new addition to the group.

Fortunately, the duchess's reception room was not a smoking room, for then, as now, I found it impossible to sing in a room full of smoke. To amuse themselves the ladies decided to make me smoke a cigarette and drink champagne. The grand duke Alexis, standing at some distance, observed my discomfiture and came to my rescue, pointing out to my tormentors that I was not accustomed to Russian practices and that I had to sing in a few hours. I thanked him, laughing, and the duchess became very contrite. She begged me to forgive her—and to prove that I had, would I not sing them a little song?

Now, it is a strange thing, but I have always rather resented that phrase, "a little song." For me it has always been more difficult to sing "a little song" than a whole opera! One has not time to warm up, nor really to hold one's audience, before it is all over—a most thankless task. When one is invited to a reception or a dinner one must eat to honor one's host, but I could never eat before singing. On a night I was to sing I had my principal meal at half past three, perhaps taking a raw egg in sherry half an hour before the performance. But when invited to someone's house a singer can safely expect to be asked to sing. In later years I took more authority upon myself; I lost my timidity and found an efficacious guard against this unpleasantness, which I shall describe with the hope that it may be of assistance to others. Upon receiving an invitation I would say, with my most pleasant smile, "Thank you very much, my dear Madame So-and-So, and may I pose one little question? Whom are you inviting? Blanche Arral the singer or Madame B. Arral?" The question was invariably surprising. I would explain that if it were Madame B. Arral I should be delighted to come to dinner, but if it was Blanche Arral the singer I would come after dinner, since I could not sing after eating. Naturally, the answer shamed into being given was always, "Oh, we want Madame B. Arral!"

Yet in those Russian days I had not arrived at the courage (or sense) to protect myself in this manner, and that day I told the duchess I would sing with pleasure for her and her guests. At these receptions one always found some good musicians—above all, good violinists—gifted with a certain musical intuition which enabled them to follow anything sung and to harmonize with the voice. I never understood how they accomplished it, as some of them could not even read music and yet were able to accompany a singer on the violin in scores they had never heard before.

Having partaken well of *zakuski*, I was glad to find the violinist beside the piano. I had studied two songs much in vogue—the still well-known "Ochi chornaia" (Black Eyes) and another called "Pevunia Ptichka" (Little Bird), which I sang in Russian. The violinist aided me considerably, for I was handicapped by the caviar and vodka; nevertheless, enthusiasm was high. Everyone crowded around with that Russian childish delight which is so charming and flattering, and the grand duke Alexis took a rose from a vase, presented it to me, and said, "This is a sample of the thousands I would lay at your feet." The duchess led me out and stopped in a little anteroom. She detached a gold bracelet in the form of a snake with the head set in diamonds and rubies, clasped it on my arm, and embraced me. I demurred at this rich gift and she said, "Oh, this is only a bagatelle!"

As it was late, she delegated an officer to escort me home in his carriage with two spanking horses, and I arrived in a state of dishevelment. To my disappointment, Sidonie had not been invited to this reception. "Etiquette," Gunsbourg explained enigmatically, but I suspect it was because these ladies did not want too many witnesses to their private behavior. Sidonie was distressed at my late return and was resolving a course of action when finally I appeared. That night I ate nothing, as I was billed to sing *Faust*. But my energy returned with the music; I felt improved for my little spree, and it is doubtful if I ever sang Marguerite better.

Continued accounts of flowers and applause grow monotonous. My excuse is that I have attempted to portray the luxurious enthusiasm of those Russian audiences of the early nineties.

While still on the subject of the duchess of Leuchtenberg, the story of the grand duke Alexis must be related. When he presented me with the rose, he and his hostess laughingly exchanged a few words in Russian. It was noticeable that the duke was more than a guest in this house, but it was not until later that I learned the sad story of these two people. Though very much in love with Alexis, the duchess had been ordered by the czar to marry a man much older than herself. It was said that Alexander III had set his heart on marrying his brother elsewhere, but Alexis remained faithful to his love, the duke of Leuchtenberg being but a figurehead in his own house. This situation endured for a number of years. The duchess and the grand duke traveled together openly in Europe. But alas! Finally Alexis cast his eyes at some of the pretty young French actresses attached to the imperial theater Michel. One in particular replaced the duchess in his affections. Her name was Madame Baletta—La Belle Baletta! She was not an actress of the first importance, but her patrician bearing suited her for the roles of grande dames and courtiers. It was also said that she resembled the duchess of Leuchtenberg in her younger days, so the grand duke remained faithful to his ideal of beauty, if not to the same embodiment of it. Unfortunately, La Belle Baletta's husband, Monsieur Larteur, who also belonged to the troupe at the theater Michel, adored her. They had a son; but instead of a home life, Baletta preferred the gaieties she had tasted with the duke. Her husband divorced her, but it killed him both as an actor and a man.

I should like to remember only that which was glittering and luxurious of those days, but this would not give a faithful picture of the beautiful and terrible Russia I knew. Side by side with the luxury was another element—indescribable, dark, menacing, and evil, even among those who were outwardly most frivolous. My happiness in Russia did not last. In that superficial and lighthearted society, so plainly riding for a fall, there was an element entirely foreign to any similar class in other countries. Only in Russia could the infamous monk Rasputin exist and obtain the power he acquired.

My impression of Grigori Rasputin was entirely uncolored by the light which now clings about his memory. At our first meeting he could not have been more than twenty-two or twenty-three and his life before him; yet already he counted as a personage in Petersburg and was both hated and feared by those who did not worship him. While nothing in his public actions or personality could foreshadow the ignoble role he was to play later on, or the devastating effect he was to produce on the life of the unhappy Nicholas II and his family, there already existed in Petersburg an undercurrent of fear and distrust, particularly among the servant class. I had gained some notion of Rasputin from hearing the account of a visit to his monastery by a chambermaid in my employ.

One day while rehearsing for my appearance at the theater Michel, Sidonie and I fell into conversation with a woman who was seated beside us. She turned out to be a self-appointed godmother to the entire company, a Frenchwoman, named Madame Devaux, who spoke Russian fluently. I sensed that it would be well to be on good terms with Madame Devaux. She had belonged to the troupe ever since the theater opened for French plays (the theater itself dated from 1833), and she was in the good graces of those inside and outside the theater. Her duty was to take care of the new actors upon their arrival from Paris and to install them in their homes. Her knowledge of Russian made her indispensable in a great many of the contingencies which were bound to arise. No actor at the Michel could escape the offices of Madame Devaux.

Sidonie made a great hit with her and we were honored one day with a call. She proposed taking Sidonie shopping to the Gostinnoi Dvor, the Russian bazaar, where everything conceivable might be purchased. At my insistence Sidonie accompanied her, and to tell the truth she was very charming and friendly. However, I had warned Sidonie to be very circumspect and above all not to mention Prince Peshkov.

One day when she called she asked if I knew Father Lagrange of the French Church. This question surprised me, as I had called on Father Lagrange and he told me he had spoken to Madame Devaux of me. Madame Devaux's inquiry seemed to be a trap in which to catch me. I was already beginning to acquire a certain amount of cunning from my surroundings: I felt confident that Father Lagrange had not spoken to Madame Devaux of my personal business, so I told her I had visited him and found him charming. I added that I intended to return the following Sunday, my only free day of the week, as Father Lagrange had *The Life of St. Cecilia* in his library, a book which had been published by my father and which I had not seen since childhood.

Madame Devaux was very much interested in my explanation and invited me to call on her some day when convenient. Then she suddenly asked if Father Lagrange had not spoken to me of Rasputin, the famous monk who performed miracles. I vowed complete ignorance of this personage. "Oh, you must meet Rasputin!" she cried. "All the actors go to visit him. He is a saint! He has great power! There is nothing he cannot do! If you want," she added, "I will take you one day to his monastery!"

Compromising, I replied that I would have to examine my free time.

Sidonie told me later that Madame Devaux had asked her if there was truth in the rumor of my engagement to Prince Peshkov. I admired her direct method of attack, but it availed her nothing; Sidonie merely said that I spoke little to her of my private affairs, being very much occupied with my work, but that she thought the prince was devoted to me.

"Then," said Madame Devaux, "tell her that the prince's family will be set against it; if she marries him she will be in danger, even for her life."

The good lady was playing a double game. Afterward I became convinced that she was in the employ of Rasputin.

On Sunday, Sidonie and I went back to Father Lagrange. He was a very erudite priest, as are all Jesuits, and a most agreeable and charming man, tall and with a very imposing presence. He had a beautiful voice. I had heard him preach and he had impressed me more as an orator than as a preacher of the word of God. I did not like his long black beard, of which he was very proud, but he had the most interesting hands I have ever seen. Without reason for my prejudice, I have always connected well-cared-for and beautiful hands with people of delicate and sensitive character.

He received us most cordially in his study, a large room furnished in quiet elegance, the walls covered with handsome books carefully catalogued and arranged. Opening a bookcase, he took down a volume and placed it in my hands. My heart contracted. I recognized again the book my poor father used to show me when I was a small child. Sidonie was moved too, but my eyes clouded and I began to weep. Father Lagrange put his arm on my shoulder and said, "Dear child, those are good and beautiful tears; do not try to check them."

But he did not know I was weeping at the thought of the sorrow I had brought upon my father by disregarding his wishes and going on the stage. I opened the book and read on the first page, "To his friend . . . Bishop of Liége, written and published by Jean Gregoire Lardinois."

"Father," I said, "this book has settled me in my purpose. In memory of my father, and because I know it is what he would have wished, I will marry Sergei Peshkov and give up the stage as soon as my contract with the theater Michel has been fulfilled."

Sidonie embraced me, and Father Lagrange said that he regretted I could not be married in his church but that the pope would recognize the orthodox marriage. He promised to come to my home after the service to give me his Catholic benediction. It made him happy, he said, to meet a young singer who had kept good religious principles and honored her parents. He regretted his inability to hear me sing.

I said it would give me great happiness to sing for him at the church or in the convent. He accepted my offer with great pleasure, for thus he could invite a guest who had expressed a great wish to hear me, someone who possessed much influence in Petersburg. I regarded him with curiosity. "Some day he will have more power in Russia than the czar, and above all, if you marry a Russian, you must make friends with him. It is the monk, Rasputin."

Without knowing why, each time I heard the name Rasputin I experienced an indescribable feeling, and I admitted this to Father Lagrange. He smiled and observed that I must be very impressionable. "But who has spoken to you of Rasputin?" he asked.

When I told him of our conversation with Madame Devaux, his expression changed. He said quickly, "On no account must you be introduced to Rasputin by her, and I counsel you to have as little to do with her as possible. Above all, do not go with her to the monastery. I cannot say more now, though some day I may. But your intuition about Rasputin is of no importance. You have nothing to fear if you meet him through me." As we left he added, "I shall count on your visit in the near future, when I know on what day Rasputin is coming. I shall not tell him you are to be here because probably Madame Devaux has already promised to bring you to his monastery, which he would *much* prefer."

At these words we departed. Poor Sidonie was most anxious to discuss this whole mystery of Rasputin with me alone. We were both perplexed. For the first time in my life I sensed danger, and all I desired was to never meet this famous Rasputin.

10

UPON OUR RETURN to the villa we found a telegram from Sergei announcing his mother's consent to our marriage. In three days he would be in Petersburg. Now that I had made up my mind to marry him, I wanted him near me. I felt need of his protection. Such was the sinister and magnetic power of the name Rasputin. I searched for an excuse to avoid meeting him without wounding Father Lagrange, who appeared so honest and sincere. I hoped Sergei would return before I received Father Lagrange's invitation to the church, but on Monday a note arrived asking me to come with Sidonie to the church on the following day at three o'clock.

When the time came, Father Lagrange awaited us in his study. He was glad we were punctual because he wished to speak with us before the arrival of the monk. He explained that Rasputin spoke very little French but understood it perfectly. Though he spent most of the year in the country with his father, he came into the city often, his missions shrouded in mystery.

Rasputin declared himself to be inspired by God. He had many disciples drawn from all ranks of society whom he taught that one must sin in order to be forgiven, and the greater the transgression the more glorious the pardon. "I am all-powerful and it is only through me that you can be saved; and for this you must be united with my soul . . . and body. This virtue which I give you will become a source of light and will destroy all sin."

This dangerous system of finding salvation naturally led to all sorts of orgies and savage practices, but his teachings had gained great popularity among those of real intellect. He acquired the reputation of a holy man and said himself he was *un homme saint*. The doors of many great Russian families were open to him—later even those of the imperial palace.

Father Lagrange thought it best to explain all this to us so that we might better understand the man we were to meet. I declared that I feared him already and would prefer not meeting him. "As long as I am present, he will play no dangerous game," said Father Lagrange.

At that moment the door opened and Rasputin entered.

He stood at the threshold, looking first at Sidonie and then at me, astonished to find strangers present. His eyes were powerful and penetrating! It was as if they actually made a physical contact with their object. I distinctly wished for a trapdoor through which to vanish like Doctor Miracle. With an effort, I collected myself.

Our host advanced, smiling, and said, "Madame Fremaux and Mademoiselle Lardinois." Rasputin made a gesture with his hand, perhaps meant to convey a blessing, and without removing his eyes from me, spoke in Russian. Father Lagrange answered in Russian, explaining our presence. The monk's eyes sobered at once, becoming very peaceful and dreamy, with the calm of a young tiger. Then he glided forward (he really did not seem to walk with human steps) and, arranging his long robe so that it touched my knee, seated himself beside me.

At first glimpse he had appeared tall, svelte, and with a suggestion of great physical health. Now, seated beside me, he seemed to have contracted and diminished. His hair, greasy and unkempt, fell limp and dank over his shoulders. His beard was thin and long, looking more like a goat's whiskers than human ones, and he stroked the end of it as he listened to his host. His manner was nervous, and his black robe, which looked as if it had been slept in, displayed his long yellow hands in startling relief. Further, I must state that if indeed he was the saintly person he declared himself to be, then I had a very clear notion of the odor of sanctity!

Having learned all he desired to know of my history, he said to me in very bad French, "I am a holy man and I can make you very happy." Sidonie stirred uneasily and said it was time for us to go, but Father Lagrange reminded me of my promise to sing. He added that there was a small harmonium in the refectory and if I could accompany myself on that it would give him great pleasure.

There was nothing to be done about it and we all trooped out to the refectory, where Rasputin again seated himself beside me, at the harmonium. As I began Gounod's *Ave Maria*, he buried his face in his hands as one in prayer. I did my best under these disagreeable circumstances, and when I had finished, the monk lifted his head and I saw that his eyes were filled with tears. He rose and kissed my hand. I felt a few sticky drops and as soon as possible I wiped them away with my handkerchief.

"You have the voice of an angel," he said in his broken French.

Turning to Father Lagrange, he began to speak rapidly in Russian, which Father Lagrange translated. He had been much moved by my singing and begged that I would come to see him again before I left Russia, adding that he felt I was in danger from which he alone could save me. It was plain that Father Lagrange himself had grown rather nervous, for since Rasputin understood French, he had to translate exactly what was said. I repeated the excuse made to Madame Devaux, that I would have to examine my free time and hoped the opportunity to accept his invitation could be found. Father Lagrange accompanied us to the door, thanking me again for having sung. I felt Rasputin's eyes upon me but bowed my farewell without meeting his look. It is unnecessary to state that the opportunity to call upon Rasputin never arrived.[43]

Sidonie herself now became impatient to leave Russia. She had received several letters from home urging her to return. Having had a good view of the luxury and superficiality of Russian life, she was no longer certain of what advice to give me. We were on the *qui vive*, until that evening a telegram arrived from Sergei announcing his return the following day.

He hastened to the villa at once, so happy and lighthearted that I did not wish to tell him of our meeting with Rasputin. In fact I told no one. I had heard Gunsbourg declare that Rasputin was an ignoble personage, and I did not even mention our visit to Father Lagrange.

Sergei wished our wedding to take place before my return to Paris, but to this I did not consent. I wanted to be away from Russia and Sergei for at least two weeks in order to think over the situation undisturbed. Then if he still desired to marry me he could fix the date. For this reason I did not wish the engagement to be made public until after my return from France. Only ten days remained before we were to leave, and Sidonie occupied herself with packing and making final arrangements.

One day Sergei arrived at the house in a dreadfully upset state. It had reached his brother's ears that Rasputin was boasting that I had promised to go to his monastery and sing for him and his entourage. Sidonie answered this challenge, saying it was true we had met Rasputin at Father Lagrange's, as we had gone there for information concerning Russian marriages; the monk, through Father Lagrange, had asked me to visit him but I had certainly made no promise to accept the invitation. We had not had time to tell Sergei all this and moreover there was nothing reprehensible in calling on Father Lagrange, our spiritual adviser. Sidonie spoke with such heat as to preclude all further argument. Much perturbed, I sat down some distance from Sergei and for the first time sulked in his presence.

Sergei explained to Sidonie that his brother was much against this marriage. Russian custom decreed that the eldest son, as the head of the family at the death of his father, should remain unmarried until all his younger siblings, especially the sisters, are settled. Sergei's one sister had refused several offers of marriage, declaring she never intended to marry. It was mainly because of this that Sergei had gone to talk the matter over with his mother, and she had said that if he thought he was making a happy marriage, he could count on her blessing. His father had been dead fifteen months and the family was no longer in mourning, but in any event the marriage would be a quiet one.

It was no recommendation to know Rasputin, the evil genius of all who knew him, but it was plain to see we had been unable to avoid meeting him. Clearly, Alexander Peshkov was attempting to make trouble.

My brain was in a whirl. Rasputin, Alexander Peshkov, Sergei, Sidonie —a discordant jumble of people and emotions had given me a frightful headache. Sergei left after making us promise to join him for dinner at Cubat's. There was little time in which to dress. "Quick!" I told my sister. "You must make yourself beautiful, and so must I. This will be an engagement dinner!" Poor Sidonie, she tried to be gay, or to make me think she was, and I, with distressed and disturbed thoughts, attempted to follow her example.

We reached Monsieur Cubat's sumptuous and pretentious restaurant to find Sergei awaiting us. He had engaged a small private dining room. "This is the first and last time I shall ever doubt you," he said, and he kept his word.

The unpleasantness of the afternoon was entirely forgotten, and we all did justice to the delicious dinner prepared by Cubat, who was in on our secret. Flowers were everywhere, but with dessert came the real surprise. Cubat opened the door and Prince Lobanov and Count Kamarovski came in, each carrying a large box of orchids. Sergei now seemed really happy, and as I looked at him he drew from his pocket a small leather box. Taking out a ring, he put it on my finger and then kissed the finger, another Russian custom. The ring consisted of two large pearls, a white one and a black one, below which a heart-shaped diamond hung, flexible: it was a queen's jewel!

There was no music that night. Cubat's restaurant, unlike San Markan, had no Gypsy singers. He had kept up the tradition of an exclusive French restaurant but had succeeded far better than any restaurant in Paris. It was a great recommendation to be able to say "I dined at Cubat's," for Cubat did not extend his hospitality to all comers. To find a table one had to be recommended by one of Cubat's distinguished clientele; otherwise, he regretted politely that there was no place vacant, that every table was reserved. This happened often, even in full view of a large expanse of empty tables. No unaccompanied woman was ever admitted.

Cubat, a man of education, had originally been chef at the imperial palace, where he not only composed the menus but was also the czar's official taster, sampling every dish served at the imperial table. The czar was afraid of being poisoned, so it was necessary to have a most trustworthy person in this post. Cubat had been engaged when he was brought to Russia, and with the czar's permission he sent for his fiancée and married her in Petersburg. At the expiration of his contract with the czar's majordomo, he asked to be allowed to retire from his post in order to open a restaurant. He made a great success. Madame Cubat herself told me the story. She was a handsome woman and also a clever manager. The tables were numbered and she devised a special system to keep track of the names of the people sitting at them. On entering, each guest received a card bearing his name and table number and was conducted to his designated place. It was no simple matter to distribute the clients, for a nobleman must not find himself seated near the table of a rich merchant. For this reason it was necessary to send word to Cubat by four o'clock of one's intention to dine, or before ten in the morning if one desired luncheon. Without this warning there was a risk of finding oneself next to a merchant instead of a prince! But Madame Cubat was usually able to prevent this catastrophe.

At last, after receiving felicitations and good wishes, it was time to go home.

Some distance from the villa we perceived that the windows were lighted. As we approached I recognized the silhouette of Gunsbourg on the terrace, who, seeing the prince's carriage, began to make his wide, despairing gestures. This reassured me, for I knew his exuberance well. Without any greeting while we alighted, he cried out, "Where have you been? Why didn't you leave word with your maid where you were going?" Sergei said something in Russian which calmed him immediately and he continued, "Here I have an imperial command—Clara Lardinois must play *Miss Helyett* at Tsarskoe Selo on Saturday. We have only two days for rehearsals. I must change the bill at the Arcadia, and the theater is sold out. It's terrible, terrible!" He flung himself down in a chair.

And so, having reached home already with an extra load of emotions and fatigue, I was obliged to discuss plans for an hour with Gunsbourg while Sergei listened anxiously to the details. At last Gunsbourg left. He had not noticed my magnificent ring until he reached the threshold.

"Who gave you that wonderful ring? But a *black* pearl! Imagine! Don't you know black pearls bring bad luck? You will weep as long as you wear it!"

A chill ran down my spine. Sergei spoke furiously to Gunsbourg, mostly in Russian, the only word I caught being the French word "diable," and Gunsbourg left abashed.

As though to prove his prediction, I began to cry. Sidonie scoffed at the words of "that foolish man," and Sergei promised to bring me a new ring in the morning. I protested that I was not superstitious at all, only tired.

Nevertheless, I had frightful nightmares. On every side hung great black pearls and all of them were shedding tears! And at recurrent unhappy moments, my mind for years harked back to poor Sergei's beautiful gift.

11

THERE WERE NOW but six days left before our departure for Paris. Sidonie assumed charge of our packing and was waist-deep in trunks and bags. Sergei hardly left us. The unpleasant experience with Rasputin still hung as a distant cloud on the horizon, and I suspected that even Sergei was vaguely uncomfortable because of Gunsbourg's tactless remarks concerning the black pearl, which I continued to wear. He insisted that I wear with it a little circle of diamonds which had been blessed at the altar of the church of Notre Dame de Kazan, and he gave me a small icon in silver and enamel of Notre Dame de Kazan as well. (As I write these lines this icon lies before me, almost the only tangible thing which I possess of Russia.) Sergei was a believer, and his faith in the icon inspired me also. He explained to me the Russian custom of keeping quantities of icons in the houses with lights burning before them night and day. How much more of Russia I had to learn!

Saturday morning a special train was chartered to take the company for *Miss Helyett* to Tsarskoe Selo, which is but twenty-two versts from Petersburg, a distance of forty-five minutes. The musicians traveled with us; the orchestra had been divided, half remaining at the Arcadia to play the evening performance.

We had not yet been to Tsarskoe Selo, though it is of course one of the sights of Russia and was the favorite summer residence of the imperial family. The aspect of the whole place recalled vividly the times of Catherine the Great, who did much to implant a picturesque and eighteenth-century air to the palace and grounds, which I am told remain unchanged today.

That day, however, I had little time for sightseeing. While Sidonie visited the celebrated Old and New Gardens, we were obliged to rehearse.

The small private theater of the palace was a gem. The color scheme was gold relieved with white, in the Chinese style. While we rehearsed the curtain was drawn so that we did not see the auditorium until the performance began. The glittering uniforms of the men, all white and gold like the theater itself, the crystal chandeliers brilliantly lighted, the jewels of the women—all produced a fantastic picture.

I did not see the dressing rooms of the rest of the company, which were on the other side of the stage, but mine, on the same side as the imperial box, consisted of a good-sized anteroom with a smaller dressing room beyond. Everything had been arranged for the comfort of the company; even an excellent meal for all had been prepared. But I retired to the chaise longue in my dressing room, where my maid brought a cup of bouillon and some sherry. Soon I heard footsteps in the outer room, but as I was undressed I could not investigate. On arising I found the whole room a mass of blossoms from the palace gardens and learned afterward that flowers are never presented on the stage at imperial theaters.

Miss Helyett had been selected for our performance because of its simple mise-en-scène and small chorus; it is a comedy with incidental music by Audran.[44] The director of the court theater told Gunsbourg that Their Majesties wanted me to interpolate some extra songs of a light, gay character. Poor souls, they had little opportunity to hear anything of the sort and must have grown weary of the heavy music which alone was played in the imperial theaters. I selected a number of songs in a lighter vein as a change from the usual imperial fare. To bring these numbers into the plot with some semblance of sense, we concocted a short scene that gave me a pretext to sing my numbers in the last act. Gunsbourg warned me of the royal custom of no applause; but when I had finished Aleksandr Aliab'ev's "The Nightingale" in Russian and my Bird Waltz, the whole imperial box made a gesture of applause without actually bringing hands together, and to this spectral encouragement I gave my encores. Playing before the czar had an added difficulty because one must not turn one's back to the imperial box. This often necessitated a complete reversal of the stage business, and as much of the action as possible had to be specially arranged to take place in the corner of the stage nearest the imperial spectators.

Between the acts the czar's brothers, the grand dukes Vladimir and Alexis, came backstage to see me and to give me the message of Their Majesties' pleasure. As I had no change of costume in *Miss Helyett* there was plenty of time in the *entr'actes* to visit, and I was brought champagne and treated as an old friend, a startling contrast to the stiff demeanor demanded of everyone on the other side of the footlights. No one but royalty was allowed behind the scenes and so Sergei was obliged to remain in the audience.

At the conclusion of the performance the Russian anthem was played as usual, and something happened which had never happened before: the czar stepped to the front of his box and three times gave the signal to raise the curtain.

Afterward, Sergei joined us on the train and took us to supper at Cubat's. Time was growing short. Two nights later my farewell at the Arcadia was to take place, a long and difficult program, and then the journey to Paris. I wonder now how I ever had the endurance to accomplish so much and with so little breathing space between appearances.

The next day being Sunday, it was possible to rest. All I had seen and heard lately had so confused me that my thoughts leapt from one thing to another, and I looked at my beautiful black pearl and felt apprehensive for the future. I asked myself what it was that had changed my usual joie de vivre into something very like despair. At the time when I should be happiest, I had only a heavy sense of doubt and mistrust.

Into the midst of my soul searching, Gunsbourg burst like a blast of wind with the information that a rehearsal must be held for the gala performance the next day. He insisted we go through the business of receiving the flowers and presents; nothing must ever be left to chance in the theater. And so I had to go.

After the rehearsal Sergei took us to the Hermitage to dinner. At dessert a messenger brought a letter for him. I saw that he looked nervous on recognizing the handwriting: it was that of his brother Alexander.

He translated the message: "A telegram has arrived from Mother asking us to come at once. We are leaving at ten o'clock. Meet us at the station. We shall have your necessary luggage. Do not fail us under any pretext."

It was then nearly nine o'clock; there was hardly time for Sergei to reach the station. His mother lived four hours from Petersburg and there were only two trains a day. I could not resist glancing at my black pearl. It must be something very important indeed that could cause Madame Peshkov to summon her children at such short notice. She might even be dying! Perhaps Sergei would not be able to return for my farewell at the Arcadia, the performance which was to be the crown of my successes of the summer. Even so, I hid my anxiety.

Sergei summoned an izvozchik (hired carriage), but not before giving orders to his own coachman and valet to remain at our command until his return the following evening. In the next room we could hear the Gypsies singing and dancing. Another night I would have been happy to listen to them, but now their curious rhythms added to my gloom. As soon as possible we left the Hermitage, telling the coachman to drive to the Point. Poor Sidonie was also troubled and unhappy. She knew more of the world than I and understood the struggle which possessed me.

After a restless night came a telegram: "All well. My thoughts are with you. Train arrives at nine o'clock. I shall come to the theater at once." It was then ten o'clock. Arising happier than I had been for some time, I thought solely of the business of the evening.

Gunsbourg, excessively nervous, rushed from our villa to the theater a dozen times, insisting on each arrival that I go to the theater with him. Finally, when it really *was* time, he came once more and told us to take the same path we had taken the night of the performance for Admiral Gervais. He explained that we must elude the public in the garden outside as they were ready to make an ovation when I appeared. He wanted them to pay their admissions and do any demonstrating inside the theater.

Good and consistent man! He seemed a tower of constancy in those frantic hours and did not forget his own best interests in the midst of my turmoil.

The actors were in their dressing rooms when we arrived, and while dressing I constantly heard moving feet and whispers in the corridors outside. As I usually had many changes to make, my dressing room had been enlarged to include a second room in which I could move freely. I had a habit of singing as I dressed, to warm the vocal cords, and found that to sing before going on the stage not only gives a warm tone to the voice but puts one better into the spirit of the theater; it is not then such a jolt to sing without preliminaries. Bouchez, the great Belgian baritone, also a Liégeois, sang in his dressing room for an hour before a performance; Pol Plançon did likewise. On the other hand, Emma Nevada never spoke in her dressing room at the Opéra-Comique. Marie Van Zandt made a few light vocalises, but only to see if the timbre of her voice was pure. Madame Miolan-Carvalho had a habit of singing "Mimi-mimi-mimi" very high in the head. One night in her dressing room, not knowing her habit, I looked about and said, "Where is the cat?" Laughing, she cried, "Not in my throat!" Talazac's method was to imitate a cat exactly: "Meauhou, meauhou." The brothers De Reszke sang "Ning-ning-ning-ning" on all tones. Naturally, like a good little monkey, I imitated them all, and found that the "mimi" of Madame Miolan-Carvalho gave a bell-like tone to the voice; but I liked best the "ning-ning" of the De Reszkes. This, I think, opens the head cavities to create a vibration and pure, exact tone. I asked Madame Marchesi her opinion of this puzzling question of exercises, and she answered, laughing, "They are all good if you have confidence in them!" So the question turns itself into another question. Although I have strayed far from my subject, I cannot resist adding that now, fifty-five years since my debut, I try my voice first on "Mmmmmmmmmmmm." Next I vocalize with a sustained tone beginning on middle G and rising in the head to F sharp, then return to middle G without going into the chest. And my voice, at my age, is absolutely without fault, without a hole, as is usually found in voices which use the chest tones.

The evening of my farewell, I asked Sidonie to find out what was happening on the stage, but she returned with the information that the door was locked. Monsieur Berthier, the stage manager, had told her that he had orders not to open before Monsieur Gunsbourg arrived, and as he spoke she heard members of the chorus laughing at our predicament. It was plain some surprise was in preparation. As at Tsarskoe Selo, the curtain was lowered at the rehearsal. I continued to dress, wondering whether Sergei would reach the theater in time.

Finally, informed that the Garden Scene from *Faust* was about to begin, I was released from my prison. I noticed no difference backstage except that the corridors were very dimly lighted. Nonetheless, I could have found my way about in the dark at the Arcadia, and I took my position for my entrance cue. Suddenly the entire theater was illuminated—the backstage, the auditorium, the wings blazed into brilliant color—and at my entrance, the entire house rose. The auditorium was swathed in garlands of flowers, flags, and ribbons, the boxes were smothered in wreaths, and the chorus filled the stage, each bearing a basket of blossoms. The orchestra struck up the Russian national anthem, followed by "La Marseillaise," and I stood before the footlights, immovable. I was overwhelmed.

Conceiving an idea, I raised my hand: "Your demonstration of kindness touches me so deeply that I am unable to express the sentiments in my heart. I beg you for five minutes indulgence, that I may collect myself; for I wish to prove by the performance tonight that my colleagues and myself are truly proud and deeply touched by your appreciation."

The curtain fell on these words, and I found myself foolishly crying in the arms of my faithful Sidonie, who was crying too. Gunsbourg was beside us, and after a few compliments he said, "This is only the beginning!" Suddenly, he asked me where the prince was. I had no time to explain, for the orchestra began the prelude to the Ballad of the King of Thulé; I hurried onto the stage. At first my voice trembled and failed. The house was quiet and cold now, ready for the business of the evening. With a great effort I threw myself into my work and soon felt my powers returning. The King of Thulé was followed immediately by the Jewel Song, and by the end of that aria I was in excellent form. The applause began again and I gave a sign, begging silence. The remainder of the cast was on the stage now and we continued the act.

Next on the program came the first act of *Mignon*, in which I sang the title role. When the act was over I fell into the arms of Sergei, who was too overcome to speak. But Gunsbourg did not allow me to lose time or strength in emotions, so I was obliged to hurry into my costume for the last act of Jacques Offenbach's *Orphée aux enfers*. This had been chosen because it required the presence of the entire company on the stage. I liked the role of Euridice, and my costume—a long, white, silk Grecian robe with a blue cincture—was most becoming.

Because of the time spent in the demonstrations, it was late and Gunsbourg cut the act in half. He advanced upon the stage, looking very impressive in his evening clothes, and addressed the audience.

So many years have elapsed that I find it difficult to recall his words, but he catalogued my achievements of the summer, not omitting the part I played in the festivities of the Franco-Russian Alliance, and sent the audience into another frenzy of applause.

Then began the presentation of gifts. A superior officer occupying the imperial box presented me with a small jewel case tied with a large ribbon inscribed in letters of gold, "Miss Helyett—Clara Lardinois—Souvenir of Tsarskoe Selo," with the arms of the czarina. The case contained a brooch with the imperial crest in diamonds. The chorus advanced with more presents; they themselves bestowed upon me a piece of silver, and the members of the company combined to present a Caucasian belt in silver and turquoise. I was astonished by the long procession, which ended when a number of the chorus set down a large box-shaped floral object at my feet. Gunsbourg indicated to me that something moved inside, for the laughter and noise had prevented my observing it. He opened the box and brought forth a tiny ball of yellow and white fur no bigger than my two hands: a Russian griffon with a gold chain and a plaque on his collar, engraved "Mouchka Peshkov. Aimez moi comme je vous aime!" The poor little creature nestled at my feet. I took him in my arms and held him during the twenty or more curtains; and for many years, he never left me.

My summer at the Arcadia was over.

⟿ 12 ⟸

AT ONE O'CLOCK I found myself in our small dining room. Thanks to my good Sidonie and faithful companion Betty, the table was laid with my favorite dishes and set for two. After the excitement and fatigue of that night, Sidonie felt my need of solitude. Few could experience the nervous and physical ordeal of such a performance and continue with a supper party without complete collapse. And yet I felt Sergei had been disappointed and even hurt that I had refused to dine with him and his friends that night.

I was up in the morning, and after noon arrived without Sergei I began to wonder whether he had been wounded at our refusal to sup with him the previous night. Just then his carriage drew up. Without waiting for the horses to stop, he leapt out and up the porch, taking me in his arms. He begged my pardon for his insistence of the evening before and said that his friends understood my excitement and fatigue. He carried with him all the morning papers recounting the "Unprecedented Soirée de Gala at Petersburg," but before we could read them Mouchka took refuge beneath the hem of my morning robe and barked in excitement.

"Good," said Sergei. "That is my wish—that he will allow no man near you."

We discussed the journey to Paris. He had engaged a special compartment for us on the Orient Express. I was somewhat worried about traveling with Mouchka, and recounted the history of poor Toto on my trip to Paris as a little girl. Sergei regretted he had not been with us on that occasion! The Orient Express stopped three times daily, and all the passengers crowded the platform of some little wayside station to promenade and stretch their legs, furnishing at the same time an extraordinary display of dukes and countesses to the gaping peasantry. Good Sergei had arranged everything for our comfort, and he gave Sidonie an envelope containing our tickets. When she asked to reimburse him he answered, "My dear sister, won't you allow your future brother-in-law a little pleasure?" Accepting the tickets, she observed that we needed a third ticket for Betty.

He grew concerned and asked if Betty could not stay in Petersburg to help prepare our new home, as she knew the tastes of the future princess of Peshkov. At that name I confess my heart sank. Clara Lardinois would not be recognizable so disguised.

After lunch he left, but not before it had been arranged that Betty was to remain in Russia. She had many friends in Petersburg, having come first to Russia with the Spanish dancer La Belle Otero, whose service she quit in order to enter mine. Sergei had hoped that Sidonie would return with me for the wedding, bringing her husband, but she was very doubtful of this plan. Sergei could not leave his post at court, so our marriage had to take place in Russia.

Gunsbourg, evidently watching from his villa to see Sergei leave, immediately came over. He was anxious to know all details of the wedding, but I gave him no satisfaction because I did not want the papers informed of our private affairs.

My next visitor, the director of the imperial theater Michel, was armed with contracts to be signed. I did not have to return to Petersburg until the fifteenth of November. However, though all our plans had been made, I was reluctant to sign the contracts except in the presence of Sergei; so I asked him to leave them with me, promising to return them to him from Paris. People with contracts are loath to part with them, but Monsieur Michel had perforce to do so.

That evening, our last in Petersburg, Sergei dined alone with us. The season at the Arcadia had given me little opportunity to see him; he had even proposed to me through Sidonie. In fact I knew him very little, and now that I had turned again into a private person and was no longer a professional singer, I took the whole matter much more seriously. I realized that I was actually engaged to the prince de Peshkov, and that I was not sure of my love for him. "Love" was a word used glibly by the heroines I so often depicted on the stage. It was difficult to connect their emotions with real life.

Sergei had asked Sidonie's permission to see me alone after dinner. This request angered me, and I wondered why he had never made the suggestion until after our engagement. Now that I found myself about to become his wife, I almost feared him. He was serious and impressive, fifteen years my senior. I had heard tales of other Russian officers who had married women of the stage, and the sequels had never been very happy. The more I cogitated, the angrier I became. Perhaps Sergei's kindness existed only in Sidonie's presence. Alone with him in Petersburg, not speaking a word of Russian (and now I thought I must learn it at once) might be somewhat different! I became more and more excited. I spoke loudly in front of the mirror in the salon. My face grew red. I raised my hand defiantly to my reflection and said, dramatically, "Not so fast, Prince de Peshkov! We aren't married yet!"

Sidonie was behind me, standing on the threshold and looking at me with tears in her eyes. I was ashamed of myself.

"Clara," she said, "it isn't too late. The prince is a man of honor. If you do not love him enough to marry him I shall take it upon myself to explain your feelings." But I promised to hear what he had to say that night and to conceal my thoughts from him. She would remain in her room nearby.

Sidonie lectured me, saying, "Chase these unpleasant ideas from your head and weigh the alternatives before you: to be respected and loved by someone anxious to take care of you, or to go on with the excitement of the theater and the tribulations and disappointments which every singer must experience, popular and adored though she may be!"

The thought that I was to find myself alone with Prince Peshkov was perturbing, and when I heard his carriage stop outside the balcony I wanted to escape by another door. He must have brought some packages, for I heard Sidonie thank him effusively. She called and I entered the salon, Mouchka in my arms. He was alone.

With a penetrating look, he slowly came forward and put out his arms. I shall never forget the reproach in his fine blue eyes as I gently pushed him from me. Quickly recovering myself, I explained that it was because Mouchka was in my arms. He put the dog in a chair and, taking my hands, drew me down beside him. It was here that Sidonie and I discussed this interview an hour before. My knees trembled and my heart beat fast.

"Clara adorée," he said, "do you love me a little?" His voice trembled. My eyes were downcast and he begged me to look at him and answer frankly. "On your answer depends the happiness or sorrow of my life."

I obeyed and, regarding him openly, said, "I do not know!"

"Then tell me if you love another."

"Oh, no!"

Then, smiling, he explained what I knew so well, that there had been little time or opportunity for him to make me love him. But he was certain he should be able to do so when we were married. And he was right, poor Sergei! He proved to be the kindest and most considerate of husbands. His natural voice, usually strong and vibrant, was low and soft that evening. I had taken Mouchka onto my lap again, and Sergei and I talked at length. When our hands met, I did not withdraw mine. I felt at peace, for suddenly my fears were settled, and I was truly happy in his company. That evening he was wearing a redingote; I had never seen him before except in his uniform, and it was a novel change. Time passed so quickly that I was more disappointed than otherwise when Sidonie called out that supper was served. If Sergei had asked again whether I loved him I would have answered from my heart, "Yes!" but he was satisfied. And Sidonie saw at that moment that I truly loved him.

That evening marked our true engagement and my supreme happiness.

We discussed our future plans. Sidonie and I would go directly to Paris. I would give a farewell dinner to my friends, dismantle the apartment in the boulevard Haussmann, quickly visit my mother, and return as soon as possible to Petersburg. Sergei impressed upon me the importance of obtaining my birth certificate, since the orthodox marriage contract is written and signed on the back of it—a marriage which could be dissolved only by death or a special annulment.

My fatigue had vanished, and Sidonie was obliged to remind us of the hour and of our approaching journey. All coldness melted between Sergei and me: we parted like engaged people. The next day was a busy day for both of us, and it was improbable that we would meet except at the station.

In leaving Petersburg there was a weight of depression upon me, and Sidonie herself seemed pensive. Two and a half months had metamorphosed the young girl who left to fulfill an engagement in Petersburg into a woman engaged to become the princess de Peshkov. In retrospect the influence and excitement of my happy musical successes, the hurry and bustle of life in a gay world, and above all the swift courtship and proposal of Sergei, appeared an ephemeral dream. I felt like the heroine of a splendid and magic play on which the curtain had just fallen. But several hours later I was called upon to realize that the comedy had not yet ended.

Gunsbourg had taken care to notify the Petersburg press of the day and hour of my departure, the result being that the train seemed too small to hold the flowers received from all my new friends. Sergei had never appeared as solemn as he did at the station. As the train prepared to pull out he kissed my hand, saying in a low voice, "À bientôt, Douchka!" A military band blared forth the Russian anthem, and those in the station gave the military salute. My heart swelled to the music, bringing tears to my eyes, but at the end of the advancing parade was Gunsbourg, his beaming face and clownish grimaces forcing me to laugh. The train rolled away toward Paris.

In settling our luggage, presenting the tickets, and so forth, we had no time to give this phenomenon much thought, and it was dark by the time we had dressed for dinner. Our compartment was in the middle of the train and consequently felt little or no vibration (compartments in the Orient Express can be no more comfortable today). Petersburg was always filled with uniforms so that one grew used to them, but it was Sidonie who observed that the staterooms next to ours were full of officers, and by the profusion of gold braid and decorations, she deduced that they belonged to the court. It proved to be the grand duke Alexis and his suite. I then appreciated Sergei's solemnity at the station, and the reason for the Russian anthem.

I was sure poor Sergei would not have selected the grand duke Alexis as my traveling companion.

Before the second service of dinner, and to pass the time, I played my zither (with which I always traveled), using the soft stop. When the bell finally sounded, I opened the door, forgetting Mouchka. The little demon scrambled out of his basket and disappeared down the corridor. Laughter mingled with Mouchka's high-pitched bark. Hurrying out, I saw the grand duke in the corridor, Mouchka's small head appearing out the pocket of his cape. "Have you lost something, Mademoiselle Lardinois?" he asked, returning my runaway dog and observing that he was a very fine specimen. He added that he was happy to find that we were traveling together, and hoped to hear me play the zither again, an instrument of which he was very fond.

The train was scheduled to make a short stop during the evening, and I knew a little airing was indispensable to Mouchka. Still, I did not relish the thought of promenading my dog outside the window of the grand duke, so when the stewardess offered to do so for me I accepted her suggestion. When we came to the station, a telegram was delivered from Sergei, sending me the kiss he could not give me in Petersburg.

The next day I did not want to play the zither, since I had been overheard the day before; but there was no sound from the imperial stateroom and the stewardess informed us that the duke and his suite were in their smoking compartment, so I sang and played softly again. It was frightfully hot. We were obliged to open our door into the corridor, drawing the curtain across it. An officer knocked with a message from the grand duke, asking if we would not do him the honor of taking tea with him at four o'clock. Punctually, we presented ourselves; it would have been impossible to refuse even if we had so desired. Perhaps there was tea in that compartment, but I saw only bottles of champagne and glasses, cakes, and flowers.

"Excuse me," said our host, indicating the surrounding bower of flowers, many of which looked familiar. "I had to press your flowers into service, since where there are pretty women, flowers are indispensable!"

Every day on the train after that we enjoyed the company of the grand duke, and we remained friends until his unhappy death in Paris some years later in the arms of La Belle Baletta.

13

THE RETURN to Paris was the expected anticlimax, except for the reunion with old friends. Instead of an inspiring spring, it was autumn with its prophecy of death. At six o'clock Paris was already alight. But it was good to see it all again; we felt we had been gone for years.

We prevailed upon everyone who met us to dine with us that night. I had sent a telegram the evening before to Melanie, asking her to have dinner prepared, and I hoped there would be enough for all. We were surprised not to find Alexis, my servant, at the station. When our carriage entered the courtyard of our apartment house and he did not appear to help with the luggage, I suspected trouble.

Melanie's niece Louise opened the door. She explained that Alexis and Melanie had gone to Belgium to see Melanie's sick mother. We asked for some details of the invalid. The poor girl suddenly realized that something was wrong and called her husband, who gave the same account. I inspected the rooms; everything seemed in order. I called for my little black cat, Fauvette, but Melanie had taken her away with her. This was a shock for I had looked forward to seeing Fauvette. And I now suspected that Alexis and Melanie had left with no intention of returning.

However, we all sat down to dinner. Though there was plenty of food, there were not enough knives and forks with which to eat it. Henri had to remove and wash them after the first course. A hasty inspection proved that nothing remained in the buffet. With the exception of the service on the table, every piece of silver I owned was gone. All the linen, my collection of antique gold statuettes and coins—in short, everything moveable in the house. There remained very little to pack for Russia.

In our reconnaissance we reached the kitchen. Monsieur Imberton, noticing a large calendar hanging crookedly on the wall, mechanically reached to straighten it. The cord broke and it fell on the table upside down. There we beheld on the back of the calendar a crude, childish drawing of a farmhouse surrounded by trees and chickens, under which was scrawled, "The house we shall build with Madame's money"—surely as naïve a proof of guilt as ever a fleeing thief left behind.

Before I had properly digested this state of affairs, Ferdinand Xau arrived with his star reporter to interview me for *Le Journal*. After giving an account of the summer, adding that I would return shortly to Russia to marry Prince Peshkov, Xau, though a small man, grew two feet in an instant. He leapt up, grabbed my arm, and dragged me into the middle of the room, crying, "It isn't true! You couldn't do so terrible a thing!" He was transformed. "Don't you know, *ma petite malheureuse*, that you will close the doors of all the Paris theaters to you forever?" He waxed more and more eloquent. He stormed and threatened like Raoul Gunsbourg. Could I abandon the public that made me? Had I forgotten what had happened to the Divine Sarah herself? hissed at after her return from a tour in Germany? and Réjane? and Yvette Guilbert? "I am one of your best friends," he said, "and I am here tonight to give you one of the most important articles an actress ever had in *Le Journal*. But I cannot mention you at all now, knowing this. I can only write—" And words failing him, he continued with wild gesticulations.

At last, Léon Couturat succeeded in calming him by suggesting that since he was the only journalist in Paris who knew of my return, and as I was leaving with my sister for Brussels the next day, it would be wiser not to mention my presence in Paris at all. Perhaps within two weeks I would change my mind. "Look what you have done," he said. "She is in tears." Indeed, with the stress of the occasion, this was the truth. Leaving them all, I hurried to bed.

"My black pearl," I observed to Sidonie.

"You can give it to *me* any time you like," said Madame Imberton. "It is the most beautiful one I ever saw." It was probably true, and Sergei Peshkov, who gave it to me, loved me devotedly. I was ashamed of my distress.

After closing the apartment for good and visiting my mother in Brussels, Sidonie again accompanied me to St. Petersburg. The return journey was not as gay as the last; there was no grand duke on the train to lend a touch of glamour and romance. My surprise and delight were great, however, on beholding Sergei suddenly step onto the train at the first station across the Russian frontier. His affectionate greeting convinced me of his devotion. In the excitement of the last weeks I had forgotten about the little house he had once promised to prepare for me. When I asked where Betty was and he answered, "Chez vous," I tried to hide my embarrassment with a laugh.

At the station in Petersburg the horses I had grown so fond of awaited us, but they were harnessed to a new carriage, on the door of which were my initials and the Peshkov coat of arms: a wedding present from Sergei.

As we halted before a house in the Quai de la Cour, my heart missed a beat. This house we were about to enter held our destiny, Sergei's and mine. I had a conviction that it would be a happy one.

It was dark as we entered the hall. All was a confusion of welcoming flowers. Betty stood waiting to attend me, and I noticed she seemed to possess a new air of elegance and respect, reminding me that I was to become a princess. Sergei drew me into the music room, where a superb piano stood open and waiting to be played upon. Later, returning through the entrance hall, I observed that in the blaze of lights and flowers I had been too dazzled to notice an icon hanging in a shrine with candles and flowers before it. At the sight of the unfamiliar image a vivid realization that I was to become a Russian, with all that this implied, overcame me. Every room in the house was devoutly furnished with a similar, though smaller, version of the same icon. I knew Sergei was religious, but these inescapable shrines with flickering candles, so bizarre and oriental, told me suddenly in how foreign a land my future lay.

The moment we were alone Sergei drew me to him and asked with emotion if I was glad to be with him. My heart was full of gratitude and love. As I was about to say yes, he suddenly held me away from him and peered closely into my eyes as though to read my inmost thoughts. I began to cry! It is impossible for me to explain why—and I know I seem to be weeping most of the time in these pages—but the strange and solemn look on his face, the exotic air of everything about, unexpectedly disturbed me. Ashamed, perhaps even frightened, I slipped away and ran to my room.

He followed me, calling, "Droushka! Droushka! Whatever it is, no matter how cruel to hear, I beg you to tell me the truth!" But now I was unable to answer him.

He stopped a moment and then came up to me and said, "I fear what I have heard is true. You have left your heart in Paris." I was so astonished that a little cry escaped me. I had never thought that any such suspicion was in his head. It explained his behavior. Sidonie had heard the cry and came running. Sergei was pacing up and down outside the room, and I could find nothing to say. She took the matter in hand and found out the cause of the trouble. He told her he wanted to hear the truth from me, for surely there must be some mistake.

I found my tongue and answered, "Yes, there is a mistake, for if you will believe any tale you hear of me then you haven't the confidence that a husband should have in his wife, or that any honest woman has the right to expect." And I went back into my room.

Betty was waiting for me there. The door being ajar, she had heard some of our conversation. She gave me an explanation of Sergei's words. I might have guessed the trouble myself had I not been taken unaware. It was of course a plot of Alexander Peshkov's, who was doing everything in his power to prevent our marriage. He had even approached Betty with an offer of money if she would tell him of anything disadvantageous to me, but the faithful and honorable girl had indignantly protested that he might be proud to have me for a sister-in-law.

Soon Sidonie returned, laughing, and told me I must go and right matters, for Sergei was very unhappy. Alexander had said my romance involved a singer, and Sergei had learned the story of Arthur Cobalet. To what lengths Alexander Peshkov must have gone to dig up that long-forgotten and mild little tale of poor Arthur!

Sidonie assumed her severest tone: "Now you must be serious; you are no longer a *petite fille*. I promised Sergei you would dine with him and everything would be serene." As a further encouragement, she warned, "Alexander Peshkov will be happy if he knows he has succeeded in making you both miserable the day of your arrival. *Perhaps he has a method of spying in this house.* You are in your own home, and you must do the honors of your return."

Spy! It was not the first nor was it to be the last time I was to hear that word in Russia.

I went back to the salon and put my arms around Sergei. If his own family was using its power to ruin his happiness, and he was braving them all on my account, I determined to prove to him I was worth the trouble. A good bottle of wine and a delicious dinner can do much to raise the spirits. Indeed, I remember our little dinner *à trois* that night as a particularly gay and agreeable meal. As he left the house, Sergei vowed before the icon never to doubt me again.

I determined to see all of my new house at once; and so, like the good Belgian housewife I hoped to become, I paid a visit to the kitchen, finding the four servants seated about the table having their supper. They were overcome with astonishment to see me enter the kitchen, for in Russia the mistress never under any circumstances appeared in the domestic quarters of the house. The cook, Augustine, a French girl, had been procured for us by Betty. I felicitated her on her excellent cooking, and then, as the servants were drinking beer, I told Betty to open a bottle of wine. It was the celebration of the beginning of a new home for all of us.

The house was in the Quai de la Cour, as I've already mentioned, also known as the Quay of the Winter Palace, which was not far away. The next house was the palace of the grand duke Vladimir, to whom I had already been presented. Beneath our windows flowed the incomparable Neva—at this time of the year without its beautiful blue, for autumn in Petersburg is cloudy and damp. Nevertheless, the view of the river was delightful. Due to the narrowness of the street at this point, only wide enough for three carriages to pass, it was easy to see over the low stone parapet to the life on the water. From the window was visible one end of the bridge, which led to the Kameneo Prospect and the tomb of Peter the Great. As I saw all this for the first time, a boat passed slowly up the river below me. I seemed to be at Liège again, watching the *bateaux mouches* on the blue Meuse—blue all through the year. The sight of a handsome carriage drawing up to the house next door brought me to myself again. It was that of the grand duke.

The next day Sergei arrived while we were at lunch, bringing some newspapers which announced my return to Petersburg and our approaching marriage. He could stay but a few minutes. Hardly had he left us when there was another ring at the door and Alexander Peshkov was announced. Sidonie and I were in the hall putting on our cloaks to go for a drive. Alexander seemed very nervous and begged me to receive him. I replied that I preferred to speak to him when Sergei was present, but Sidonie thought it best that I admit him now. He followed us into the salon and I could not help observing that he looked abnormally pale. I had hardly invited him to be seated when he asked if I had seen the papers announcing my marriage to his brother.

"That marriage," he said, "can never take place. You must break it off yourself. We have nothing against you, but you will ruin the family and Sergei's position at court. If necessary we will prove that my brother is not responsible for his actions; and if you persist, the marriage shall be annulled."

I jumped to my feet. Sidonie quickly touched my arm to restrain me, but Alexander Peshkov's last words consolidated my stand. "I am sorry," I said, "that you planned to come here to surprise me in Sergei's absence. I beg of you not to repeat your visit without him, for you will not be received." I withdrew, leaving Sidonie to have him shown to the door. He said nothing further and, taking his hat, left the house.

Alexander Peshkov was my implacable enemy.

Given that our carriage was waiting, I suggested that we go for our drive at once. The horses stamped impatiently at the door, and the coachman held them by the bridle. As he understood only Russian, I gave the order "Arcadia!" without thinking. I was happy to see again the scene of my great success. Only now, the season over, the villas were empty and the avenues abandoned. It was a disheartening sight. From the few carriages on the road, people regarded us curiously; a few recognized us and bowed. On we went, two helpless foreign women driving in the Novaya Derevnia and only beginning to realize what it meant to become Russian, not speaking the language and suddenly finding ourselves confronted with some strange system of espionage and intrigue. Even the coachman who drove us had about him a peculiarly unnatural air. He was enormously fat, with a large black beard, and swathed in a cape that made him look still larger. Both a large size and a generous supply of whiskers were necessary for any coachman in Petersburg who wished to appear elegant. It was said that it took two strong men to hoist the coachman of the imperial family onto the box.

When we reached home I was anxious to know whether Sergei had returned. As we stepped out of the carriage, Betty came running to tell me that the director of the Mikhailovsky and his wife were waiting for us in the salon.

Monsieur Michel and his wife were delightful, friendly, and obliging. He was a tall, angular man of a particular type, and he himself performed from time to time, specializing in parts known as *comique à froid.* Madame Michel was small and vivacious. They had brought magnificent flowers with them, as is the Russian custom. The object of their visit was to arrange with me the works that were to be produced especially for me and the extra music that was to be added to the performances I was to sing. The general director of the imperial theaters had told Monsieur Michel that the court wished to hear me in *Mam'zelle Nitouche,* one of the most popular successes at the Arcadia, and in several operas besides, all of which I was to sing while supported by the Russian company singing in Russian. This seemed to me impossible, but I was told it had been done successfully from time to time, latterly with Battistini, who sang only in Italian. At the end of our conference Sidonie came in with tea, served in the Russian manner in tall glasses with lemon and sugar (we call them *mazarins*). As I was already at the prospect of work, the disagreeable impression of the afternoon disappeared. It was now the eighth of October. Rehearsals for *Mam'zelle Nitouche* were scheduled to begin in about a week.

Thus I would have a good week to settle down before beginning work, which was why we had returned to Petersburg as soon as possible. However, I had not counted on the intervention of Alexander Peshkov.

Poor Sidonie had grown very uneasy. She still feared, I think, that I would seize the late unpleasantness with the Peshkov family as an excuse to break off the engagement, though I assured her that I had no such intention and loved Sergei sincerely. We were both more and more anxious for him to arrive, feeling so helpless and at sea about the whole business. The telephone rang and Sergei's agitated voice said he would not be able to come to dinner but would arrive as soon as possible. I dared not ask for particulars—the telephone was in a place where all the servants could hear us. Unconsciously, I was already growing circumspect in my own home.

Dinner was a lugubrious meal that night. Sidonie and I were both preoccupied and uneasy, and we were relieved to hear the doorbell ring just as we were drinking coffee in the drawing room. Sergei dashed in without waiting to be announced as was his usual formal custom. His mother was growing quickly worse, and he was obliged to leave for the country immediately. Alexander had been to see her the day before but had not told Sergei till that same day. It was clear to both of us that Alexander had upset her to such an extent that she had grown weaker as a result. Sergei had planned to take me to her two days later (my birthday) but now he had to leave alone.

Because of this I could not tell him of Alexander's visit of that afternoon, nor that the date was set for my debut at the Mikhailovsky. My heart was heavy. Though I had not met her, I had great respect for Sergei's mother. She had proved herself our ally against the other members of the family.

Sergei left for the station in a few minutes. Just before leaving he said, "If Alexander Peshkov calls, don't receive him." He never knew of the visit; I never told him. His mother's grave condition, there could be no doubt, was the result of the evil things Alexander told her about me. The next day we had a telegram announcing her death.

Among the countless things which have perished in Russia, this imperious attitude toward family, this riding roughshod over people's happiness even to the extent of causing death, is surely one that nobody can regret.

⟵ 14 ⟶

T WO OR THREE DAYS after the death of Madame Peshkov, my first
bulletin came from the Mikhailovsky Theater and I had to go to
work. Sergei was still absent, and there was little hope of seeing
him for some time.

We opened with *La tournée Ernestin*, which was finally chosen because
it was a spectacle piece and required the services of the entire company.
It was a so-called *pièce à tiroir*, meaning that disconnected acts and scenes
could be inserted or withdrawn following the exigencies of the moment
and the talents of the cast. The Mikhailovsky was a permanent French
theater with a French company and director. Included in the company
was Monsieur Andrieux, who considered himself a star of the first magni-
tude; and indeed, he had a right to do so, for his popularity in Petersburg
was great. My appearance was not to his liking at all. La Belle Baletta
and her husband, Monsieur Larteur, were likewise in the company. Larteur made a great hit in *La tournée Ernestin* with the song "Ta Ra Ra
Boom De Ay," which amused the czar. Years later I heard it in a far distant part of the world, sung by Lottie Collins. Another member of the
company was my old friend Madame Devaux, who played duenna roles.
She pestered me to go to late suppers with Baletta and others. Under the
circumstances it was of course quite out of the question. She assured me
I was making a big mistake, but even had I been quite free to do so I
could not forget Madame Devaux's dear friend Rasputin.

We played only three times a week, so I was free to appear in the other
imperial theaters, of which there were two, not counting the celebrated
Bolshoi for ballet. Accordingly, I sang a great many times at the Mariin-

143

sky Theater, particularly in *Mignon, La traviata, Roméo et Juliette,* and *Faust*; and at the Maly Theater (Little Theater), where *The Beggar Student, Orphée aux enfers,* and *Giroflé-Girofla* made up the repertory—the older and newer true *opéras comiques.* Unlike the other theaters, there was no permanent company at the Maly, only various transient troupes. It was here that Bernhardt played, and Eleonora Duse, who made a great sensation in *La dame aux camélias.* I believe Battistini sang here also. As the company was Russian, I had some trouble, despite assurances. The solos were my comfort, and during them I braced myself for the nerve-racking ordeal of the concerted numbers, in which my cues were in a language I did not understand. My colleagues tried to help wherever possible, but familiarity with the music was my great aid. What I feared most was some unexpected contretemps or a ridiculous and incongruous effect, and this I did my best to avoid by trying to arrange the *color* of my voice to harmonize with my fellow singers in the duets. Though the whole spirit of Russian is opposed to French, when sung it is a surprisingly soft language, and the two blend together without unpleasant sounds.

The imperial theaters were collectively under the management of one man who occupied a high military position; in short, he was so great a dignitary that, though he signed all our contracts, none of us ever came face to face with him.

The management was very severe. Rehearsals began punctually; no one would dream of being late. Indeed, backstage one felt all the etiquette of a court. The elegance too was extreme; the dressing rooms were not only furnished in luxury but also had large salons attached to them for receiving one's visitors. There was never any bustle, confusion, or unpleasantness at the imperial theaters. All was serene, severe, and governed by a curious military exactness. I have never seen its equal elsewhere. The artists' foyer was large, out of all proportion, and here the members of the company and the great world mingled for long, sociable intermissions. A *buvette* opening onto the foyer served every imaginable refreshment. These long intermissions had the undesirable effect of breaking the thread of the performance and getting both audience and actors quite out of the spirit and atmosphere of the theater, a most inartistic situation.

The audiences were certainly brilliant. The imperial family attended both the Mikhailovsky and Mariinsky Theaters, and evenings in which the imperial box was occupied were always gala events. On those nights an electric atmosphere surcharged both the audience and the company. All was more tense and exciting; everyone was pitched to a higher key. Of course, the applause had to await a signal from the imperial box, and we bowed only toward it, ignoring the rest of the house. The Mariinsky had a capacity of two thousand, the Mikhailovsky only nine hundred. Curiously enough, the imperial family no longer attended performances at the Maly Theater. I believe the building was considered too old and tottering—it did not matter if it collapsed on *us*—and here it was more difficult for the secret police to take precautions against assassins.

The prodigality displayed on benefit nights beggars description. One piece of silverware was nothing, not worth mention: boxes the size of small trunks fitted with complete services of solid silverware, even large silver samovars, were presented on the stage. The munificence was impossible to believe. My benefit night was the only performance Sergei attended all winter. Because of his mourning, he went nowhere in public. Sidonie and I only dined with our most intimate friends.

The cold was intense, the ground covered with snow which deadened sound to a wonderful extent. In the streets only the jingle of bells on the horse's harnesses was heard, as people, invisible beneath mountains of fur, sped past in their troikas or hurried through the streets. It was a battle to keep from freezing to death (and anyone who has spent a winter in Russia can understand why the Russians consume so much vodka). The houses were all closed by at least three doors, and in the more fashionable districts each of these doors was guarded by a porter. "Na chai!" (For tea!) was the constant cry when one attempted to call on a friend, with a hand in one's purse searching for small change, bribing one's way in. I do not believe the evils of tipping ever reached such a state as they did in old Russia. The Soviet Union abolished it completely, and a good thing too.

In spite of continued work at the Mikhailovsky and guest appearances at the Mariinsky, life was very monotonous, for I could not dine with my colleagues, being a fiancée in mourning as it were. However, the companies at these two theaters did not altogether understand my situation.

It was a pleasure to sing at the Maly Theater, where among other things I created Karl Millöcker's *The Beggar Student* in Russia.[45] It was curious to sing and speak in French with the rest of the company performing in Russian; at the other theaters, of course, the audiences were re-cruited from the court and the aristocracy, and so everyone spoke and sang in French.

In *The Beggar Student* occurs a charming duet in act two. After a few performances, I sang the refrain in Russian with the tenor—which ren-dered the good Russians mad with joy. For my encore I used to sing Aliab'ev's "The Nightingale" or some other song in Russian, and the au-diences came back night after night just to hear this part of the perfor-mance, which caused the receipts to mount and made me popular with the managers.

At a small dinner at my house, Sergei announced our wedding day for the following month, 9 May. After this he attempted, unsuccessfully, to have my contract with the imperial theaters annulled. It had two more years to run.

I now turned my attention to my wedding dress and other such con-cerns. Madame Izambon, the court *couturière*, brought me a dress from Paris. I had so often played a bride on the stage that my dearest wish was to avoid completely the look of an operatic bride. Every day large pack-ages of gifts arrived more and more frequently at the house, and finally the great day dawned.

The custom in Russia forbade the bride and groom to meet on the wedding day except at the church. I spent the afternoon at my toilette with Madame Izambon's help. Downstairs the employees of Cubat pre-pared the wedding breakfast, and I could hear the horses at the door champing and neighing to take us to the Chapel of the Court Pages.

At last it was time to leave. I peered into the mirror anxiously but reached the conclusion that there was nothing at all of a comic opera bride about me. Just as I started downstairs, Sidonie appeared with a package from Sergei that was to be presented at this particular moment. I opened it and found a jewel box containing a magnificent set, consist-ing of a necklace and tiara of pearls and diamonds. They were a magic dream. I hastily put them on but dared not look again in the mirror.

My two witnesses, Prince Lobanov and Count Kamarovski, were wait-ing in the salon. They had another gift from Sergei, an ermine cloak which they put about my shoulders. Young officers of Sergei's regiment were a guard of honor in the anteroom, and three carriages decorated with flowers were at the door. We started off. As a neighborly gesture in honor of the wedding, the palace of the grand duke Vladimir next door was illuminated and remained so till we returned from the ceremony.

The Chapel of the Court Pages was likewise ablaze. Even with only our most intimate friends in attendance it seemed crowded, though in my state of excitement everything dazzled me. The Belgian consul was present, as was the French ambassador, the duc de Montebello and his staff, and numerous members of the imperial theaters, including various directors and officers. But beside Sergei stood only a cousin to represent his family. Alexander Peshkov, who lived in Petersburg, was "in Europe." The chapel organ boomed, and the choir began to chant a litany in Russian. Prince Lobanov conducted me into the nave where Sergei stood

Clara Lardinois. Courtesy William R. Moran.

and we moved to the altar, Sergei on the right and I on the left, with our witnesses behind us.

The high priest of the cathedral of Notre Dame de Kazan began the service, aided by the chapel priest. Their jeweled robes, as well as the gleaming metal on the officers, actually hurt the eyes, while Prince Lobanov and Count Kamarovski held the massive crown above our heads, relieved every few minutes by other members of the wedding party. For a long while the priest went mumbling on, performing various offices of which I understood nothing. Only when I heard the name "Princess Sergei Nikolaevich Peshkov" did I realize it was all over.

We traveled to Moscow for the two weeks of our wedding trip. One can never forget one's first view of Moscow, especially if the sun is gilding the golden domes and minarets of the many churches there. One evening we attended a performance of Offenbach's *Orphée aux enfers* at the Hermitage Theater. A French company was playing, and to my delight the role of Euridice (one of my favorites) was sung that night by Mademoiselle Méaly, a French girl who had in a very short time risen to a high position in her profession. Not long before, she had been a member of the chorus in my Paris production, and later we had been sister stars at the Casino de Paris. Recognizing me in our box at the end of the first act, she threw the bouquets she had received up at me. Of course, this started confusion and neck-craning in the audience, and the director came before the footlights to explain, politely expressing the wish that they would soon hear me in Moscow. He then came to our box accompanied by three gentlemen in elaborate uniforms. From the respect our companions accorded one of them, I understood him to be a personage of great importance. He spoke to Sergei and then said he hoped to hear me soon in Moscow, kissed my hand, and departed. He made a strange impression on me, for though he was a man of imposing figure and bearing, his eyes were peculiarly hard, perhaps even cruel. The director explained that he was the most important man in Moscow, the chief of police; but Sergei seemed to know him both by name and reputation, and I saw that his reaction agreed with mine.

On our return to Petersburg, Sidonie left for home, laden with presents from Sergei for herself and her family. His kindness touched her deeply and she left lighthearted, convinced that my happiness was sealed.

The summer passed quickly in a little cottage Sergei had taken which was not far from our first home in Russia, Arcadia. In October, with the opening of the imperial theaters, my work was to start afresh at the Mik-hailovsky. Russian contracts were sacred things.

Only one rather odd occurrence that summer upset Sergei.

I was in the habit of going horseback riding with various friends through the shady bridle paths and alleys around Arcadia. The summer weather was lovely and we rarely missed a day. One day my mount acted very strangely and soon began to balk, shy, and rear. We decided he must have a stone wedged into his shoe, and the groom inspected his hooves, but they were in good order. A moment later he reared abruptly and be-gan to froth at the mouth. I dismounted at once and we took off the sad-dle, finding under it, so arranged that it pointed directly into the horse's back, a good-sized nail. It had been hammered carefully into place under-neath the skirt to be invisible from above, and projected only enough to wound the horse while being ridden. We never discovered who did this, but Sergei was certain it was not the groom.

One day I received a call from the director of the Mikhailovsky with news which was to me (and even more, as it appeared, to Sergei) unwel-come. Monsieur Michel had with him a letter from His Excellency, the director of the imperial theaters, and enclosed was another from the di-rector of the Hermitage Theater in Moscow, who was anxious to have me open his season with two weeks of guest appearances. I said I was sure my husband would not let me go, since he himself could not then leave Petersburg. But Monsieur Michel called my attention to my contract, which stipulated that I must go wherever the director chose to send me.

Since we could do nothing but accept the inevitable, Betty and I set out for Moscow. We had had the good fortune to reserve in advance the apartment in which Sergei and I had stayed the previous spring, and this made me feel a little more at home.

The director of the Hermitage Theater was a second Gunsbourg, hav-ing had brilliant success as an impresario, and I soon knew he was doing everything possible to make the season a gala experience. We had a great many rehearsals, which occupied much time. For recreation and a little fresh air, Betty and I took long walks about Moscow whenever possible.

After our second or third sally to revisit the sights, Betty observed one evening that she was sure we were being shadowed. She had more than once noticed a tall, remarkable-looking man at some distance.

After every performance I received a mysterious basket of red roses with no card attached, which I knew could not be from Sergei, who always enclosed a little note. The evening before my farewell appearance I received an invitation to a reception and supper at the palace of His Excellency, the chief of police, for the following evening. I immediately declared to Betty that nothing would induce me to go, but she assured me she had heard at the theater that this was the custom, an invitation His Excellency tendered to all visiting artists. I spoke to the director, telling him that, being alone, I could not accept the invitation. He was horrified and with wide gestures assured me that I could not affront His Excellency. The invitation was in the nature of a summons—a royal command. If I disobeyed, it would injure not only me but also my husband. His Excellency was a most influential man in Russia, and many high dignitaries and other important guests were present at these receptions. I inquired then if it was he, the director, who had sent me the roses without a card. When he left he was still unable to control his laughter.

After the performance His Excellency's carriage drew up at the stage door. I told Betty I would not remain long. The director presented me to a strange, military-looking gentleman and informed me that this man was commissioned to take charge of me. Unlike most Russians I had met, he spoke no word of French. Much against my will I entered the carriage, my silent companion following, and we drove off. As I settled myself in the carriage I observed two men pass quickly, giving me a curious look. Moscow was growing decidedly unpleasant.

The horses were lashed and in a few minutes we drove up to the steps of a magnificent palace. The approach was truly fairylike. In the vast gardens behind the palace, as far as one could see, were trees illuminated in many colors. The entrance hall was superb. Two rows of dignitaries, one to the right and one to the left, saluted me as I went by; it was almost like the Chapel of the Court Pages once more. And as obsequious hands removed my ermine cloak, a door at the end of the hall opened and His Excellency appeared, arrayed in a gold chamois uniform glittering with decorations.

He came forward with welcoming words and kissed both my hands.

Anxious to know the reason for this amazing display of pomp and luxury, I was at first unaware of his presence. He placed my arm in his, and thus together we entered a beautiful room where a long table stood laden with *zakuski* and covered with bottles of wine and liqueurs. Looking back now, the whole scene, indeed the entire situation, appears incredible, ridiculous; then, I was really both alarmed and astonished. I could hear through a distant door men and women laughing and talking and a Gypsy orchestra playing loudly and then dying away into a soft accompaniment. It is one of the most vivid memories of my life and hardly seems more of a dream now than it did at the time.

But the doors were suddenly shut against the reassuring noise, and left alone, His Excellency began making polite speeches about the pleasure it gave him to welcome me to his house, and *unaccompanied*. We walked about the table, helping ourselves to caviar and other delicacies while I tried to think of a plan of escape. He conducted me to a sofa and served me champagne, bringing me the glass with a courtly bow. I inquired, with an effort at ease, if his other guests had already dined. He replied with the same disagreeable smile I remembered so well from the previous spring, and sat down close beside me. I then made the unpleasant discovery that if he had not supped he had at least already drunk.

I should like to be able to say I made some wonderful remark which cleared up the whole situation, but what I did was to make a sudden movement with my foot and upset my glass of champagne down the front of my dress. Springing up with a cry, I ran to a large glass door, tore it open, and flew into the garden. The trees with their many-colored lanterns looked more unreal than ever. I heard His Excellency call several times, but ran blindly on. I confess I was thoroughly frightened! All at once I saw one of the men who had passed the carriage outside the theater talking loudly with one of His Excellency's guards, and his companion was coming toward me. He took me by the arm and led me through a covered entrance back to the street while the other man continued to harangue. A carriage stood there and I was thrown, rather than assisted, into it—without my cloak, but happily likewise without His Excellency! The two men followed me. All I understood of their talk was the Russian word "orders" and the name "Sergei Nikolaevich."

The next morning the cloak was returned with another bouquet of roses and a diamond bracelet. Needless to say I sent the bracelet and roses back at once. My two guardians, whom Sergei had sent from Petersburg, did not leave me again. As for my soirée with His Excellency, I did not tell Sergei the true version of that until we were safely out of Russia.

The following September, Sergei and I left for Brussels. Sidonie had written me that Mother was not well. I had been gone from home too long, and now Sergei was on leave and my contract with the imperial theaters had run out. We gave up the house in the Quai de la Cour and put most of our valuables in storage, including all except a few of the magnificent jewels Sergei had given me. I took Betty with me.

Sergei had a vacation of three months. Our plan was to go directly to Brussels to meet my family, and then Sergei would leave me there while he made a flying trip to Constantinople to see his brother Feodor, who, as I have already said, was military attaché to the Russian embassy there.

He stayed a month in Brussels, and I was very happy to see the good impression he made on my family, all of whom became devoted to him. At the end of the month he planned to leave for Turkey and asked again if I did not wish to come with him. I decided against going because the purpose of his trip was in part to arrange family affairs, and knowing the attitude of the Peshkovs I decided it would be more tactful and helpful to remain in the background; besides this, my mother was not yet well.

So Sergei left for Constantinople alone early in October 1894, traveling with only a few pieces of hand luggage. He planned to stay only a week with his brother and, as it was a four-day trip each way, be back in Brussels in about two weeks.

The first few days after he had gone I received letters and telegrams telling me of his progress and then of his arrival in Constantinople. He met his brother and seemed to be pleased with the results of the trip, though anxious to return. But then two days went by without any news of him. The last word I had was of a proposed trip to some spot not far from Constantinople, but there was no mention of the name of this place, nor was the exact reason for the necessity of the trip given. His letter was postmarked "Cirkadje Station," a small town in the direction of Siberia and not far from Constantinople.

At the end of the second newsless day I sent a telegram to Sergei's brother at the Russian embassy. Had Sergei not kept me so closely informed of his movements I would not have grown uneasy, but because I knew his habits the silence was inexplicable.

The next day I had an answer from Constantinople. "Sergei has met with an accident." That was all. Frantically, I telegraphed for further news but received none.

Then I went to see a Russian count who was living in Brussels and whom we had met on the train coming from Petersburg. I knew he had been in communication with Sergei and might possibly have news. As it turned out, he had none. But at my request he sent out a telegram, and soon received an answer. Sergei was dead and his body had already been sent back to St. Petersburg.

15

THE DAYS that followed are not a blank in my life, but I am unable to recount them.

Sergei was not dead—I refused to accept the terse words of that telegram as the truth. I could not give up to despair on the word of Feodor Peshkov. In those terrible moments and without anyone to assist me, I threw myself on the mercy of the Russian count who had sent the telegram.

This count and his wife were fairly important people in Petersburg, but I did not know exactly who they were or even why they were living in Brussels. Brussels is a famous city for exiles and for people who for any reason find it inexpedient to live in their native places. Rather than living in seclusion, however, the count and countess entertained a great deal. They had entertained Sergei and me in Brussels, and at this time they had among their house guests Jean and Edouard De Reszke, whom I met here for the first time. For various reasons, I felt a certain distrust of the count but not particularly of the countess. I knew she disliked me and I suspected she liked Sergei perhaps too much, for she had demonstrated bad taste and stupidity by disparaging me to my husband. But now in my trouble and despair I begged the count to help me. He inquired what friends I had in Petersburg whom I could trust, and I thought of Prince Lobanov. He was one of Sergei's closest friends, and he had always been a kind friend to me; indeed, he was a witness at our marriage. The count telegraphed him and received a letter in answer. It merely confirmed the report. Sergei's death had been announced in the Petersburg papers; he was already buried in Petersburg; and the prince advised the count to warn me not to return, for the present, to Russia. No further information was given.

Sergei was dead. I had to accept that testimony.

I decided to leave at once for Petersburg—alone, if no one would accompany me; but the count insisted I remain in Brussels. He went with me to the Russian ambassador in Brussels. From him I likewise only received admonitions to stay away from Russia, though he promised to write to Petersburg in an effort to learn more.

But the days went by without any news, with only the repeated assertion that I must be patient. Finally I went to him and demanded a passport for Russia. He said that for my own good I must not entertain the idea of going to Russia, and when I closed my ears to this I discovered that he had no intention of giving me a passport. He did not refuse in so many words, but I saw that this was his decision.

By now I had come to the conclusion that the count was not to be trusted, and I told him no more of my plans. I little doubted that he was in communication with Feodor Peshkov. At last I realized I could not look for help from any of these people. There seemed to be a conspiracy to keep me ignorant concerning the death of my husband. I received a letter of condolence from Prince Lobanov which contained no information, merely the warning to remain in Brussels. I wrote to Monsieur Michel of the Mikhailovsky Theater, but he was out of Russia and the answer came from the south of France. No help there either.

After a talk with the family lawyer, I decided to go to my sister Clémence in Romania. Her husband was now district attorney for Craiova, the second city in Romania, and there might be a chance of help there. From Craiova it was not far to Constantinople, and I was fully determined to go there if necessary, as it might be possible to learn something there if all else failed. But I felt something must be done. I thought of my friend Ali Raiff Bey, one-time military attaché to the Turkish embassy in Brussels, who now enjoyed a high position at the court of the sultan of Turkey, and from whose family I had received many invitations to visit Constantinople.

In the middle of December I left for Craiova in secret with Betty. No one outside my immediate family knew of my departure or of my destination, for in truth I felt I was not safe anywhere if ambassadors themselves could only warn me to stay in seclusion in Brussels.

My brother-in-law Michel, on hearing a detailed account of the whole tragedy, did not conceal from me his belief that the situation would be dangerous if I were to return to Russia. He could not understand my wish to go to Constantinople. The customs of the Turks and their habits of thought were not understood by Occidentals. I told him how I had first met Ali Raiff Bey, what sort of person he was, and that any day I expected an answer to the letter I had written him from Brussels.

Clémence had married when she was very young and I was still a small girl, so I had not known her well, but it was a great consolation for me to be with her again. She was an excellent pianist and much interested in painting, and under happier conditions I could have remained with her for an indefinite period. She had a lovely home. It was delightful to meet for the first time my Romanian nieces and nephews, but I could not compose myself for a leisurely visit with Sergei's death uppermost in my mind and the mystery still unsolved. I thanked her for her invitation to spend a longer time with them and promised to accept it—but later, when my mind would be at rest.

At the end of the following week Ali Raiff's answer came, saying his mother and sisters would be delighted to receive me. In the meantime Michel had made investigations and learned that my Turkish diplomat's family was beyond reproach and most respectable; and following the instructions in the letter, Betty and I set out for Constantinople.

I had some difficulty in persuading Betty to come with me, but Michel finally convinced her it would be a pleasant voyage, only forty-eight hours on the Black Sea. We were to take a boat from Constanţa, the port for Bucharest, to Pera, the European port for Constantinople. With Michel's help I got a passport immediately, made out under my maiden name. He accompanied us to Bucharest and put us on the train for Constanţa, making me promise to keep them informed by letter of all my adventures. He also gave me a number of letters of introduction, including one to a confrère of his who lived in Pera. Luckily, after we left he had the inspiration to write to the Belgian consul at Pera to inform him of my arrival, for Michel had very little confidence in the Turks.

When our ship finally docked at Pera we were obliged to stay in our cabins until the arrival of the Turkish officials. At last three men appeared, and after reading my passport attentively they began questioning me on the purpose of my journey. Unprepared for this and certainly not wishing to tell them the truth, I merely said I had come to visit the family of Ali Raiff Bey. The men began to talk excitedly in Turkish and I became very ill at ease, when suddenly Ali Raiff presented himself at the cabin door. He spoke to the men, who retired with military salutes. Ali Raiff was aide-de-camp to the sultan.

He regretted having been late and therefore unable to dispense with some of the formalities with which I had been troubled, but the boat had arrived early. His two sisters were waiting in their carriage on the quay. With a few words he attended to all our luggage and conducted us from the ship.

The primitive wharf and the strange noises of the crowds which had collected about astonished me. The crowds were mostly composed of women and children, the women in long somber cloaks, their heads hidden by hoods to which were attached heavy veils that concealed all except their eyes. The men were dressed in European style except for their fezzes of red felt, which the law required. I did not have time to notice much else, for the carriage was close at hand and there sat Ali Raiff's two sisters. They were similarly dressed in veils and cloaks. They greeted me amiably but in very bad French. Ali excused them, telling me that in Turkey women generally speak only their native language. My uneasiness was still greater when the carriage, having gone through a number of very narrow streets bordered with houses which looked like prisons, entered an immense courtyard surrounded by high walls. The great gates, which opened as if by magic at our approach, closed quickly behind us with a sinister clang. I began to regret, too late, that I had come to Constantinople—above all into Ali Raiff Bey's family, who lived in the Turkish town of Istanbul, which was separated by a large bridge from Pera, the European section of the city.[46]

Betty looked at me with large terrified eyes, but I soon decided that because the life I was now seeing was very different from that of western Europe, it was foolish to give way to regrets and misgivings; this was a new adventure and must be considered in that light. So I was determined to accept in the best possible grace this curious Turkish hospitality.

A second gate opened carefully and shut behind us, and here I had another surprise. A long flight of double stairs rose before us. When we dismounted, the two veiled sisters invited us to climb the left side while Ali took the right. I learned soon that the left side led to the women's quarters, the harem, to which the men never came except on particular invitation; the right side led to the men's quarters, the solemneck. We followed the ladies and were ushered into a large room furnished in true harem style, with divans all along the walls and many large cushions and little tables in the center of the floor.

At once several young slaves came forward to help us off with our outdoor clothes, and now for the first time I saw my hostesses face to face. The elder was dark and swarthy of complexion but had very lovely eyes, inspiring confidence. She seemed intelligent and kindhearted, and it was clear she had some conception of the strangeness of my new experiences. Unfortunately, she lived at a considerable distance from Istanbul. Both sisters were married. The younger was really beautiful, and unlike most Turkish women (particularly those of the lower classes), she was fair. Her hair was dark blonde and her eyes blue, yet she retained something of her oriental heritage. I soon discovered, however, that she was as stupid as one could imagine and of no use whatsoever to me.

We were invited to sit down and make ourselves comfortable, which we did. After we exchanged banalities for a few moments a door opened at the end of the room and a number of slaves entered in a procession. The elder sister said hurriedly to me that this signaled the approach of their mother, and when she appeared I was to do exactly as she and her sister did. A tall majestic lady followed the slaves, dressed in semi-European costume with a flowing loose garment with wide kimono sleeves over it. At her appearance my two hostesses fell to their knees and I hastily did likewise, signaling Betty, who was stout and unsupple, to follow my example, which she did with groans. Ali Raiff's mother came forward and held out her hand, which her two daughters kissed. Lifting the hem of her loose robe, they kissed that too, and you may be sure that I entered into the spirit and did a good job of it myself. The tall lady seemed pleased at this; she smiled and placed her hand on my head as a token of welcome. She sat down cross-legged on a low couch, and we sat on cushions close by. Slaves came forward with thick Turkish coffee and little sweet cakes, an indispensable ceremony in Turkish homes when any guest is present. While we ate and drank, several young slaves performed a sort of dance, playing curious music on primitive instruments, small guitar-looking objects and little tom-toms.

Knowing no French at all, my hostess spoke to me through the intermediary of her elder daughter, whose name was Xenia, wishing me welcome and inquiring about my journey from Romania; she smiled pleasantly and said several things which were translated to mean that I had found favor in her eyes. At length Xenia rose at her mother's suggestion to show me my "quarters."

We were led through a number of small corridors which opened into rooms. Young slave girls and boys flitted silently past doorways on their various errands, and this we soon discovered was a good sample of Turkish domestic life. One never felt alone or private for a moment—a dark, silent shadow might be confidently expected at any time to interrupt one's meditations or one's toilette, though the Turks paid no more attention to this than we would to a housefly buzzing past an open door.

The quarters selected for us consisted of a large, empty room with an alcove. A series of tall windows, which took up one entire wall and looked out over a garden with trees and fountains, relieved the prison simplicity; and these windows were hung with mousharabia curtains and blinds, permitting one to look out and yet be invisible from the outside. When I say the room was empty I mean just that, for the furniture consisted only of a few low cushions on which we were expected to squat cross-legged. Betty, who was growing more morose and despondent by the minute, inquired about the beds. At this, Xenia smiled and said they had no European beds. She opened an armoire and indicated two rolled-up mattresses within, informing me that at sundown a servant would take them out and unroll them on the floor, putting them back in the morning. She wished to assign an adjoining room to Betty, but quickly I said that she was used to sleeping in the room with me (a lie), and therefore the present arrangements were perfect. So, after being informed that at dinner I would meet Xenia's father, we were left alone.

Betty immediately broke out into lamentations and complaints as she surveyed the bare room, the doorways without doors, and the thin mattresses we were expected to sleep on. As for the toilet arrangements, their elemental state quite beggared description. Hot water was a great luxury in Turkish houses, and seldom used. Cold water was brought in high jars, and with the use of basins in the alcove we made some attempt to bathe for dinner. My luggage had not come from the wharf yet, so I had nothing but what I already wore.

Taken all in all I was rather depressed by the whole affair, but I reprimanded Betty, regaling her with words of courage I did not actually possess. These were adventures of travel, it was foolish to sit always at home with comfort and peace, the world was large, and so on; but I felt considerably annoyed at Ali Raiff for not having warned me in his letter of what to expect in his house. He knew occidental ways and had often been a guest at my father's house in Brussels. I could not help feeling he was guilty of negligence and ignorance for allowing me to come so unwittingly into a life so different from my own.

Nevertheless, the novelty of everything about and the promise of more to come (soon fulfilled) allowed me to put a bold face on our adventures. I was sadly amused at the thought that several of my roles were those of Turkish and Arabian slave girls, particularly in the operas *Le grand mogol* and *Ali Baba and the Forty Thieves.* For this reason our surroundings were not altogether as novel as one might have expected, the main difference being that on the stage, when the curtains fell, I went home to a comfortable bed and all the amenities of Western civilization, while now I was having a taste, without intermissions, of the genuine article.

Three knocks on the door—the signal of a male member of the family—interrupted us. By experience I soon learned that the father knocked once, the two smallest boys, aged twelve and fourteen, twice, Ali three times, and the two brothers-in-law four times. This system was devised in case the women were entertaining female guests; it gave them time to cover their faces before signaling to the servant who guarded the door to pull aside the heavy portieres. The portieres, as well as the heavy curtains at the windows, were useful to take refuge behind if by chance any ladies outside the family were caught unveiled. In this case the intruding gentleman could retire to give the ladies time to cover their faces.

Ali came in at my invitation, and I was relieved to see him in the mood of the young diplomat who had received the hospitality of my family in Brussels. He came forward smiling and, taking my hands, told me how happy he was to find me in the bosom of his family. He said I had made a great hit with his sisters, as well as with his mother. This last fact I privately put down to my success in genuflecting and kissing the hem of her robe so wholeheartedly. He assured me that his father would be equally pleased, and I wondered if I would have to kiss the hem of his robe too, for that evening there was to be a family dinner at which I would meet the father as well as the two brothers-in-law.

Ali spent some time explaining to me the manners and customs of the country, while Betty busied herself arranging our personal possessions in the two rooms allotted us. Having read my letter, he was au courant with my misfortunes, so I explained my true reasons for coming to Constantinople, pronouncing that I must go to Pera the next day to see the lawyer who was a friend of my brother-in-law in Craiova. Ali appeared somewhat displeased at this and finally said that I must be patient for a few days. Furthermore I was made to understand that because I was the invited guest of a Turkish family I could not possibly go out alone or wear European dress. Ali's father was a minister of the sultan and Ali himself one of the sultan's aides-de-camp, and so over the whole family a strict watch was maintained. The sultan was in constant fear of assassination, especially by some European plot.

"So you see how dangerous it is when we have a European visiting us," Ali said, "and how much we have to depend on your tact. I count on you not to make any move without first consulting me. All boats docking in Constantinople are surrounded by spies: easily fifty per cent of the people in the streets of Pera are spies. In the shops the women who serve you are spies. In the restaurants, theaters—in fact, everywhere. You must be watchful of your speech, and it is mandatory that you be accompanied by a Turk who is well known. Many people are arrested without knowing why, for having spoken a word or dropped unwittingly a chance phrase concerning the sultan."

This was consoling information!

"Why didn't you tell me all this in your letter?" I demanded. "For what purpose did I come here if I cannot take one step by myself?"

One can imagine my state of mind. If Feodor Peshkov learned I was in Constantinople, what might he do? I was much alarmed, and it seemed as though I would be as helpless here as I had been in Brussels.

"For my peace of mind," I told him, "I must see that lawyer in Pera."

Ali begged me not to take things *au tragique.* He promised to assume all responsibility for us, but his duty bound him to obey the laws of the land. He took a pad from his pocket and asked me the usual questions about myself and my family and my reasons for coming to Turkey, which we decided to put down purely as a visit. The same questions were asked of Betty. Brisk and business-like, he closed his book and awaited the momentary arrival of the officers of the censors to whom we would be obliged to give all this information.

⟿ 16 ⟾

SOON IT WAS EVIDENT that not the least of my troubles in Istanbul was to be my little dog Moushka. Betty carried him in a basket with a coat thrown over it, and so far no one knew I had a dog. As soon as we were alone Moushka was let out, whereupon he instantly took refuge under the long seat which practically surrounded the room. When Ali appeared, Moushka began growling as if uncommonly disturbed and could not be quieted or coaxed from his retreat. Ali frightened us by informing us that dogs were forbidden in *musulman* homes, and caused further alarm by adding, "If one of our native dogs sees your pet, he will be gone in one gulp."

It was against the law to kill a dog in Constantinople. Wild dogs ran free in the streets of Istanbul, prowling like scavenging jackals, living in cellars and abandoned holes, with each pack haunting a certain section of town. If a dog belonging to one clan encroached upon the domain of another, a bloody battle ensued. In general they kept to their cellars or slunk along in the shadows of the buildings, but if they took up a position in the center of a narrow street, carriages had to avoid them carefully or risk heavy fines in case one was killed. Although it was necessary to protect the lives of these dogs, it was unnecessary to feed them; and as they received little food, they became a wild, ferocious, marauding, savage horde akin to wolves. They increased in such numbers that the government was compelled to put a large colony of them on an island in the Bosporus, but here they made such an unearthly clamor that they were shipped back to their old haunts. Ali told us to hide Moushka for the time being, promising that on the following day he would see what he could do.

Ali's father, Ali Raiff Pasha, did not return to the house every day. He had his own quarters at the ministry and lived there certain days in the week. Ali, as aide-de-camp to the sultan, went to the palace every three days and remained on duty all night. I was assured that the pasha, though in appearance very severe and forbidding, was at heart a kind man. He spoke French fairly well, though he preferred to speak English, a language I did not speak at all. That evening he was coming home especially to do me honor.

As it was necessary to inform me of everything, I learned that it was not the custom to speak much at meals, though afterward, when the family retired to the reception hall to take coffee, all was life and animation. When I inquired if I might wear my only evening dress, Ali laughed and said his father was used to meeting European women in Pera. Betty left the room for a moment, and I explained to Ali that she was my companion, not a maid, and I wanted her with me wherever we went. "That is as you wish," he said, and he put his valet Bilal at our disposition. Bilal was a Negro, born in Constantinople, but I knew him well from the days in Brussels, where he had learned French. Both Betty and I were reassured to have him as our personal servant. Betty, I could see, was growing more and more ill at ease in a *musulman* house: both she and Moushka were all that was unadaptable. She refused to leave the dog, so Bilal served her meals in our quarters. When the pasha was absent I could do likewise.

Ali left very amiably, wishing me happiness while in his home and promising to aid me all he could. In leaving he warned me to be ready at five o'clock, the hour at which his father was expected.

At five o'clock I was ready, wearing my only evening dress, when Ali appeared and conducted me to the dining hall. A gong sounded three times. Xenia had sent me, by the hand of a little slave, a large veil similar to those she and her sister wore, and Ali explained that I must wear it lest we pass some male domestic of the house on our way to dinner. So for the first time, I entered purdah, and we started off.

In a small anteroom outside the dining hall the ladies laid aside their veils. Xenia and her sister were waiting for us here; the rest of the family had already assembled within. Before we entered, there was a discussion between Ali and his sisters, and I realized their gesticulations were aimed at my veil, the subject of the argument. Foreign women did not visit *musulman* families, and certainly not with their faces uncovered. Xenia and her sister were not pleased that their husbands should see my face. Ali won the day, however, and told me to take off the veil. I obeyed, and we all four entered the hall.

Ali Raiff Pasha stood in the center of the room. His two daughters went forward and kneeled to kiss his hand. When I advanced to do likewise, he stepped toward me, raised his hand as a sign for me to desist, and then extended it courteously in European fashion. It was surprising to find him a tall, handsome man in his late forties, with very polished manners. He wore a black beard scrupulously cared for, and his eyes, as is usual in Turkey, were beautiful. He was dressed in European fashion, with a very long redingote, but he also wore the invariable red fez and tassel.

In the middle of the room stood a long table, and the pasha and his wife sat down at either end. I was seated to the right of my host, with Ali at my right. At either side of the mother sat her young sons. The two brothers-in-law, who merely bowed to me distantly, were on our side, with their wives opposite.

So far all had gone smoothly. The pasha addressed a few polite remarks to me in French in a pleasant, low voice. But as Ali had warned me, there was little conversation at the table, food being the only purpose of the gathering.

A small retinue of slave girls in gay costumes (I noticed they were also wearing soft slippers, though they usually went about barefoot) flitted silently around the table. First we had bowls of soup, thick and peppery but good. Next came the usual Turkish dish, a mixture of meat and vegetables hashed together and rolled up in large leaves. The Turks hash all their meat dishes except roast lamb, which is cooked entire and then hacked into generous hunks. Knives are not used at table, but we had spoons for the soup and curious two-tined forks. For dessert small sweet cakes of every shape and vivid color were served—these were excellent. And for drink there was a punch made of fruit juices and an unusual, rather strong wine or other alcoholic concoction.

In the middle of the meal I suddenly became aware of a soft, high-pitched voice intoning a chant, which drifted in the open window. It was a curious song consisting of very high tones. Immediately, the whole family rose and, facing Mecca, bent over until hands nearly touched the floor. I knew at once it was the signal for evening prayer, sung from the minaret of a nearby mosque, and so I was able without confusion to bend over in the same devotional attitude until the song was ended. Then we all sat down and silently continued our dinner. When we were finished the pasha gave a signal and we rose. He signed for me to follow him, and we passed through another door into a large, light room where a bevy of young slaves dressed in costumes of unexpected splendor danced and played while we took coffee.

It seemed hardly possible that I was seated next to so high and important a Turkish dignitary as Ali Raiff Pasha in the familiarity of his own home, an opportunity which few European women had enjoyed.

Though he had never been to Europe, the pasha evidently had many relations with Europeans outside his home: his dignity, ease, and suave oriental manners were truly impressive. During the dance of the slaves both the men and women smoked cigarettes. Turkey and Russia were the only countries I had been to in which women smoked at this time; indeed, in Turkey smoking seemed to be the beginning and end of their emancipation.

The pasha said that his son had informed him that I sang, and he hoped that I would consent to allow him to hear me. He then inquired what I most wanted to see in Constantinople. Unabashed, I answered, the sultan's palace. Looking at me attentively, he asked, "Would you not be afraid to be kept there?" and laughed, adding that he would see what arrangements could be made.

Soon after this a gong sounded, signaling the arrival of a visitor, and Ali was sent to find out who it was. He came back with the information that it was another pasha, and all the gentlemen withdrew. Left alone with the ladies, I was informed by Xenia that her mother had planned for us all to go to the Turkish baths the next day, as they were anxious for me to enjoy the experience. The words "Turkish baths" conveyed to me only the well-known establishment of Hammam in Paris, which I assumed was an authentic one.

Shortly after, I begged leave to retire, and Ali was sent to conduct me back to my quarters in the harem. I was glad to see him again for a moment alone, as I was anxious to learn when a visit to Pera could be safely arranged. That night he was on duty at the palace, and there was no knowing when he would be free again. Though Ali knew of the death of Sergei I had not given him my complete confidence, and now I told him that I wished to go to the Russian embassy to see Feodor Peshkov without his being aware of my identity. All Ali could say was that he would put inquiries afoot. He had already made arrangements for Bilal to take Moushka to a secluded courtyard during the day. As for Turkish baths, he said it was the custom to spend one day during the week in them. They were in the nature of a social gathering place, like a club, or even the opera; it was there that I would meet all the female friends of the family. With this I had to be content.

Before we parted I told Ali how charmed I was by his father. "I know well that my father is a charming man—you must be careful!" he said as he left me at my door. We both laughed, though my laugh was a trifle forced.

To assure ourselves the door was tightly shut, there being no lock or key, Betty suggested we put some cushions and a little table against it so that if anyone tried to come in during the night we would be awakened. I pointed out that Moushka was a sufficient guard. This was unnecessary, however, as I hardly slept at all, between the night watchmen who every hour tapped out the time with their clubs and the truly "strange beds," as fortune-tellers called them. Even with thick mats under the mattresses, these did not take the place of good beds. Large bags of white cotton were used in place of sheets, and there were several blankets and cushions. One reassuring thing was the light in a corner of the room which burned all night, as was the custom in *musulman* homes.

As soon as it was daylight Betty rose softly and, thinking I was asleep, crept to the door. On opening it she was startled to see Bilal stretched along the floor outside, asleep on a mat. If we had known of his presence we would probably both have slept better. As I heard her whispering I called her and learned that she wanted to take Moushka out to the courtyard as she had done the previous evening, before the family was up.

Bilal served us breakfast in our room, a custom of Turkey. A Turkish breakfast is a thing I have ever since missed. The coffee is delicious and is served with a pitcher of heavy fresh cream as well as milk. The bread, butter, and preserves, all made at home, are excellent, and there are varieties of fruit and cakes too; indeed, it is a little banquet. All this cheered us up considerably, and I told Bilal to come back when he had learned what time the ladies intended to leave for the baths.

A soft scratching at the door announced that the servant wanted to clear away the beds. The cupboards for the mattresses, we discovered, contained windows; thus the bedding was aired all day. In spite of their bizarre (to us) customs, we were glad to see the Turks followed laws of hygiene. All this clearing was done rapidly and systematically, with the economy of gesture of a Pullman porter making up a berth, and like the porter, with a fixed and pleasant smile. Those little doll-like girls were charming, smiling silently and gliding about on their small bare feet.

Instead of Bilal it was Xenia who finally came. She was in an expansive mood and asked gaily if we had slept well, laughingly realizing the mats must have been a strange experience for us. She said that her father had told her particularly to take good care of me. "You've made a conquest of him," she said.

Betty was invited to join us but hastily declined the host with the excuse of a headache. I knew the real reason—Moushka.

Xenia prevented me from wearing a hat, saying she had a *charchaff* or me and that to go out in Istanbul with them I must be dressed in the Turkish mode. I followed her to the reception hall, where her mother and sister waited. They put the *charchaff* on me, and the authentic veil, but as there was no mirror in the room I could not see the effect. The slaves stood around staring curiously; and I could not blame them, as it must have been a novel sight. As we started out, I felt more than ever that I was playing a role.

In the carriage I took my place beside the mother. Because the baths were not far off, we drove about so that I could see a little more of Istanbul. We saw the famous mosque, so ancient that the minaret from which the singer announced the hour of prayer looked as if it would collapse on the city any minute. Xenia explained that no repairs could be done, as this would be sacrilege. The women in the streets, especially those of the lower classes, reminded me of Brussels at carnival time, when everyone wore dominoes and masks.

At last we arrived before a great gate, which silently opened, and we could see a number of carriages in a large courtyard.

We descended some stairs into a good-sized room where a number of huge, fat Turkish women seemed to be awaiting customers. They were dressed in long sleeveless blouses or chemises, with turbans of gay colors on their heads, and bare feet. My companions spoke to a woman who appeared to be the chief, and she immediately began to undress me, as others did my friends. I was rather alarmed to see that my friends had all their clothes removed and unabashedly stood waiting for me, naked as fish. I asked Xenia if I could not have a robe to cover myself. She laughed gaily and said that I must have no shame, for it was the custom and I was about to see all the ladies naked in the bath. I said firmly that it was not *my* custom, and I wanted at least a large towel, as I feared catching cold.

So they gave me a large towel, while the others were given smaller ones, and I followed my companions into an immense room. In the center was a large pool, and two smaller pools for those who could not swim. Around the pools were benches of marble and many exotic plants, but I was unable to admire the beauties of this picture, so shocked was I. Old and young women, pell-mell, without a stitch, crowded the entire apartment. Some were being worked over by masseuses, while others lay prone on marble benches smoking cigarettes or drinking coffee. And an unselected crowd of Turkish women in the nude is no treat to the eye! In fact it was a horrid experience. The friends of my companions crowded about to examine me, the first opportunity they had been given to get a good look at a European woman, and their intellectual curiosity went so far that they began to poke me here and there as though I were a chicken in a kosher market. It was intolerable.

I told Xenia that I did not feel well and would dress and wait for the others above, but after a few words the entire family decided to dress and go home with me. While we were dressing Xenia explained that I had witnessed one of the established customs of Turkey. Turkish mothers were arranging the marriages of their sons. Young men could not see their destined wives, but their mothers, after a few visits to the baths, could give them full details of their fiancées, so they could avoid disappointment later on!

When I got home I found Betty in a more nervous state than ever. As I took off my *charchaff* in the hall she almost wept. "Oh Madame, you are not going to stay here a long while? Because I want to go back very soon to Europe!" I could not understand her sudden determination, but

Xenia laughed and said it was a surprise of her father's, and when we reached my quarters I found the rooms had been completely transformed as if by magic. A European bed, some chairs, dressing table, washstand, mirror—all complete, and in the next room the same for Betty. I exclaimed at the sight and assured Xenia that this was not at all necessary—we were very comfortable, and could not stay long in Istanbul in any case. But the pasha had given the order and that was that.

When we were alone I reassured Betty that in spite of the permanent look our quarters had taken I had no intention of lingering longer than absolutely necessary in Turkey, and that I wanted to leave as much as she did. "Ah, but this isn't all!" she wailed. "There's a piano now in the reception hall!"

Before I could well assimilate all the implications one might put on the pasha's hospitality, Ali came to speak to me. As soon as I saw his face I knew he did not have good news. He had made some discoveries through the employees at a club in Pera, a club frequented by European diplomats and their friends, and to which very few Turks went. Wishing to detract attention lest the Porte consider his visits strange, he had learned little as yet. Nevertheless, he had some valuable information.

Feodor Peshkov was in Petersburg, though his family in Pera expected him within a few days. Sergei, on his arrival in Constantinople, had lived a week with his brother, but one day took a room at the club, lunching alone there every day. In the evenings he dressed and went out, sometimes returning later with his brother, but often returning alone. The waiter to whom Ali spoke did not understand Russian, so he learned from the brothers' conversation only that a strained atmosphere existed.

One day Sergei had said he would be away for a day or two and gave instructions to keep any mail that might come for him. At the club he had written many long letters but always took them himself to the post office. When he left he carried only one small handbag.

Several days later Feodor Peshkov came and spoke for a long time to the director or manager of the club, but the waiter knew little more. Knowing there was said to be much gambling for high stakes there, Ali had asked if Sergei had played. The waiter was embarrassed by the question but finally professed ignorance; his work was finished at ten in the evening, and if there was gambling it was late at night.

Hoping to fall into conversation with the manager himself, Ali went into the smoking room, where he saw him reading the papers. The manager came forward and cordially asked if there was anything he could do. Ali asked him to take coffee with him, which he did, passing across to him the French papers. Thus it was made easy for Ali to turn the conversation to his old friend Sergei Peshkov and to voice his regret at not having seen him when he had lately been in Constantinople.

"Ah," said the manager, "he was a charming man—much more agreeable than his brother. Since you were a friend of his I can tell you what happened. When he came here I believe he had been quarreling with his brother. He seemed extremely nervous, smoked a great deal, and in the evenings when he went into the card room he drank much champagne and played for high stakes. His luck was poor, and though his brother was in Pera he cabled to Petersburg for money. When it arrived he asked me to identify him at the bank, which I did. He received two thousand rubles. It was my night off and I went home early. The next day I was surprised to learn that he had left with the word that he would be back in a day or two."

Ali learned from a guest at the club, a Russian traveler who was passing through Constantinople, that Sergei had lost heavily the evening before. He asked a number of times at the office if his brother had not sent any letters or telegrams that might have come to the embassy for him, but none had come, and the next morning he left with only a small handbag.

"Three days later Feodor Peshkov called on me," the manager continued. "He was very agitated and told me he had come to pay his brother's bill. I was surprised and asked if his brother had no intention of returning. 'No, there has been an accident,' was all he said, and as he seemed unwilling to speak I did not ask any further questions. But it all seemed very strange to me.

"After taking what his brother had left in his room, he departed. As he quitted the building I saw a dragoman wearing the uniform of the Russian embassy hand him a telegram in the street. He opened it hastily, read it, put it in his pocket, leapt into his carriage with the dragoman, and drove quickly away. I feel sure the telegram contained bad news. A week later the foreign newspapers announced Sergei Peshkov's death in dispatch from Petersburg, and Feodor Peshkov left suddenly for Russia.

"If Sergei Peshkov was your friend," the manager added, "I must tell you that the whole affair appeared suspicious to me." He ended by saying that all he had told Ali was, of course, confidential. Ali assured him on this score. He wanted to question him further but feared the manager had already observed his intense interest in the account of poor Sergei's last days. He went out by the side entrance to attract less attention.

Poor Ali! He continued speaking, seated beside me, his eyes lowered. I could see he suffered in telling me his sad discoveries. I tried to control my emotion so that he could relate all he knew without interruption, but I had reached the limit of my strength; when he turned at last to look at me I was so pale that he called Betty. She came running, and at last I gave way to my sorrow and tears. I did not notice that Ali had taken my hands and was kissing them in the Turkish manner which signifies true devotion—on the palms. Betty was weeping too, though as yet she did not know the reasons for my desolation. I withdrew my hands, thanked Ali for having obtained the precious information, and asked if I might dine alone in my quarters that evening.

This was arranged, my excuse of having developed a headache at the baths serving me well, combined with the fact that the pasha was not expected that night. Ali asked if he might not return later to talk further, which I was glad to have him do, as I was now determined to write a letter for him to deliver to the lawyer in Pera, the friend of my Romanian brother-in-law at Craiova.

Left alone, I removed the traces of tears and lay down, Betty staying beside me with her sympathy and affection. What I feared, however, soon happened. Xenia asked if she might come in and then enthusiastically suggested such remedies as the Turks used for headaches. I refused her ministrations, assuring her that a good night's rest would completely restore me.

"Oh, I hope so!" she cried. "Because we are planning to take you tomorrow to the great Turkish bazaar of Istanbul and then go for a drive through Pera. And besides, Father is coming to dinner tomorrow night and is very anxious to hear you sing. Ali has told us you are a famous singer, and we do not have any opportunity to go to the theater. In Pera there is a little theater for traveling companies—mostly French and Italian, with a few good Armenian performers—but we cannot go to the theater at all, even covered."

All this was said in very bad French, but I well understood that the next night I was expected to entertain my hosts. I feared that it would be impossible, as Turkish music is utterly different—baroque, and with a distinct scale, accompanied by tom-toms—and if they expected an exhibition of this they would be sadly disappointed.

At the sound of the dinner gong Xenia finally left. She was expecting her husband that evening, so I had the great luxury of being left alone for a while. Betty, who knew only that I had learned something from Ali, sat down silently in a corner with Moushka and left me undisturbed with my sad thoughts. Ah, I felt I understood everything then. Sergei and his brother had engaged in arguments and discussions about me, and probably about their inheritance as well. In a moment of anger Sergei had left his brother's house and taken a room at the club, of which he was a transient member. The letters I had written him were intercepted by Feodor Peshkov, and perhaps he thought I had not written at all. I had received the letters he wrote me because he had posted them himself—all until the last fatal one, postmarked "Cirkadje Station." But what had happened so soon after he wrote that letter was as dark a mystery as ever. Had he gone off on a little trip with his brother? Had he lost much playing cards? Had he gone on a yachting trip on the Bosporus and been drowned? In writing these lines now, so many years after, the sorrow and horror of those days return to me and I live through them again. At the time, one thought held me, and that was to confront Feodor Peshkov and make him answer for his brother's life.

Poor fool! How could I hope for vengeance when I was unable even to learn the truth about my husband's death? I was wholly dependent on anyone who could tell me anything. Now, in another world and another civilization, it is hard to believe in all the deceptions and despair that my investigations brought me, the loss not only of a good and noble husband, but the loss of all my happiness, and even my safety. From the day Sergei died my life changed completely, and what I am today is the absolute outcome of that inexplicable tragedy. At every door upon which I knocked for information or advice, all I ever learned was that Russia was a dangerous place and I would do well to stay away from it. I never went back. I never knew what had become of my husband. Of Russia all that was left me were those short memories of another world.

17

I HAD BEEN IN Constantinople for about two weeks and realized I was making no progress.

That night I gave Ali a letter to deliver to the lawyer in Pera, asking him to let me know at what time I could be sure of finding him at his office. Because my time was not my own, there was no hour in which I could be certain that I might leave the house to pursue my own inclinations unmolested. I was really little better than a prisoner.

The next day the lawyer's answer came, saying that I might call any afternoon between the hours of three and six o'clock; yet there remained no prospect of my being able to go to Pera—at least not alone. I was taken with the ladies to the Turkish bazaar, which was most interesting, or would have been had I not a more absorbing interest to fill my mind. We saw the tall buildings of Pera and drove out of the city, where I had my first glimpse of the Yildiz Palace, the fabulous residence of the sultan, Abdülhamid.[47]

That night the pasha dined at home for the second time since my arrival. All occurred as on the previous occasion. We adjourned to the reception hall following the meal, only now there was a beautiful new piano in it. After coffee and the monotonous music to which the slave girls danced, I saw that the moment had arrived for me to entertain my hosts.

I did so with some trepidation, for though the pasha was sophisticated and more or less cosmopolitan, his womenfolk were untouched by the outer world, and I had no guiding knowledge of what they might think of my curious European music. First I played a few compositions, to which they all listened in respectful silence, and then I began to sing.

With modesty, I may say in all truthfulness that my singing created a sensation, at least with Xenia and her sister and mother. I had hardly begun when they jumped up from their seats and crowded around the piano. Such sounds as I emitted, they said quite frankly, they had never before heard. They peered into my mouth to see what it could be that produced such strange, *loud* noises. All fear that I might annoy or offend them with my music was quickly dispelled by their eager attentiveness. A magician taking rabbits out of a hat could not have entertained the Turkish ladies more. I felt myself a phenomenon.

Ali left us to entertain some young officers in the solemneck. Shortly afterward the ladies withdrew, leaving me alone with the pasha.

Now the time had come for me to express my gratitude at the great hospitality accorded me in furnishing our quarters in European fashion. I assured him that it was unnecessary, as my stay in Istanbul was to be fleeting. The pasha replied that his only wish had been to make me comfortable in his house. Then he asked why I had come to Turkey.

"I have been visiting my sister in Romania," I said, "and as it is not far from Craiova to Constantinople, and as I am anxious to see the world, I wrote to Ali Raiff and asked him if you would be gracious enough to receive me."

The pasha, in his smooth and courtly manner, responded that he knew how kind my family had been to his son when he was stationed in Brussels, and it gave him great pleasure to be able to repay in a small degree that hospitality; but he could see no reason why I should have to leave so soon.

"I am afraid that my presence here is somewhat disturbing to your family," I said. "I do not wish to interfere with their customs—and too, it is essential that I attend to a matter of business which cannot be undertaken while I am a guest of your wife."

The pasha expressed distress and graciously suggested that it would make him very happy to secure a large and comfortable apartment for me in Pera. This seemed a curious declaration. I searched about for some good excuse, growing more and more uncomfortable. Finally I said that such an idea could not be thought of. Of course I should be delighted to remain in Istanbul for the duration of my visit, but my sister and her husband were waiting for me in Craiova. The pasha looked at me in a curious manner, and I wondered what was passing through his mind. The atmosphere of the house was growing upon me, and I privately decided to leave as soon as I could do so gracefully.

"You spoke once of wishing to see the palace," the pasha said. "I have spoken to the grand vizier. You doubtless know the wives of foreign diplomats are the only women admitted to the palace. There is only one way for you to enter it, and that is as a professional artist. The sultan has a private theater, and a French company is now playing in Pera. An entertainment can be arranged in the palace for the company if you wish to join it as one of the players."

Since my entire fortune was held in Russia I realized there were only two alternatives for me to accept for the future: to return to Brussels and live with my family, which after so many years of professional life seemed impossible, or to continue my musical career.

Stories of the fabulous riches of the sultan, of his magnificent palace that was so difficult to visit and his great harem, were known to everyone and inspired the imagination; if I could possibly see the inside of the palace, it would be a chance too good to miss. Plays and *opéras comiques* with Oriental or Asiatic settings were popular at the time; I had appeared in two or three myself, and so I was curious to verify my ideas on the subject. I told the pasha that whatever could be arranged by the grand vizier would please me.

Another thing that made it impractical for me to remain long in Istanbul was that I had a small dog with me. The pasha waved aside this consideration, saying the only reason dogs were not generally kept was because of the wild dogs that infested the streets.

The rather marked attentions of the pasha began to make me a little suspicious and very uncomfortable. Returning to my room, I decided to leave for Craiova to ask my brother-in-law for his advice. However, having risked so much in making this trip, I did not wish to lose the unique opportunity to visit the celebrated harem of the sultan, which the whole world spoke about sotto voce and which was considered inaccessible. Perhaps even more than this I was curious to see, face to face, the terrible Abdülhamid, he who had ruthlessly deposed his brother Murad V in 1876 and had been ruling Turkey ever since, a legendary figure.

Knowing of the French company playing in Pera, I was very anxious to at least see the outside of the theater and was glad to accompany the ladies there the next day. Ali came with us. He found a moment to tell me that he would dismount before the door of the Romanian lawyer, whose office adjoined a pastry shop where his sisters would doubtless go for coffee and cakes, and that he could deliver the letters and rejoin us.

The carriage stopped outside the pastry shop, a rendezvous for the haut monde of Constantinople. Here I observed another Turkish custom. Instead of helping the ladies out of the carriage, as was the practice in Europe, Ali stepped down from the carriage and walked away while we followed—at a respectful distance! A Turk never walked in the street with a member of the female sex. Since Turkish women all looked alike, completely disguised with their *charchaffs* ("By night all cats are gray," as the Spaniards say), this etiquette prevented gentlemen accompanying the wrong lady: otherwise it would be too easy!

Ali disappeared into the lawyer's office and in a few minutes joined us at the pastry shop, after which time we went for a drive through Pera. Passing the theater, I was pleased to see announced a repertory of standard works, all of which I had sung.

That night the pasha was absent, conferring with the manager of the theater and the grand vizier. After dinner the ladies retired and I was left alone with Ali. I took him partially into my confidence, telling him I must leave as soon as possible for Craiova. He understood my meaning and assured me against all fear. The pasha, a man of the world, was seeking to make himself agreeable, and he told me not to forget that my present experiences might be of much value to me if I decided to continue my career. He was seated beside me on the divan, the slaves softly playing their curious music. Now, the Turks have very beautiful eyes, and Ali, who was no exception, took me by the hand and stared into mine. He assured me of his devotion and protection and announced a secret as yet unknown to his family. The post of military attaché in Berlin was vacant. He had asked for it and was almost certain of an appointment.

"And now that you are free . . ."

Good heavens! My thoughts can be better imagined than described. I hope to be forgiven for appearing to have made my charms irresistible to the Turkish gentlemen, but my being foreign and therefore something of a novelty may have been responsible. Far from being reassured, I felt even more uncomfortable at this new complication.

Reaching my room, I assured Betty that all was going well and that we should leave sooner than I had planned. I wrote some letters and retired for the night, my mind a little more at ease. We were awakened early next morning by the arrival of a note from Ali saying the pasha had arranged a little voyage on the Golden Horn. It was Friday, the Turkish Sabbath.

To prepare for this fête I had to pass again through the hands of the ladies of the house. Instead of the gloomy *charchaff,* I wore a kind of hat covered with white veils, arranged about the face to leave only the eyes visible. This attire was called a *yachmac,* and it too was not altogether novel: I had worn a costume similar in every detail in *Ali Baba and the Forty Thieves.* In spite of the sadness of my state I could not repress a smile, for never had I thought to relive in private life the comedy of the theater.

It was a splendid day. Between its uneven shores the Golden Horn was dotted with little boats rowed by natives in strange national costumes. These boats, each with a tent erected on the deck, bobbed on the waves as far as one could see. The soft noise of waves lapping against the gunwales of the boats as they passed, the Turkish music produced by the slaves who sat on the decks playing stringed instruments, the heat and gold of the sun, the women veiled all but for their eyes: this was an experience never to be forgotten, and that day, Turkey, which I was beginning to find less and less pleasant, showed itself in its brightest colors.

Though heavily veiled—or perhaps *because* heavily veiled—the women of Turkey gave the effect of being very handsome, and they, in common with the women of Egypt, had raised the art of coquetry to a high level. They carried little fans, and when they saw men glancing at them they instinctively knew how to use eyes, fans, and gestures to make themselves all the more alluring and mysterious. They were the world's adepts at flirting, all because of the enforced wearing of the veil.

The occasion of the day was a battle of flowers. Passengers threw flowers at the occupants of other boats as they passed. As the little bouquets fell on the decks they were picked up by servants who were there for that purpose. Ali gallantly said the reason we received so many flowers was that I was on board. (Turkish women used cosmetics to make their eyes look larger, but mine were large naturally.) On our return the pasha was much pleased with our success, the receipt of many flowers being a great compliment to his house.

After dinner I gave Ali my letters to post and he left for the palace. Soon the ladies retired, leaving me tête-à-tête with the pasha. He sat close to me and told me with enthusiasm that all was arranged for Monday. He warned me that it would be a tiring day, for in order to visit the harem I should be obliged to go to the palace early. The director of the French company was coming to Pera the day before the performance to arrange the program. The pasha spoke of his trouble in securing the consent of the grand vizier to allow a woman's appearance on the palace stage. It seemed I was destined to be the first woman to play at the Turkish court. When touring companies appeared there, a man played every female role. In China also I was to see this as the usual practice, though the Armenians were said to be the most successful at female impersonations.

I was effusively grateful, and the pasha replied that it was his only desire to make me happy in his country. He had hoped to arrange for me to live in Pera, but at the moment the city was crowded and he was much occupied with affairs of state. However, he had arranged for us to witness the maneuvers of the fleet which was preparing to depart. This was to be a historical occasion—poor Armenia!

The next morning Xenia came with the information that the pasha was to meet us at a special place. I had already learned from Ali that trouble was brewing again with the Armenians, and our faithful Bilal told us before leaving that Ali had returned from the palace to accompany us.

When we descended into the courtyard to the carriage, disguised as usual in our *charchaffs*, Ali was awaiting us. The windows were down, everything had an air of intrigue, and a Turk in a special uniform I had not formerly seen was seated beside the coachman. He had a truly terrifying look. Ali informed me he was a member of the special police force attached to the pasha. After passing through a great number of tortuous streets, we arrived at a wharf on the Bosporus and there boarded a rather large boat rowed by a number of seminude Arabs. Here the pasha met us, guarded by two more policemen. I regretted having come. Even though far away, the noise of guns and cannons was deafening. But at least this made speech unnecessary—in fact, it made it impossible.

The pasha signaled and the boat shot out like an arrow into the water, only coming to a halt a short distance from the great warships, which were covered with flags and crowded with sailors. There were very few boats like ours about. Ali explained that only high dignitaries were permitted to take part in the departure of the fleet.

Suddenly, without warning, the cannons of the departing boats gave a salute. A moment later the water eddied all about us and our boat bobbed on the waves. I might well have believed my hour had come! Our boat was flooded. I remember giving a cry, but I knew no more until I recovered on the divan in the reception hall, smothered in blankets, Betty weeping and trembling beside me. My three hostesses, soaking wet, had returned to their apartments, and a doctor had been summoned.

Rising immediately, I demanded to be allowed to return to my room. The domestics of the house, old and young, crowded speechlessly about me, and my one desire was to be alone. However, I had to go through with the visit of the famous Turkish medicine man—or woman, rather—for, of course, it was an "annum." When she arrived I was in bed covered with even more blankets, for I had suffered a chill. She looked at me solemnly from her dark eyes and, making a sign to an aid, ordered water to be brought. Washing her hands but without further warning she removed all my clothes and began to massage me from head to toe with a terrible strength, causing me to cry out in pain. Suddenly, however, I observed that I was no longer cold, as blood coursed through my veins once more. In finishing she anointed me with some sweet-smelling oil and insisted I take several small pills. Through all this poor Betty stood like a statue, hardly knowing whether or not to interfere. Finally, the good annum sank to her knees on a small rug her assistant had laid out for the purpose and began to pray. The assistant had lighted some incense as well, and only when it burned out did the annum rise, make a few mechanical signs over me, and hurry away.

By now the little pills began to take effect and I was soon asleep.

Unfortunately, I had at last to wake. How long I lay in that enchanted sleep I do not know, and even now in attempting to describe it I regret being unable to renew the experience. Some marvelous and mysterious drug must certainly have been given, but whether it was opium, hashish, or a more unusual herb, I never learned. When I finally aroused from my private utopia, Betty stood over me, telling me that Xenia had been in to make inquiries and warned her not to wake me, saying I would be perfectly well after my sleep. Bilal brought our meal and with it the news that the pasha and Ali were detained at the palace.

It was already late. I was glad that Betty and I were to be alone in order to plan our departure, for it was evident that escape would be the only method of leaving the country. To begin with I told Betty to make a *char-chaff* like mine, for if she attempted to leave in European costume we should be discovered—and probably just when the boat was about to sail.

The appearance of the French company at the palace was fixed for two days off, and through Ali it had been arranged that Betty and I should go alone to the theater for a rehearsal with the company. Xenia helped Betty make her *charchaff*, and we started off in the carriage with Ali, leaving Moushka in the care of Bilal, to Betty's despair. As soon as we were alone I told Ali of my wish to call on the Romanian lawyer after the rehearsal. I told him that I expected to do so alone with Betty, while he remained in the carriage, and promised not to stay long.

I cut the rehearsal as short as possible. Knowing that Ali was in the carriage behind the theater, Betty and I took off our *charchaffs*. Seizing two hats belonging to members of the chorus, who were still in rehearsals, we left by the front entrance and hurried down the main street of Pera to the lawyer's office. Betty waited for me in the hall below and promised not to move or to speak to anyone. I hurried up the stairs as fast as I could.

Fortunately the lawyer was in. My sudden appearance, my paleness, and my excitement rather amazed him; he made me sit down, fetched some brandy, and waited for me to speak. "I wish to leave Turkey on the first boat out of Constantinople," I announced. "Please get me two tickets and have my passport arranged by the Belgian consul, because this is going to be a flight." Naturally the poor man was astonished. I explained that the pasha wanted me to stay in Constantinople but that his son would help me leave. He promised to do what I asked and gave me letters from Brussels and Craiova which I had arranged to be sent to his address. Thanking him, I slipped them into my pocket. He told me that Feodor Peshkov was due back in Pera in two days and advised me to be very prudent in my actions, as he could not say what the man would attempt in order to have me in his power. I promised to be careful, and hurried away.

Betty, trembling in the hallway below and not knowing which office I was in, reproached me for not having taken her with me. We hurried back to the theater and were glad to find the rehearsal still in progress, which enabled us to restore the stolen hats, don our *charchaffs*, and join Ali in the carriage.

Ali too was in a nervous state, not knowing where I had been. I could not understand so much excitement over what seemed very simple. I had been rehearsing all that time—officially, at least. As we started back to the house Ali told me that his father would return that night. He warned me to be very circumspect and not give the least inkling of our plans. In fact, I was counseled to play a part and appear very happy and content in Istanbul. This was Betty's first outing, and as she stared about her, Ali took me by the hand, whispering that he must have a few words alone with me during the evening.

On arriving in the courtyard I heard another carriage quickly following us. I barely had time to enter the house before catching a glimpse of the pasha, who jumped from his carriage and spoke to Ali in a louder voice than I had ever heard him use. Without turning back I told Betty to come quickly to our room, fearing that the pasha would question us. Had our tales differed it would have been inartistic, to say the least! My one fear was that we had been followed from the theater and the pasha knew already of our visit to the lawyer. I instructed Betty to say that when rehearsing I had become thirsty and we had hurried off to the pastry shop without taking time to cover ourselves. Oh! By now I really was afraid of the pasha, for it was clear that my presence in his house might seem suspicious, and God only knew what might happen. It was impossible to speak to Ali before dinner, so I had no idea what he had said to his father. There was hardly time to change my dress. I decided to ask Xenia to come to my room.

"Oh Xenia!" I cried innocently. "Do you know what we did?" I raised my voice so Betty could hear me. "After the rehearsal at the theater I was so thirsty that we took two hats belonging to the choristers and went to the French pastry shop for some *chocolat*! I knew that Ali was in the carriage waiting behind the theater and could not see us, and I felt like a little girl running away from school!" Xenia laughed gaily, and I laughed equally as gaily with her.

"I must tell this to the pasha!" she cried. "He will think it very amusing." Then she grew serious and informed me that I had really done a very risky thing. If an officer of the secret police had seen us we would have been arrested and questioned. Ali should not have left us alone, but had we worn our *charchaffs* we would have been safe in going to the pastry shop.

"Perhaps it would be wiser not to say anything about it to your father," I suggested.

"Oh, he has probably learned all about it already from the police," Xenia said easily. "I heard him talking to Ali in a rather loud voice in the solemneck. I will go down and try to see Ali for a minute, then attempt to return to tell you what they both said."

She left me in a terrible state of apprehension, and I dreaded every moment to hear the dinner gong sound. Soon she returned, running, to inform me that Ali had told our story about the pastry shop. The pasha answered that he had been informed that the police had seen two women in European costume hurrying through the streets of Pera, but they entered the building next door to the pastry shop. "Ali told me to warn you after dinner, when we are in the reception hall, to tell your story of the pastry shop to the pasha as a great joke." And Xenia hurried away again.

Shortly afterward I went down to the table with a very gay air, but no one at the table was gay at all. Everyone had his nose in his plate; one could hear a fly buzz. Even the little Arabs slid more silently about in their sandals. Only the pasha carried his head high, and with such a severe expression that I lost my appetite on seeing it. I turned my head toward him and smiled sweetly. His expression changed so suddenly that it frightened me more than any expression he had previously worn. Everyone seemed to be waiting for a word, which he finally pronounced in Turkish. All heads raised and everyone attempted a forced smile.

In that moment I decided to flee that house at the first possible opportunity. Had it not been that I must sing next day at the palace, I should have abandoned all my baggage right then and left this place that struck such fear in my heart.

All was as usual; the ladies retired to the reception hall. The pasha tapped me lightly on the cheek and shook his finger as at a disobedient child. Then he said that Anum, his wife, had asked if I would not sing a little for her, since she could not hear me at the palace. He added, "I am going to scold you the day after tomorrow. You were in great danger this afternoon." Then he laughed and conducted me to the piano. I had eaten little at dinner but enough to make it most unpleasant to sing. Xenia sat next to me while the pasha spoke to his wife and kissed the palm of her hand. I asked Xenia in a low voice why Ali was not with us. It appeared that the pasha was angry with him for not having watched over me more carefully, and for this reason Ali was not permitted to join us that night. He was punished like a little child, and I was watched over like one too! I was heartily sick of Turkey, Russia, and all countries filled with spies and secret police.

After singing a little I begged permission to retire in order to be well rested. The pasha informed me that he would be unable to see me the next day but would tell Ali where we were to meet after the performance in the palace. "I shall be there to see you, but you will not see me."

I thanked him effusively for all his kindness. He kissed my hand and said, "There is a surprise reserved for you after the performance. Then you can thank me." When I looked up quickly to question him, he put his finger to his lips.

As I was the first to leave the room, I made the Turkish salute to the ladies. Bilal stood at my door with a note from his master which said he could not come to see me due to his father's suspicions. "I shall see you tomorrow and tell you of my intentions. You are right. You must leave on the first boat that sails after tomorrow. I think I have discovered my father's plans."

18

As it was now the eve of our flight, no wonder this night was a nerve-racking one. Our preparations must be made in secret: if we aroused the suspicions of the house I dared not think what obstacles might present themselves, and there were already complications enough. For several days past, Anum and her two daughters remained alone. Likewise, Xenia no longer dropped in to see me as previously. She had at last come to suspect that her father and brother entertained a different attitude toward me than they were wont to have toward other visitors.

Our problem was to carry as many pieces of luggage as possible, including Moushka, when we went to the palace, under the pretext that all would be needed at the performance. With this excuse ready if necessary, I packed my best dresses in a large hand valise. As to the trunk, there was no use thinking of that.

Sunrise found us already up and dressed. Bilal, who had slept outside our door as usual, knew that something was brewing and went to inform his master we were awake. The strained atmosphere of the house was truly horrible—the ladies staying pointedly away, the pasha strange and inexplicable (as well as unpredictable), Ali laying elaborate plans to outwit his father—and I was the unwilling cause of all. I really tremble today when I think of those nightmare hours.

A soft rapping at the doorframe surprised us at our packing. Pulling aside the curtain, I let it fall behind me to screen the room. It was Bilal, and he made a sign that he wished to enter and speak. He informed me his master would soon follow and I must leave the door open to prevent any noise.

Ali arrived shortly, setting Bilal to watch the passage. I learned that when we left for the palace we were not to return to Istanbul. I had done well to pack all I could; it would be our only chance to salvage our belongings. The ladies were going to spend the day at Xenia's country house —partly to prevent my using their carriage to drive to the palace, as Anum was very jealous of my going to the sultan's court. As soon as they had left and the coast was clear, Bilal was instructed to hire a fiacre to convey our luggage to the lawyer's office in Pera.

Bilal was delegated to prepare our breakfast. My instructions were to eat nothing that he did not serve himself. We must be ready to leave one half hour after the ladies so providentially departed for the country. The cabdriver, already arranged for, was personally known to Ali and could be depended upon to drive us directly to the lawyer's office. We planned to lunch there, and at exactly three o'clock Betty and I, in our *charchaffs*, were to be waiting at the gate of the Yildiz Palace, leaving Bilal to take care of Moushka. I had to be in full toilette on my visit to the harem. After the performance, in the evening, I was to partake of nothing—not even champagne, unless the bottle was opened in front of me. Above all, if I met the pasha I must show no anxiety of any sort. That night I would be safely lodged in the consulate. Ali was in service for the night but had arranged to be relieved in order to see me through.

I asked him if he were not running into grave danger by helping me this way. He replied that he was not thinking of consequences, as he felt it was his fault that I had come to Istanbul at all and must now assist me in this dilemma. His mother was very jealous of me, and his sisters sympathized with her, which made it impossible for me to spend another night in their house. After telling me all this, Ali hurried back to the solemneck.

Briefly I told Betty that we should be on our way to Romania the following day. She was so happy she burst into tears.

Only one thing troubled her after learning the outline of our plans, and that was the idea that she leave Moushka at the lawyer's office while she accompanied me to the palace. On one occasion she had taken Moushka outside the garden walls in the company of Bilal, and a most serious catastrophe had only just been avoided when a large number of savage dogs surrounded them almost at once, snarling and growling. I did my best to reassure her, and hastily we finished our packing and made ready for flight.

About this time a good deal of activity became noticeable in the house. The horses in the courtyard neighed, impatient to take my hostesses off. Bilal came in with our breakfast, not so elegant a meal as when it had come from the kitchen but at least innocent of any suspicion of drugs or worse.

By this time, in the stress and excitement of the moment, I had almost forgotten my reasons for making this trip at all. There was surely something mysterious in the fact that the only man who could have given me any details of the death of my husband had left Turkey a few days before my arrival, and now, to escape the pasha, I was forced to leave the country the day before his return. In the midst of my sorrow and anxiety, all my plans were culminating in a perfect fiasco. And at the very peak of the strain, I looked forward to finding myself face to face with the redoubtable Sultan Abdülhamid, of whom everyone spoke in horror—the bloody tyrant of Armenia, the ruthless usurper of his brother's throne! I can say in truth that *The Arabian Nights* contained nothing more incredible than this wild situation in which I found myself.

At last the women drove away, and half an hour later Bilal came to our quarters for our luggage. Ali had told the fiacre driver to wait outside the solemneck so as not to arouse the curiosity of the female domestics. Betty and I, ready in our *charchaffs*, followed our deliverer by new and intricate passages through the house and out to the fiacre, without one backward glance. Bilal jumped up beside the driver and we started off. Only after we had crossed the Galata Bridge leading out of Istanbul to Pera were we able to breathe freely.

The lawyer awaited us anxiously in his office. Ali had explained the whole situation to the man, and informed us he had begun to think the pasha had planned a coup for the last moment.

We were made to remove our *charchaffs*, and I fell into a chair, too distrait to connect my thoughts. The room next to the office was at our disposal for the time being. We were instructed to lock ourselves in and not open the door to anyone who refused to give his name. The lawyer was obliged to hurry off to the Franco-Belgian consulate, which occupied a single building, to make further arrangements for us to spend the night and to prepare for our departure by a boat which was leaving the following day.

Before we locked the door Bilal made an ostentatious salaam and asked permission to speak. He said, "Bilal want to go to Europe with Madame."

"But Bilal," I told him, "that is impossible. You must stay here with your master. He will certainly need you after we have left, and besides, he has told me he expects to go to Europe soon. Then we shall all meet again."

His large white eyeballs gleamed and his shiny teeth flashed in his black face. "Bilal very happy. Ali Bey love Madame very much. Bilal too. Bilal unhappy here. No friends . . . servants laugh . . . speaking French. They say 'Monsieur Francis.'"

I gave him a little tap on the back in token of friendship, as I had seen Ali do, and said, "Surely Bilal will return to Europe with his master and we shall all meet again."

At last I was free to lie down on the sofa in our new prison while Betty inspected our surroundings. She displayed interest in a balcony which gave onto an inner court, a spacious little recreation spot like a veranda, screened from the curious by mousharabia curtains, which were customary on all the windows in Istanbul. I realized what she was searching for when she opened Moushka's basket and hurried him onto the balcony. I fell asleep wondering how I should ever be able to muster my strength and assemble my jangled nerves for the ordeal that faced me in singing that night for the sultan.

At one o'clock Bilal scratched in his peculiar way at the door and brought in a basket of provisions from the pastry shop. A few minutes later the lawyer arrived with a young secretary attached to the consulate, who brought a message from the French consul. The consul excused himself for not coming in person but said he feared his personal visit might attract the attention of spies who ran the streets of Pera, and it would not take much to come to the notice of the pasha. As we were not on French or consular soil, nothing could be done for us in an emergency yet.

The salon at the consulate would be put at our disposal for the night, but unfortunately we would have to spend the night on chairs, as the consul did not live there himself and the building was not furnished with living quarters. The most trustworthy guards, however, would be assigned to us, and the consul would be there in person to receive us. He was invited to the function at the palace that night but of course could not communicate with me. It was impossible to know at what time I would arrive at the consulate after the performance, but both the front and rear entrances of the building were to be guarded. Our instructions were to observe principally that our carriage drew up well to the steps under the *porte cochère* before we descended. If we left the carriage in the street we would still be in Turkey and beyond the power of consular protection. Realizing our precarious position, the young secretary did his best to cheer us, saying that so long as we were at the consulate we were as good as in Europe.

At length we were warned by our host to prepare for the palace. Ali appeared upon the scene, breathless with haste, just as we were about to leave. He drew me aside and whispered that he had just learned from his own spy (everyone of importance in Constantinople had a private spy!) that the pasha had hired a private dining room in the best hotel in Pera and had made arrangements for a midnight supper to be served that night. A single bedroom had been taken on the floor below. This was the "surprise" the pasha was preparing for me. This was where he planned to drive me after my performance before the sultan.

There was only time for a few last-minute instructions: drink no coffee and avoid champagne not opened in your presence, tell Betty to be careful to show no anxiety while she waits for you, be prudent and play your part. This was all I heard, for the carriage was waiting below. Bilal was to accompany us and then return to guard Moushka until sent for from the consulate. At three o'clock we were at the gates of the Yildiz Palace.

Even though every passing minute brought nearer my longed-for escape from that terrible country, I could not help being interested in the life of the poor women who lived under the domination of the Terrible Turk, Abdülhamid. From the center of Pera the massive walls of Yildiz Palace were visible high above. Though called a palace, it had the sinister aspect of a prison, an impregnable fortress, for with the exception of a few small turrets one could see only a high wall dominating the peak of the mountain. As to what transpired beyond those walls one would be reluctant to inquire. It was impossible to forget the sultan or the ruthlessness of his reign.

The drive up the mountain was truly superb, with its ever changing view of the mighty Bosporus.

At last we reached the plateau, to my great joy and also to the satisfaction of the poor horses, who had galloped almost the whole way up and were covered with sweat and foaming at the mouth. We stopped at numerous sentry posts for inspection and showed the pass Ali had given me. Our arrival seemed to arouse the curiosity of the guards, policemen, and variously uniformed soldiers whom we passed. Finally we came to the last sentry, in front of an immense gate, where I noticed a number of eyes peering at us through peepholes in the wall. Here we had to leave our carriage and enter a charming calèche drawn by four horses. The windows of this new vehicle were screened by mousharabia curtains so that we could look out as we drove along without being seen. The great gate opened. We drove through an enormous park, in which were a number of little chalets or kiosks, and came to a halt before a curious-looking building that was larger than the others. I had noticed that each little kiosk in the park was surrounded by a small esplanade, on top of which stood two huge guards, immovable as statues. Immersed in staring at everything we passed, Betty jogged my elbow and said, "Look Madame, are those men statues?" They really might have been, except that I saw one or two turn their eyes toward us as we passed. I controlled my laughter and hushed Betty. Ali Bey had warned me that once in the palace grounds we were not to speak or make any remark about anything we saw because the walls had ears. That they had eyes, I had already observed.

As the calèche stopped, several guards in Arabian costumes suddenly appeared and helped us out. A superior guard, whom I took for a eunuch, conducted us into the building, leading us to a large reception room furnished with divans, tables, and chairs in European style as well as Turkish pillows. Before I had time to speak to Betty, a portiere was whisked aside and two young Arab servants, brilliantly dressed, came forward, followed by a lady. She made a sign to the servants to help us remove our *charchaffs* and then, in perfect French, said, "Welcome, Mesdames, to the palace of our great sovereign, Abdülhamid." In saying this she bent down to the ground, touched it with her hand in a gesture of lifting up a bit of earth, and raised her hand to her lips, forehead, and heart—a salaam I had practiced enough at Raiff Pasha's and which I now did after her. Betty got rather mixed up in attempting to follow our example, but the lady was looking at me and fortunately did not see her. This lady, appointed my hostess for the day, was a Frenchwoman from Marseilles. She was dressed like the pasha's wife, with a long redingote over her dress. Her age was uncertain but she was still very handsome. I believe she had been in the palace for many years, for she must have had to go through a long apprenticeship to reach her high position of confidence at the head of the sultan's harem. Her manners were charming and she did her best to put me at ease, perceiving well enough that I was nervous. She smiled, though her smile was more sad than cheerful, and taking me by the hand assured me that I had nothing to fear, as I was the first foreign woman her sovereign had permitted to visit the interior of his harem.

"You must have a very great influence at court," she said, a questioning inflection in her voice. I did not respond except by smiling. She explained that she had been chosen by the master of ceremonies to be at my service during my visit. She hoped I would treat her as a friend and ask any questions that I wished, as she had been ordered to answer anything I might inquire about. I looked at her closely and asked, lowering my voice and trembling slightly, if I would see the great sovereign, Abdülhamid.

"Certainly," she said, and told me I was to dine with the sultana, who normally ate alone, as did the sultan himself, except at special state dinners in honor of foreign ambassadors and distinguished visitors. She explained that these dinners, though of the best European cuisine, were always cold and dreary affairs. Turkish women were not even permitted at the table! And given that the sultan spoke no language but Turkish, Europeans had a very dull time at the court. Even more curious, the sultan was a total abstainer, and so, though the table was always set with a complete collection of glasses for every sort of wine, none was ever served! Thus, though it was a great honor to be invited to dine at the palace, dinners had grown rarer and rarer because of a lack of guests. As we spoke, the Arab servants seated themselves behind an array of palms and began to accompany our conversation with the low murmur of their instruments.

Betty, seated all this while on a low chair, began to stir and cough to attract my attention. I had introduced her to my hostess as my faithful traveling companion, and the lady, seeing Betty's nervousness, asked if I felt sufficiently rested to visit some interesting sights of the palace. She said that to see everything thoroughly would take several days. My baggage had already arrived and was in the dressing room reserved for me at the palace theater. Betty, she explained to me, could occupy her time arranging my costumes in the dressing room, and her dinner would be served to her there.

As we left the room two eunuchs standing on each side of the door joined us without a word. One walked ahead, followed by the lady of honor and myself, then Betty, and the other eunuch drew up the end of the procession. These two eunuchs had evidently been assigned to guard us as long as we were in the palace, for they never quitted us except to guard the door behind which we might be. The lady, seeing I was curious about this, told me that even the sultan never walked in his park without his confidential eunuch, who went ahead to make sure no one was on the path His Majesty had chosen for his promenade. The ladies of the seraglio never walked in the park except at certain fêtes during the year, and were obliged to cover themselves as well. It was unlikely they would ever encounter any officers or other men, she explained, so they wore only long veils. And my hostess went off to get her own veil, and to bring one for me.

It was a moment's relief for Betty and me to find ourselves alone, even though I felt that eyes and ears were not far off. Making a sign that she should not speak, I told her in a low voice not to be nervous and explained that I had to visit the ladies, that she could not accompany me but should instead occupy her time arranging my costumes as she was accustomed to do at the theater, and that she must remember we were only a few hours away from our liberty. We became aware of tramping feet on the stage of the theater—and a number of familiar voices speaking French, a comforting sound to both of us. It was the stagehands, come to arrange the scenery for the performance. Soon the French troupe would arrive and Betty would have no need to feel lonely, though she must stay in the dressing room and speak to no one, since she could be heard through the partition. She promised to do as I said and warned me to be careful with the little pocket containing my jewels, which I always wore concealed in the bosom of my dress. I could not repress a smile for her faithfulness. She was convinced we were in a robber's den. If she could have seen the jewels belonging to the sultan and his wives, she might have had less concern for my few baubles!

Almost at once my friendly companion returned with the veil, arranging it herself over my head and face with the speed that comes from long practice. The result pleased her, for she clapped her hands with delight and said, "Oh, it is good the sultan will not see you with the *yachmac*! I would be afraid for your liberty!" Though she laughed heartily, the little pleasantry did not serve to reassure me very much. She suggested we start out at once, as there would be little time left for me to change into my costume after dining with the sultana. How I would be able to sing seemed more a mystery than ever, but I followed her, leaving the desolate Betty imprisoned in my dressing room.

We hurried through a number of salons and winter gardens filled with magnificent plants and little murmuring fountains. Stopping at last, she told me we were about to enter the state banquet hall where the sultan and his guests were to dine in my honor before the performance. "Not many," she said. "A few foreign ministers, ambassadors, and prominent members of the Porte." As she spoke we entered a truly magnificent room. The table was already set—and so luxuriously, in the European style, that I might have thought myself at the Palais des Champs Elysées, a guest of the president of the republic. The silver service, the gold plate, and the sparkling crystal glasses were all complete, but I thought it certainly a low trick to play upon Europeans, to place every glass for wine and liqueurs before them but leave them all empty. I inquired if the sultan did not speak at all and was told that the chief dragoman of the palace stood behind His Majesty to act as interpreter, and that some diplomats spoke a few words of Turkish. It struck me that the function must be a particularly trying ordeal, and I was heartily glad that women did not come to table in Turkey. I was informed that the sultan set an excellent table, and the palace chef was the finest in the world.

"But what does His Majesty drink?" I risked asking.

"Water," the lady answered. "But what water!"

And as we hurried on to other sights she explained the story of the sultan's horror of intoxicants.

Like all Turks, the sultan was superstitious. He had suffered from dyspepsia for many years, and all the doctors he had consulted advised him to be very careful of the water he drank. Once, years before he became sultan, an old Gypsy warned him of the danger he ran, as much from diseases such as cholera and other plagues as from assassins, but said he would be safe so long as he drank only the water from the fountain of Kiat-Hane, a small village north of the Golden Horn. Since that time he had drunk nothing else, and all in the palace were made to do likewise.

"You will drink it this evening yourself," she said. "It is very agreeable —slightly carbonated." She added, "There are many stories about that water, but I cannot tell them to you now." And I realized the reason was that the guards were within earshot.

"What would happen if the fountain dried up?" I asked, wondering aloud. That, she confessed, was the danger, but the sultan employed a regiment of men and women, guarded by soldiers, to take care of the fountain and to make certain the water he drank actually came from Kiat-Hane.

We were now in the park, and we passed a number of the little chalets I had already noticed. Each had a large object on the front terrace that looked like a cannon but was in fact a telescope. The sultan lived in one after another of these chalets, but all were kept guarded in order that no one might know in which one he was lodged at any specific time. He rarely spent more than one night in the same chalet. We continued on to a distant corner of the park, and here, perched on an artificial rock, stood a large building which had just been completed. There had been an earthquake not long before, which had spurred the construction of this new royal abode. The sultan's great fear was fire, so the building was supposed to be both fire- and earthquake-proof.

Though the royal residence contained a famous collection of animals, we did not have time to visit the places which housed them, including the farm, artificial lake, stables (which, as indicated by my hostess, housed the finest horses in the world), and menagerie. Yildiz had all the attractions of a European city, and the sultan required a huge staff of Europeans to take care of it. Including ladies of the harem and their servants, nearly five thousand people lived at the palace at that time, besides which the sultan maintained a guard of seven thousand. For Abdülhamid the palace, in reality, was a prison fortress.

I was absorbed in this interesting account when, suddenly turning down a new alley, we stood before another magnificent building. This was the palace of the sultana and the ladies of the seraglio. The great gate was wide open, and several enormous eunuchs stood guard like bronze statues at the entrance. Like all those in the palace, it was a large low building designed for an unobstructed view for the royal guards. As we approached the gate I could not help a slight shiver. This was another prison, containing not only the sultan's legitimate wife but also a famous collection of beautiful women of many nationalities, all in a state of slavery which was naturally repulsive to the European mind.

Our two eunuch protectors silently replaced those at the gate, who conducted us through a winter garden leading into the palace. The sight was extraordinary. There were flowering trees everywhere, and even more delightful, tropical birds of splendid colors flew from branch to branch. This was the famous Yildiz aviary. The sultana was very proud of her gift for training wild birds. She was young and charming, a good musician, and spoke several languages, including French and English. My companion had no time to tell me more, as the terrace of the sultana's chalet quickly filled with young girls, laughing, dancing, and speaking with animation. Suddenly the sultana advanced toward us. A gesture silenced the crowd and they drew aside. My companion waited respectfully in the background.

I immediately gave the Turkish salute already described, but the sultana quickly extended her hand in European fashion. I could not take my eyes from her face. She was really beautiful. Her large blue eyes were encircled with kohl. Her complexion was pale and pure, and her thick brown hair, dipped in henna, encircled her high forehead in a most becoming manner. Tall and stately, she wore a long robe—open in front and displaying her dress of rich silk and brocade—that was the perfect costume to flatter her excellent figure.

She seemed very happy, but later my companion explained it was delight at seeing a European. Her love of music was sincere. Deploring the fact that the ladies could not hear me sing that evening, she drew close to me on the divan and softly, almost like a prayer, implored me to give them that pleasure now.

Her eyes were wet, and I understood more than she could tell me; I was delighted with the suggestion. She at once gave a sign to a young girl who seemed to have a superior position at the palace, and spoke a word in Turkish, the only official language at the court. I wondered where there could be a piano, when all at once the young girls who had been dancing and laughing in the winter garden—and several hundred other ladies, ranging from very young to elderly members of the sultana's entourage—grouped themselves silently about the room, while two great eunuchs appeared, pushing a grand piano onto the terrace as if it had been a chair. All this returns so vividly to my memory today that I cannot help wondering what it was that gave me the courage to sing Gounod's "Sérénade" as I did. Looking at the brilliant birds still flitting from branch to branch among the trees, I sang my Bird Waltz, which I was forced to repeat twice. But what a recompense I was given! Seeing that her chalet was in danger of destruction by my enthusiastic audience, the sultana embraced me spontaneously and signaled to my companion to let me walk down and mingle with the ladies. They were in such a state of excitement and uplift that they crowded around me in intense joy, one after the other wishing to kiss my hand, my feet—in fact they felt my dress, fell on their knees, and embraced me from head to foot. It really was an extraordinary, an *indecent* performance.

Finally two eunuchs came down to deliver me, and with my companion we were conducted into another of the buildings, one occupied by ladies who had reached an age of discretion. These were the concubines of the sultan. They showed me about their home, and almost all of them spoke French to me, begging me to promise to return. The horror of the empty, dreary lives they lived was vivid to me. Their only concern was to conserve their beauty, and that only so they would be able to please the horrible Abdülhamid: there was no other object to their lives.

I asked if they would not tell me some of their beauty secrets, and they responded with delight. One lady was chosen as the model to be worked over. A number of older women who appeared to have the position of superior servants came forward, and each contributed her share. To me the whole procedure was a revelation. Beauty culture and beauty preparations were not the great international pursuit and business that they are today, and I experienced something absolutely new. I learned that the concubines who had a very youthful air were almost all about twice as old as they looked. Some even appeared fifteen or twenty years younger than they were.

The becoming costumes which the younger ones wore enhanced their good looks but required a youthful figure. Their clothes were very light.

All wore the familiar Turkish trousers, full and gathered at the ankle, made of thin silk. Only light veiling covered the bust and served for sleeves, relieved with gay ribbons. None wore either corset or brassiere, but a narrow piece of silk crossed in front, and a larger one served for sash and floated long in the breeze. Some (doubtless those with natural curls) let their hair hang down unconfined, while others wore braids with colored ribbons. The effect was one of complete, unshackled freedom of movement—a great antithesis indeed to their actual position.

As time lay heavy on their hands, they had developed the art of rejuvenation to a degree unknown elsewhere. I learned that with intelligence and care a woman can take a good number of years from her looks, and I believe I can say that I myself am an excellent example of the results which can be obtained by using those Turkish methods of preservation.

Finally my companion informed me that the sultana was waiting for me to join her at dinner. It was now six o'clock. Though I left the seraglio with regret, I hoped to have at least half an hour of complete rest before the performance, which was scheduled to start at nine. On leaving the chalet, a large number of young girls, led by older women, advanced and began to offer me gifts. Some hung necklaces of many-colored beads and pearls, which they had made themselves, around my neck; others clasped bracelets of fretted gold encrusted with oriental stones about my arms, and hung magnificent silk scarves over my shoulders. My emotion was augmented when suddenly I beheld a large basket filled with still more gifts—perfumes and cosmetics made by themselves, embroideries worked in gold and silver and indescribable colors. I had no words to express my feelings at this truly oriental generosity. But an idea saved me, and I asked the sultana if she would permit me to send them some photographs of myself in theatrical costumes. With her permission I promised to do so as soon as I returned to Europe, and I kept my word. Among others, I had a picture of myself in the costume of an odalisque, which I sent directly to the palace. More than a year later I received a beautiful letter from the sultana herself, forwarded by my family to the distant place fate by then had taken me.

Unfortunately, though the dinner was excellent and the cuisine European, by this time I was so exhausted with the emotions of the day that I could eat very little. I had the opportunity to taste the famous water of Kiat-Hane, which was agreeable enough, but I was delighted to accept a glass of wine with dessert, served me especially, as the sultana did not drink. When I took my leave to return to the theater, she presented me with a jewel case containing a gold bracelet set with rubies, diamonds, and sapphires.

"A souvenir of your visit to Yildiz Palace," she said, and she kissed me again, wishing me happiness and success.

Poor soul! My heart was heavy for her, and I knew I should not see her again.

19

THERE WERE a few minutes of grace left me in which to take a nap in my dressing room. All too soon Betty was leaning over me, crying "Madame! Madame!" in a voice of alarm, "Courage! Wake up! Don't forget, tomorrow we shall be free!" I could well have slept forty-eight hours then and there, but I struggled back to earth. "Our handsome guard just brought this to wake you up," she said, and handed me a cup of black coffee. The words "handsome guard" coming from the lips of the suspicious Betty provoked a smile. She was in a very different mood. The troupe from the French theater was present, and she had shared dinner and a good gossip with the wardrobe mistress, so she no longer felt herself among murderers. The coffee, from the private kitchen of the sultan, accomplished its mission. (My charming guide had told me, by the way, that the sultan's kitchen was separated from the other palace kitchens and that every day he sent a portion of all the dishes served him to a different "favorite" to taste—sometimes without warning the superintendent of the kitchen himself—to insure the absence of poison.)

The word "free" from Betty, the good coffee, the sound of the orchestra tuning up—all brought me to reality, and I told her to hurry.

"All is ready in the boudoir," she said with a certain note of triumph, opening the door to reveal the chaise-longue. The costumes were spread out upon it, and I could not stifle a cry of pleasure on seeing that they were all new. Betty knew my aversion to costumes which had been worn by others, but in this case the situation had not seemed avoidable since I had no costumes with me.

A knock on the door and the wardrobe mistress appeared. I did my best to show her my gratitude, and she expressed her pleasure in having been able to do this for me, confessing that it was really due to the prima donna of the company. When she had learned she was not to sing for the sultan, her fury knew no bounds. To keep me from appearing, she had torn every costume in shreds before the eyes of the poor director, the result being that the costumer had to sit up all night with two helpers to make the necessary costumes, which fortunately only numbered two. While explaining all this, she and Betty helped me into the first-act costume, that of the Bride. It was a beautiful dress of rich stuffs and oriental lace. I decided at once to buy both costumes, as well as to give a personal present to the wardrobe mistress and her aids. Not only were these more handsome than my own costumes for *La petite mariée*, but what an interesting memento of the whole adventure they would be!

We were warned that the curtain would rise in fifteen minutes. I was nervous, as it was my custom to vocalize before a performance, choosing always the dressing room farthest from the stage so as not to be heard by the audience, but here I was directly beside the stage. Now I envied Melba and her whistling; I have never been able to whistle in my life. A few vocalises of my good teacher Madame Marchesi always did so much for me: they reminded me of her, which never failed in its effect. She was an inspiration, and her vocalises electrified me, gave me confidence that my voice was placed and all was in accord.

The orchestra began tuning their instruments. I ventured into the wings for the first time.

Since the curtain was down, it was impossible to see the auditorium. The orchestra suddenly began the overture; the chorus, only men, was already onstage. I was astonished that there was no applause, but other surprises were in store. The role of the jealous wife, which had been created by my dear old friend Marie Desclauzas, was to be played by a man in disguise (as I have already explained, I was the only woman in the piece). Indeed everything was so fantastic that I was no longer able to think clearly myself.

The role of La Petite Mariée in Lecocq's work, though agreeable to sing and accompanied by light, gay music, had nothing in the first act that would show my ability as a vocalist. With the conductor I had arranged to interpolate the Air du Mysoli from *The Pearl of Brazil*, singing it in the wings before my entrance, the flautist beside me for the cadenzas. The tenor, my betrothed in the play, was unfortunately the good, good friend of the recalcitrant prima donna of the company and therefore not particularly amiable or friendly toward me, the interloper. He had not been informed of the innovation, the director fearing another unpleasant scene. At the rise of the curtain, hearing me warble an air from *The Pearl of Brazil* offstage, he became confused and dazed. When he did realize the situation, he started to pace to and fro across the stage, not at all in his role, while the director in the wings opposite frantically gestured for him to sit down on a bench and await my cue after the air. Luckily I could see nothing of this little drama from my position.

When I finished my last note, an E-flat in my duet with the flute, I thought I should faint with the strain. Audiences did not usually wait for the end of the last note to break into heartwarming applause, but now a stony silence greeted me. At the imperial theaters in Russia the audiences never applauded until the signal came from the imperial box. The sultan, however, never applauded, and therefore his guests did not dare. When I think of that performance even now I shiver! Death was in all our souls. The performance, always so light and gay, was funereal. Those Turkish dignitaries stationed behind the sultan nodded their heads like mandarins: a Turkish sign of approbation. But even the solemn nodding heads could not bring life to the performance, and I realized that at any price I must save my reputation as far as the ambassadors and other foreign dignitaries were concerned. The second act was laid in the palace of Podesta, who is in love with La Petite Mariée. Fortunately there was a piano on the stage. Without warning anyone I suddenly added a few words to my part, asking Podesta if he would not like to hear me sing. Much astonished, he answered "Certainly" (how lucky he did not say "No"!). Secretly I looked at the conductor, who was quite plainly laughing into his beard. I seated myself and sang the Bird Waltz, and on top of that Elena Sanz's "El bolero grande" by way of contrast. Furious at that great mummy of a sultan who did not move a muscle in spite of all our efforts, I sang with more fervor and abandon than ever in my life—so much so that the sultan's foreign guests, clearly understanding the situation, could not help laughing. (I do not know if laughter was also forbidden.)

At last the much-desired end to that grotesque performance arrived. I warmly thanked the director and my associates of that doleful evening and rushed to my dressing room to change to my own dress. I was just finishing when my lady of honor arrived, much excited, saying she had been commanded to conduct me to the sultan's private salon at once. "I am very glad you are ready, as the sultan does not care to wait," she said breathlessly. As we hurried away I hastily inquired what my actions should be in his presence. The first requisite was that I must not look at him!

Before we reached the door she threw a magnificent veil over my head, which I was to keep until the two guards removed it, and made me change my slippers for new sandals. I entered the presence of Sultan Abdülhamid II.

From behind the door my friend gave a signal, and two eunuch guards led me to the throne. I walked with my arms flat against my sides like a wooden soldier, my head bowed so that I saw only the floor. The room was very dark. At the foot of the throne I made the traditional salaam very slowly, bending low, and sank to my knees on the third step of the throne, my head still lowered. The sultan raised his right hand and I looked up. I was at last face to face with Abdülhamid, of whom the whole world spoke with terror. But my astonishment crowded away every other thought, for the sultan was a double of Raiff Pasha. Though the pasha was a tall, handsome man and Abdülhamid was small and thin, the sultan had the same dreamy, deep eyes, the same look which could change in a twinkling from excessive tenderness to ferocious cunning, the same mobile mouth, the same cold smile. All this coursed through my brain in a moment. He extended his beautifully cared-for hand, and I bestowed a respectful kiss upon it. He closed his thumb over mine, a sensation I shall never forget, and smiled briefly. Our eyes met, and in his I saw a benign and gentle expression—so much like that which I had seen on the face of the pasha. It was startling.

As I attempted to rise, my two guards assisted me but did not lead me backwards as I expected. Instead the sultan signaled, still smiling faintly, and a young page advanced with a cushion on which was a small *coffre*. The sultan motioned for me to accept it. In the dim light I saw there was a small key in the lock, but in my confusion I could only bow again very low in token of my gratitude. The two eunuchs, each taking me by an elbow, backed me out of the sultan's private salon, and the reception was over.

Once outside I felt regret, for the terrible Abdülhamid, in his own way, had been most kind. That he was sultan of Turkey naturally made him an interesting personage, but for another reason he fascinated me far more. I looked up at the wall, behind which I believed I had just divined a secret—a secret which explained the great influence that had opened the intimate life of the Yildiz Palace to me. I had no sooner formed my suspicion than I realized that if anyone suspected my thoughts I might be in serious danger.

I was led through a number of rooms, my head closely covered, until we reached the hall where the lady of honor had first received me. She was waiting there, and greeted me joyously, especially when she saw the *coffre* in my hands. Betty stood waiting too, dressed in her *charchaff* and holding mine in her hands. As my charming hostess could not conceal her curiosity, I opened my casket for her and drew out a jewel in heavy gold worked with oriental enamels in various colors and with the arms of Abdülhamid in pearls. There was something else in the box, a silk purse containing a thousand gold francs, with a message in perfect French: "For your poor." *Quelle delicatesse*! I asked my friend how I should ever be able to express my gratitude to her sovereign, and likewise to herself for her daylong kindness to me. At least I could never forget them. "That may also be said by Abdülhamid and his humble servant," she answered, bowing, and asked if I would permit her to embrace me. She put her arms around me affectionately and, as I put on my *charchaff*, flung her beautiful veil around my neck "as a souvenir." The eunuchs helped us into the magnificent court carriage drawn by four white horses, which had already taken me over part of the grounds, and we parted.

Alas, our adventures were not over yet, though the night was well advanced. Soon our carriage stopped. We saw the fiacre we had taken from the lawyer's office waiting for us, and we were transferred to it. Then began the visits to the various posts we had passed in the afternoon. It was pitch black and we could see nothing. Finally, at the last post, I recognized the voice of Ali at the window of the carriage in the dark. "Remember all my instructions," he said quietly. "You have nothing to fear— I will see you later at the hotel." And we continued our way down the mountain at a good clip. I warned Betty to do exactly what the hotel manager said and to wait in her room for the next instructions. But we were not there yet, and during the drive my thoughts returned to the sultan.

I saw his face clearly again, and beside it the face of the pasha. I knew the sultan had five sons and three daughters *whom he recognized.* I felt convinced the Raiff Pasha was another son and Ali was therefore the sultan's grandson. The great position the pasha enjoyed was thus explained: his extraordinary influence at court, the fact that Ali had been military attaché at the Turkish embassy when only twenty-five years old, and that both he and his father had received a European education, unlike most Turks at that time. I felt more nervous than ever at being in the hands of the pasha. I realized that under no condition must I allow him or anyone else to see that I divined his secret. It was an unpleasant quarter of an hour, but when the lights of Pera twinkled below I took heart.

We arrived in front of the famous hotel at last, but a doorman signed for us to turn the fiacre into the courtyard. I held tight to the sultan's casket, which was concealed under my *charchaff,* and Betty, carrying my bag, followed me into the lobby. The proprietor, who seemed to be waiting for us, led me down a hall. Betty was conducted to the lift. Seeing me stop to stare after her, with a sinking heart, and seeing her look sorrowfully back at me, the proprietor explained he had no vacant room nearer mine than the floor above. I said nothing and followed him up a short flight of stairs into a winter garden. Opening a door, he led me into a room which like all Turkish rooms was dimly lighted. A moment elapsed before anything was visible, and then I might have thought myself in a private salon in the Hôtel Vendôme in Paris. The room was luxuriously furnished, there were flowers everywhere, and a table in the center was set for three.

Left alone, I removed the *charchaff* and sat down to await—what? It was very late; all was silent. Thick portieres hid a view of the sleeping city, and a heavy scent of roses and incense made me feel slightly dizzy. Soon I could hear running footsteps, then a soft rap on the door, and the pasha entered. He was dressed in a superb official uniform, his breast covered with medals and decorations. He came forward to kiss my hand. He *was* a magnificent man! I looked at him attentively and could not help picturing him as a far more resplendent sultan than he whom I felt certain was his father.

The expression on his face impressed me most. It was different than the one that had formerly alarmed me. He was sad now. Holding me to his decorated bosom, he kissed me paternally on the forehead. It was a solemn moment. He told me he knew I must be tired and invited me to take my place at the table, suggesting that I needed a glass of champagne. "But you have another guest," I said, indicating the third place.

"Yes," he answered with a smile. "It is for my son. I thought that would give you pleasure. But he had left the palace when I started out, and I don't know where he is."

Luckily the maître d'hôtel came in with the supper before this conversation went much farther, for I was most troubled and uncomfortable. A bottle of champagne was brought, and a hasty glance was enough for me to see that it was unopened. When the cork was drawn, I was glad enough to accept a glass from the pasha's hand. My brain seemed to have lost its power of constructive thought. If Ali Bey was expected to supper, all my fears were groundless. I could not fathom the depths of my fears. Though the waiter stayed constantly in the room, I was able to eat little. The pasha overwhelmed me with compliments about my performance before the sultan. I wished to tell him of the magnificent gift but thought it might be imprudent while the waiter remained in the room. When coffee was finally served I remembered Ali's instructions and took none. The pasha urged me to drink a little, saying that it would keep me awake and that he wished to speak to me afterward, but I assured him there was no danger that I would fall asleep. My nerves were unstrung, for Ali did not arrive. Yet the pasha's attitude was somehow reassuring, and I was curious to hear what he wished to say.

Finally he arose, signaling me to sit in an armchair. He picked up my *charchaff*, with which I had covered the sultan's gift. I lifted the golden box and silently showed it to him, but he said he knew all about it. Then he begged me to listen to what he had to say, as Ali might come at any moment.

"To begin with, tell me frankly, do you love my son?" He put this question in a low voice I would not have recognized as his own.

"I love Ali Bey very much as a friend, as a sincere friend," I answered. "I have known him a long while as a friend of my brother's, but I can assure you I have no stronger attachment."

"Then I can speak," the pasha said. "My life is a mystery which I cannot yet reveal to you. Though I had always desired to marry an intelligent and educated European, I was obliged to marry a Turkish girl. I did so with the assurance that my sons would be educated in Europe." He did not mention the contingency of daughters. "I have not taken any concubines, as my principles are opposed to this custom, but I promised myself that the day I met the woman whom I knew I loved, I would marry her. That woman is you."

As I searched for words, he stopped me and asked that I reflect before speaking. "While waiting, I beg you to be my guest at this hotel, with your companion. All your wishes shall be as commands." This was the most oriental phrase he had uttered. "I shall send a request to be received, and I hope you will authorize me to tell you my secret."

I was so astonished and upset by these dignified words that my only thought was that if I fled Constantinople without informing the pasha it would be unforgivable. So I told him that though I felt much honored by his confidence, I too had a sad secret, and I would never marry as long as the mystery which had broken my life remained unsolved. I came to Constantinople with the hope of solving that mystery, but without success, and I begged that if my actions appeared strange he would not judge ill of me.

Kissing my hand he said, "I await your orders."

My heart was heavy, for I felt my actions had been, or would appear to have been, questionable in the light of the present revelation. Here was a noble heart destined to suffer on my account.

He left me then. I fell back on the chair and could not control my tears; I knew, too late, that the pasha was a great gentleman.

Suddenly I heard a soft rap on the door to the bedroom I had not yet had time to explore. I was on the point of taking another glass of champagne when Ali appeared around the door. He looked as tired as I did and directed his attention immediately toward the champagne. He had heard all, had been in the bedroom the entire time!

Ali had arrived at the hotel just after his father. Seizing the opportunity, he slipped into the bedroom when his father came into the salon, while the waiters busied themselves with supper. But then it had been too late to make his presence known. Now that his father was gone he told me we too must leave at once. Betty was waiting in my room, ready.

I hastily flung on my *charchaff,* then snatched up the sultan's casket and hid it. The waiters were gone. The porter, having received his tip, probably slept. Ali summoned Betty and all three of us tiptoed down the stairs. His carriage was waiting behind the hotel and we hastily entered it. I threw myself on the cushions, close to hysteria. Dawn was near at hand, the night having grown gray; we risked being recognized at such an hour. Ali mounted beside the driver, we passed an officer whom he saluted, and a few minutes later we were at the consulate.

Bilal was there. Ali, leaving us in his care, had immediately to return to the palace. The consul was depended on to appear at nine o'clock with our passports and tickets.

Betty and I slept like the Seven Sleepers of Ephesus, but when the consul arrived we were ready, and soon we were at the dock. Before leaving the consulate I wrote a letter to the pasha on the official paper:

> Dear Raiff Pasha: My heart is full of sorrow and remorse. Perhaps you will think it is a lack of confidence on my part which prevented me from telling you the truth last night, but I must leave as I am now doing (almost a flight). This is due to the mystery of which I spoke. Believe me, my dear Pasha, that whatever happens I shall never forget your chivalry and kindness to me. I promise to write you, and I hope you will forgive me and keep for me some of your affection.

When we arrived at the dock I saw Bilal. Detaching himself from a group of Arabs, he came up to tell me that the ladies were furious with him for having helped me to escape, and had shown him the door—and now he wanted to come with us! I gave him the letter I had written to the pasha, with the instructions to take it to him at the ministry after the boat had sailed, and I assured him that Ali would take care of him.

The consul spoke to the captain, explaining that I had our passports and tickets and asking that no one be allowed to disturb us. The boat was scheduled to sail before noon, but we were informed it would be delayed. This was unpleasant news. The consul left to attend to his official duties but said he would return before the sailing of the boat to see that all was well.

Shortly after, Ali Bey arrived, but the crew had received their instructions and so he was not allowed to pass to our stateroom. Luckily the lawyer appeared and smoothed matters over. He brought with him a letter from my brother-in-law, who was waiting with Clémence for me at Bucharest. He likewise brought a newspaper. Large type announced a performance at the palace the evening before with the French company and a star from Paris, Clara Lardinois. The diplomatic corps was invited and all were present in full force with the exception of Feodor Peshkov, who was due to return from Petersburg that morning, after a trip having to do with family affairs. "We regret that this charming artist is leaving today on the steamship *Constanza* for Romania."

This time I felt all courage leave me! Ali was furious and demanded an explanation, almost rudely. The answer was simple enough. The director of the French troupe had inserted the notice himself, too good a bit of publicity to miss; and the fact that I was leaving for Romania had doubtless been overheard by a member of the company when I called at the consulate. I begged the lawyer to ask the captain how soon the boat would sail. While he was gone I told Ali of Bilal's troubles, and we arranged where we were to correspond.

We suddenly heard high voices in the passageway outside my cabin, and when Ali opened the door he found himself face to face with his father. Bilal, thinking the boat was to sail before noon, had delivered my letter at one o'clock. Though the pasha already knew that I had not spent the night in my room at the hotel but had left with Ali shortly after he did, he had been unable to find Ali anywhere. Xenia's husband, who occupied a position under his father-in-law at the ministry, had just shown him the newspaper article when my letter was delivered. Knowing the sailing of the ship had been delayed, he hurried to the dock.

The pasha said a few words in Turkish to Ali, who smiled and left the room.

The poor pasha! He looked completely bewildered but had the same expression of kindness I had noticed the evening before. He took me by the hands and asked why it was I did not have confidence in him; he could have helped me if my troubles were in Constantinople. In a few words, for there was no excuse now for me to remain silent, I told him why I had come to Turkey. I told him how, after learning all possible, I had realized that Feodor Peshkov, fearing I might surprise his secret, could only look upon me as a dangerous enemy—and I had decided to leave before he arrived. "Now that you know everything," I said, "tell me that you no longer feel resentment toward me, and that Ali will not suffer for having helped me so much."

"Ali has done his duty," the pasha said. "Why should I punish him?" Then, because there was so little time left before sailing, the pasha imparted final messages to me. I promised to keep my word and write to him from Romania. "Though so far I have not been permitted to leave Turkey," he said, "many things change, and I hope to see you before long, in Europe."

Ali knocked on the door and entered in time to see his father embrace me affectionately. Turning to his son, the pasha said, "I know everything, and I am proud of you. Embrace your friend now—you have merited it," and he tapped him on the shoulder with his favorite gesture. It was the only happy moment I had witnessed in Turkey—and the saddest. The siren blew, and my two faithful friends were forced to hurry down the gangplank.

I went on deck after them. On the dock I saw the Romanian lawyer and the French consul smiling and bowing. But my heart followed two splendid silhouettes standing a little apart—Ali and his father. As the ship moved rapidly away, the last thing I could distinguish through my tears were the figures of two of the finest men that I have ever known.

❖ 20 ❖

FTER A QUIET VISIT with Clémence in Romania, and while traveling home to Brussels, I had the unpleasant experience of waking
in the train to see a dark figure standing over me. Thinking it to
be Betty, I was not at first alarmed, but with returning consciousness I
realized my mistake and cried out. In that moment the figure was gone.

All my luggage had been ransacked, clothes littered the floor, and the
small leather bag containing my valuables, which I kept under my pillow,
had been opened. My few rings were lying about the stateroom together
with my passport. Whatever the thief had been searching for, he had only
taken one small ring. I have always thought my wedding certificate was
the jewel sought that night. Luckily it was safe in Brussels.

In February I finally reached home again. My first act was to call on
the Russian ambassador, to whom I recounted my adventures in Constantinople, but not the theft on the train. He was very suave, smooth,
and confidential, and I did not believe a word he said. On hearing my
story he assured me that Sergei had committed suicide due to losses at
cards. I did not tell him that I utterly discredited any such preposterous
theory. He went on to say that in order to get my property out of Russia
I must sign a paper, a power of attorney, giving him and his agents complete authority to act in my behalf. This I was most unwilling to do, as I
trusted no one. And when informed that I must give up my marriage
contract to facilitate proving my legal rights, I knew what had instigated
the robbery on the train.

"I believe you always carry your marriage contract with you," the ambassador said, "and that is a very dangerous thing to do because these

people will stop at nothing to procure it." He was speaking the truth then!

I was so startled to learn that His Excellency knew something he could only have learned through those intimately connected with me, that I hardly knew what to answer. I was told over and over again, "It is the only way to get your property safely out of Russia."

I pointed out that my marriage contract was the sole proof left me that I had ever been married to Sergei Peshkov. Though of course I had confidence in His Excellency, I could not be sure into whose hands that paper might fall in Russia, since so many seemed so anxious to acquire it. I could not part with it.

"Since you refuse, I can do nothing more for you," he said pleasantly. And he warned me that I might be followed as long as I still carried the contract with me. "Think it over; perhaps you don't realize . . ."

Having learned only the worst side of my desolate condition, I went home in despair. Sidonie as usual was my comfort and stay. I was thoroughly unnerved by what I had learned, not least by the fact that such personal and intimate details of my manner of life seemed to be known to His Excellency. Sidonie warned me not to part with my last link to Sergei under any circumstances. She had been in Russia and was the only person with any conception of that terrible country and my present situation in regard to it.

I was so thoroughly alarmed and upset now, so truly in the position of "neither maid, wife, nor widow," that I felt I could not stay in Belgium, or even in Europe.

About this time, providentially, Maurice Grau offered me a contract with the Metropolitan in New York. Under ordinary circumstances I should have preferred to wait until later to appear in America, but now I accepted the offer with gratitude. It was arranged that I would join the company sometime after the opening of the season, and I arrived in New York with a maid in the middle of bitter weather. To be close to the opera house we went to Morello's, an old-fashioned family hotel which has long since vanished. I at once came down with a heavy cold, and before I was completely cured I went to the opera house one evening to attend a rehearsal of *Faust*. This was a foolish thing to do. The opera house was cold and drafty and it had begun to snow.

After a time Mr. Grau came in to suggest that we all go home, as the snow was falling heavily, but when we attempted to leave the building we discovered that heavy drifts had formed under the doors. In the end I was let out of a window on Thirty-ninth Street and carried home by two firemen attached to the theater. I had never seen such deep snow; traffic in the city was at a standstill.

My cold developed into pneumonia. With some difficulty a doctor was summoned, and his treatment consisted of wrapping me in sheets wrung out in ice water. That I did not die is a miracle. When I was well enough to travel we fled from the rigors of New York back to Brussels. This time I stayed at home, accepting some engagements in various Brussels theaters for the next year or so.

Since leaving Turkey my time had been full. After my visit with Clémence in Romania I had joined an opera company playing in Bucharest, touring with it in Germany—Munich, Dresden, Leipzig, Berlin, Hamburg—and as far as Stockholm and Copenhagen, appearing both in concert and opera. I left the company at Aix-la-Chapelle to return home, where my adventures, instead of ending, had begun again with redoubled vigor.

During this time my mind was not at rest, and I had a constant fear of being watched. The Russian ambassador communicated with me, renewing his importunities to give up my marriage license, and now some members of my family began to urge me to do so. Being convinced that an attempt had been made to rob me of this document, it seemed a foolish surrender to give it up of my own free will. I received no answers to my letters to Russia, and my attempts to procure a passport were unavailing. Besides this, in Brussels I remained under the surveillance of the Russian ambassador. At last I declared that if I could not go to Russia I would at least make it difficult for them to keep a constant watch over my actions.

I packed and left for Paris to seek Roberval, the big agent, an old acquaintance of mine. I told him my story and begged him to find me an engagement somewhere—anywhere, as long as it was far enough away.

"What a pity," he said. "I've just sent a fine troupe to Costa Rica to open the new opera house at San José. A fine company, but they have a prima donna with them."

"No matter," I said. "I'll go at any price—I'll sing in the chorus. I must leave Europe at once. I'll join them by the quickest ship possible."

After cables and excitements it was arranged. The impresario, a man named Aubry, seemed pleased to have me, even under an assumed name, for I wished to cover all traces of Clara Lardinois. I became Blanche Arral (*Blanche* for my favorite niece and *Arral* due to the mistake of a printer who had produced the word *Aralc*, my name reversed). It was arranged—

Advertisement for "Blanche Arral, Prima Donna Soprano: Opéra Comique—Paris, Théâtre Royal de la Monnaie—Bruxelles, Des Théâtres Imperiaux—St. Petersbourg." Courtesy William R. Moran.

not altogether to my advantage perhaps, but I was delighted with the chance of an engagement in so remote a place as Central America.

The company had sailed directly to New Orleans, where they were to take ship for Puerto Limón, Costa Rica. In order to save time it was arranged that I should set out at once on a fast liner for New York, where I could connect with a ship going directly to Costa Rica. Part of my advance was cabled to Paris to defray my passage to New York, and the remaining amount would await me in a bank in New York. It was not a perfect arrangement, but my anxiety to leave Europe made me accept the proposition almost joyfully.

I sailed alone. My funds were too low to take a companion or maid, and Betty felt she had had enough. I reached New York in early spring and went to the one French hotel I knew about, the Lafayette in University Place, which was still run by Louis Martin, as it had been during my childhood. I had had plenty of opportunity to think over my situation and develop a few qualms, but New York seemed sufficiently large and remote to be a comforting sight.

I remember sitting down in my room on the second floor to take stock of my situation, the first plan in my head being to go to the bank to collect my funds. Suddenly I heard music coming from the next room, a violin and a piano playing a duet. The effect of music on me has always been the same. Immediately I forgot myself and my problems. The two unknown musicians were great artists. The broad, inspired sweep of the violinist, the rich, heartbreaking tones that he drew from his violin! I was completely carried away, and after a moment I could contain myself no longer. I must make music too. All alone as I was, I leapt to my feet and began, in full voice, the final trio from *Faust*.

> Anges purs, anges radieux,
> Portez mon âme au sein des cieux!
> Dieu juste, à toi je m'abandonne!
> Dieu bon, je suis à toi, pardonne!
>
> (Pure angels, radiant angels,
> Carry my soul to the bosom of the heavens!
> Just God, to you I abandon myself!
> Kind God, I am with you, forgive me!)

As I sang, the violin stopped. But a moment after, it began to accompany me, with the piano, in that inspired and dramatic melody. Then the music ceased altogether. There was a frantic bang on my door, which burst open, and I found myself embraced by a gentleman with flowing hair: my old playmate and compatriot, Eugène Ysaÿe! Close behind him stood the pianist Raoul Pugno.

"My little Clara!" cried Ysaÿe. "I would know that voice anywhere!"

It should be unnecessary to explain my feelings, with two good friends appearing so miraculously while I sat stranded in a foreign land, for it should be likewise unnecessary for me to add that no advance on my contract was waiting for me in any bank in New York. I might have been truly frantic then, with the prospect of having to return home, had it not been for my sister Angèle's fellow student, now the great Ysaÿe.

"My little Clara!" he said. "To go to that wild, savage Costa Rica! With an impresario you cannot trust! You are mad! It is very simple. Pugno and I are giving concerts. You join us, and we will make our duets into trios!"

All my plans, I thought for the moment, had undergone another complete change, and I accepted the invitation. What a pleasure it was to be associated with those two great artists and friends. We gave several concerts in New York at various clubs and in one or two great houses. It brought me some welcome money, and I was delighted of course; but when Ysaÿe approached his manager to suggest I join them on a concert tour through the United States, my new-found career was again nipped in the bud. Due to my contract with the untrustworthy impresario, no manager dared book me. True, my contract had been defaulted, but this did not guarantee a new manager against an always-dreaded lawsuit. The upshot of the matter was that everyone, even poor Eugène, advised me to go to Costa Rica and present myself to the manager by the stipulated date. Then, if he refused to have me, no fault could be attached to me.

By that time the ship I was to have caught had already sailed, and the next one was not leaving for nearly a month. In order to preserve my reputation, since I saw that I could not otherwise look for engagements, I was now anxious to get to Costa Rica. I went by train to New Orleans. Here I sought a ship bound for Puerto Limón, and with some difficulty found one.

It was a small Norwegian freighter with a cargo chiefly consisting of pigs and sheep. There was to be one other passenger, a little French Jewish gentleman who ran a photography business in San José. At great expense I sent a telegram announcing my arrival, and went aboard, bag and baggage.

We had other passengers besides the little photographer—every sort of creeping and crawling creature an entomologist might desire. Cockroaches were everywhere, including the captain's beard. There was no such thing as a cabin, much less a berth or bed. A place was fixed for me on the floor, and here I attempted to sleep, covered with veils and wrapped in every garment that might keep at bay the busy insect world. My little Jewish friend slept, fully clothed, outside my door to discourage prowling sailors, and for ten days we drifted across the Gulf of Mexico.

The heat was suffocating, and soon I thought I should lose my reason. Day after day enduring such hardships, such weather! So short a time before I had enjoyed a high position at the Russian imperial theaters and been decorated by the czar. Now, unknown, almost penniless, and using an assumed name, I found myself bound on a trip to a remote corner of civilization, a dubious and unpromising predicament to say the least. I could barely summon the heart to continue, and I finally thought of the sea as a last resort. There were no bath or other amenities of civilization on board. There was little food to eat, and what was there was filthy beyond description. Day after day battling the dirt, the bugs, the heat, and the smells, I had learned what violent contrasts life could show me, and in those terrible hours I found true despair.

As the days crawled by it became more and more difficult to keep my head and endure that unending trip. Ysaÿe and Pugno were now peacefully filling their engagements in cities laden with American comfort. I felt like the Flying Dutchman; my future seemed as shrouded in darkness and as ill-omened and unbearable as his ever did.

But at last in the distance appeared the first faint sight of the coast of Costa Rica. As we approached the high, blue mountains far inland, in whose heart stood San José and the opera house I hoped to inaugurate, my courage rose slightly. It was a perfectly magnificent sight, and now I wanted to leap overboard and swim ashore—even though I could not swim!

As we approached, the little port of Limón became discernible, with its warehouses for coffee, sugar, and bananas, its few houses along the waterfront, and its one hotel. But we kept right on peacefully sailing, past the town, past the hotel and the wharves. The town that looked so neat and comfortable grew dim. Neither my photographer nor I spoke a word of Norwegian, but at last by dint of sounds, gestures, and sheer despair we learned that something had gone wrong with our engines, and that if we stopped now it would not be possible to start them up again. It was sunset, so we were doomed to another night among the cockroaches, sailing round and round in a circle until dawn when we could maneuver into the port and up to our berth.

Day broke at length, and we finally reached the dock. Along the quays walked crowds of people, many natives half naked and carrying bundles on their heads, others dressed in white, who I hoped were the members of the company I expected to join.

We docked, and the pigs and sheep were unloaded. They were placed, a few at a time, in a great canvas sack and hoisted by a crane onto the dock. This, I thought, was truly the last straw. We were not to be permitted to disembark until after the last pig. Still, I was determined to land at once. I would not spend one more hour on that boat. I would go up in the derrick with the pigs. No—this could not be. The derrick was unsafe and might break; we must wait. But I refused to do this. The photographer was now as frantic as myself, and the captain gave in. We stepped into the canvas bag, for the moment divested of pigs and sheep, and the crane lifted us high above the decks. Thus Blanche Arral, the new prima donna from Paris, landed in Costa Rica.

I stepped out of the canvas—and into the arms of my old friend and colleague Bartel, with whom I had played innumerable times in Paris (in fact he and I had created the roles of father and daughter in *La fiancée des verts-poteaux*).[48] It was a strange and unexpected meeting! A few other members of the company were with him: Jacquin, Darman, and Bernard Bégué.[49] I looked in vain for Aubry, for whom I had been hastily planning a little speech in which to paint my ideas of his ill-treatment. I was so happy to see good old Bartel, though, having been through such days of torture and uncertainty, that I burst into tears in his paternal arms. When I was able to I inquired why Monsieur Aubry did not accompany them, but they eluded my questions. At that moment two gentlemen approached, and I was introduced to Señor Rodriguez, a charming inhabitant of Puerto Limón, and his secretary. In bad but understandable French he informed me that a room was waiting for me at the hotel, and we set out across the plaza.

Oh, what a comforting, heartening thing a good hot bath can be after days of deprivation! I retired hastily to my room, wondering whether I could ever scrub off the ten days' grime of my Norwegian freighter. A bath was prepared, and I was conducted to it. Entering the room, I locked the door and turned around, only to find myself face to face with a rearing scorpion!

The dining room of that primitive hotel had been transformed into a banquet hall. In lieu of a table cloth the table was most delightfully decorated with brilliant leaves and flowers. The sight was so charming and fresh that I applauded. The real surprise, however, was the presence of a number of the members of the Costa Rican chamber of commerce, who had their quarters at Puerto Limón and its environs. They were all proprietors of huge coffee, sugar, and banana plantations. Señor Rodriguez was likewise a leading banker of the country. He not only furnished the funds to build the magnificent opera house at San José, copied from that of Paris, but also advanced the money to bring the entire company from Paris and to order new costumes and scenery for our entire repertory. In a word, he, with a few other rich planters, was the promoter of the whole venture.[50]

Señor Rodriguez invited Monsieur Bartel, the senior member of the company and my old friend, to inform me of the position we were in. I realized there must be something untoward to explain Monsieur Aubry's behavior, and I soon found out what it was.

Monsieur Aubry—the news was broken to me between sips of champagne and bites of delicious native dishes—had absconded. He had absconded with all the advance receipts—a vast sum, since people all over Costa Rica had paid in gold for subscriptions to our season. He had, as a matter of fact, fled the country. He had insisted on complete payment for tickets in advance. Not content with the Costa Ricans, he had even journeyed into the adjoining republics of Nicaragua and Panama and sold tickets for special performances, to which these poor wretches were to come by the trainload from great distances. One of his excuses for complete payment in advance was the tale that I—poor deluded creature myself!—was in New York and had refused to come to Costa Rica until my entire salary had been sent me. The irony of it! This story painting me so adamant and pitiless, squeezing the last penny from the music-starved inhabitants of Central America, was making the rounds, being recounted to innocent natives, Indians, and planters who, hungering for opera, had mortgaged the produce of their lands and their toils for months ahead in order to have ready cash in hand. And all the while I was suffering agony and despair among the swine and cockroaches on a Norwegian freighter in the infernal heat of the Gulf of Mexico so that I could come and sing for them!

While poor Bartel explained this dreadful state of affairs to me, I could not help but see the anguish written clearly on the faces of these poor men, whose confidence had been so sadly misplaced in that swindler, that archfiend, Aubry.

I explained in a few words that I had received nothing from Aubry but the price of my passage from Le Havre to New York, and that I had come the rest of the way in my determination not to forfeit my contract —a contract which was now a worthless piece of paper if ever there was one! But I could not understand how Aubry had been able to escape the country so successfully. I was told he had often been absent for days at a time, acting as an advance-booking agent for the opera season in distant towns, and that he had given full authority to the stage manager Monsieur Darman to conduct rehearsals in his absence. In fact he had never occupied himself with anything about the theater. He had evidently laid his plans long in advance.

Aubry was a fine speaker, he dressed in the latest fashions, and his prematurely gray hair had given him an added air of respectability. He had begun as the agent for Cousenier de Marseilles, the celebrated house of liqueurs and brandies. At one time stationed in New York, he preferred more remote places without competition, where he could win success with less effort. He made the acquaintance of the French consul in Costa Rica, who was himself the agent for some French product on the side, and little by little drew him into his plot. This man, who had the reputation of being a sneaky dog, helped Aubry to succeed in his swindle. In fact I believe they found it a simple matter to deceive the kindhearted Costa Ricans, suggesting to them how fine it would be to have an opera house in their capital, describing the amusement and pleasure it would bring to their wives and daughters, not to mention the prosperity and éclat which would follow.

Their calculations, however, were incorrect. The money was gone before the building was completed (as is so often the case), and they were obliged to put the roof on the auditorium when the plans called for two more balconies. As a result, the acoustics were dreadful. And even worse, there were not enough inexpensive seats. But the poor creatures were so anxious to have their opera, as the people of New York had, that they continued to raise money for Aubry to put into his bottomless pockets, in order to bring a complete company over from Paris. This company was now in San José and numbered over a hundred members. There were twenty singers for principal roles, a chorus, a good orchestra, and even a ballet (they had insisted on a ballet). There were also scenery and costumes, all new; but these did not belong to the theater, as Aubry had only paid a little on account, the rest being paid with notes of hand, which of course he had no intention of honoring.

I may add (to paint him darker, if that were possible) that, not content with his Great Opera Swindle, he brought from France the first motorcar ever seen in Central America and here again made a pretty penny, setting himself up as the agent for that car. The principal thing, however, was that he made good use of the motor for his escape. In spite of all the search made, he was never discovered. I believe he must have dyed his whiskers and, abandoning the car in a ditch, fled the country on some small freighter.

But this sad tale could not prevent me from enjoying my first real meal in eleven days, and I did full justice to it. In Costa Rica the drink was champagne, the money was gold, and in spite of all our troubles, smiles and gaiety were the order of the day. I promised to do what I could to help us all out of our extraordinary predicament, but first we would have to confer with the whole company, some of whom must surely have made plans of their own. The poor souls, abandoned and stranded, were living on public charity in San José. That very afternoon we entrained for the capital.

The trip from the coast, high into the mountains, consumed five or six hours, though it was only 103 miles. It was surely one of the most spectacular train trips in the world. The tracks were built on high trestles running between the mountains and over the most hair-raising gorges and gulfs, which stretched away below into the bowels of the earth. The view in all directions was superb, the sensation that of being suspended high in the air, for from the cars it was impossible to see the tracks at all. Bars in the windows prevented passengers from leaning out; in case of an accident, unless the train was stopped at one of the few wayside stations, there would be no chance of getting off. A few years later a horrible accident did occur. The tracks and trestles were swept away by a great landslide after the mountainside had been weakened by tropical rains, which were so common in these countries at certain times in the year. A great number of people were killed.[51]

When we reached San José and pulled into the station, all the company was there to greet me. The members of the orchestra, in full force, played a serenade as the train drew in and came to a puffing halt; and the French consul, accompanied by a representative of the president of Costa Rica, Rafael Iglesias, welcomed me to the city. If I had been uncertain and doubtful before, this picturesque and charming welcome into the heart of this Latin American republic, under such curious, even painful, circumstances, left me determined to do all in my power to bring opera to Costa Rica, if such a thing were possible. Here were a whole company, complete and ready to perform, a new opera house, and a musical, eager public. It would be foolish to give up now.

The new French consul had an apartment engaged for me at the best hotel in the city, and he accompanied me there, giving me details of Aubry's flight and explaining what a dreadful position the entire company had been left in, being now at the public charge. I did not take very well to this consul. I knew nothing bad of him, but I could not help feeling he was not sincere. Begging permission to retire, I promised to consider our predicament and to see if a way out could not be found.

I had a restless night, the seriousness of our trouble growing in my mind with the hours. Good heavens, I was in as bad a fix as any of the others! What money I had would not last long, and I was far away from any other engagement or any chance of finding one. But the next morning, with the sun, my courage returned. I drove to the presidential palace to acknowledge President Iglesias's honor in sending a representative to the station.

Rafael Iglesias lived with his family in modest style in a pleasant, unostentatious house. I was shown into his private office, where he greeted me in a most charming and friendly manner. He was a small, slim man in his middle forties, and unlike most of his compatriots, he was fair. We had a short talk about the situation, and he assured me of his patronage and backing in any undertaking we should decide upon. I met his wife and his daughters, and we became good friends. Later I was frequently invited to the palace, more as a friend than for official reasons.

In the afternoon a meeting of the whole company was called to the stage of the opera house, and there was a great deal of talk at cross purposes. At length I arose and proposed to open the theater, the receipts (if any) serving to pay first the chorus, orchestra, and ballet, and the residue (if any) to be divided, share and share alike, among the principals. As is usual in these cases there were some malcontents who wanted the salary stipulated in their contracts. They finally calmed down when they realized we were all in the same boat and could only save ourselves by a united effort. When I was able to tell them I had already had an audience with the president of the republic, who had promised to help us in any possible way, their confidence grew. The patronage of the president meant the patronage of his seven elected ministers and the whole chamber of deputies, including forty-odd men. And that of course meant the patronage of the haut monde of Costa Rica, the rich planters, the gold and silver miners—everyone. I was chosen director of the season and installed in the director's office. It would be up to me.

How I found the strength and energy to do my work for the next two months I do not know.

We opened with *Faust* to a gala house. Scenery, costumes, everything was new. And we gave a good performance—our future depended on it! A fine esprit de corps was engendered which would sustain us throughout the season. There was much doubt as to whether the public, having once been so swindled, would buy seats all over again, but they did. Instead of reducing prices, I had boldly raised them, feeling that with the company actually on the scene the public would be willing to come at these prices. The president and his seven ministers, as well as numerous deputies and all the high life of that airy capital, were present the opening night. An atmosphere of excitement and good will keyed us all to fever pitch. After so much trouble, over so many difficulties, the Costa Ricans were having their opera at last.[52]

I soon found that the receipts were greater on the nights in which I sang, so my name began to appear on the bills three nights a week, often more. I also found that mixed bills were very popular—why, I could never imagine, for it has always seemed to me a rather unsatisfactory and inartistic thing to give acts from three operas on one evening. But the public liked it, so I announced such conglomerate performances a number of times.

Before long things were in good running order, in spite of the constant work that involved directing a company. Darman had charge of the stage, and a number of chorus members did the sceneshifting, receiving extra pay for this so that the work was well concentrated and ran smoothly. Our repertory was rather large, as there was a limit to the audiences we could draw from. We produced, among other things, such standard works as *Faust, Roméo et Juliette, Carmen* (which was very popular in spite of the Spanish civilization of Costa Rica—in contrast to Spain itself, where *Carmen* has never been popular), *Philémon et Baucis, Mignon,* and *Manon,* and such *opéras comiques* as *Le grand mogol, Le Pré aux Clercs, Le coeur et la main,* and *Giroflé-Girofla.*

In order to ensure the patronage of the great landowners—to preserve the *entente cordiale* as warmly as possible—I had to accept their innumerable requests to go and sing in various small villages for charity affairs, and this in addition to my other duties. Toward the end of the season I went to sing in a distant plantation for the benefit of a church under construction there. It took place on a Sunday evening so that all the peasants in the district could be present. I took with me a young girl named Albertine Miédon, a dresser in the company whom I had made my personal maid, and we were invited to spend the night in the villa of the chief landowner. As there was no organ yet in the church, a piano had been brought from the villa and mounted on a wooden platform. I had likewise brought one of our violinists with me, and thus we performed our portion of the program.

When the service was over, many people crowded up to see us more closely. The platform, however, had not been intended for any such weight. A sinister crackling sound was loudly audible, and down (I don't know how far) went the piano, the violinist, myself, and many others. Because I had been standing beside the piano, everyone thought I had been crushed to death beneath it. But the piano was arrested in its fall by jutting masonry and exposed beams, and I was dragged from the pit unconscious. A number of people had suffered contusions and broken bones, and most tragic of all (to one), the violin was in splinters. I was carried to the villa on an improvised stretcher, though there were no doctors in the vicinity and none could come until the morning train arrived from San José on Monday. The daughter of the house, seeing my condition on recovering consciousness, gave me what she thought to be a sedative pill. In reality it was a soporific, a strong dose of morphine, and for a number of days I lay between life and death.

When at last I was well and able to return to San José, I learned with joy that the French government had answered my cables and arranged for the entire troupe to be returned to France on the next ship. Thanks to Rafael Iglesias and his ministers, who gave their patronage most graciously, I was able to announce a grand gala benefit for the company, which would assure the brave souls of returning to their native land with a little money in their pockets.

But my situation was now as critical as ever, for I did not want to return to Europe!

Providence came to my aid at the last minute. The Costa Rican papers had loudly trumpeted our success, and the news had spread abroad. I received an offer from the director of the French Opera in New Orleans to perform for the balance of their season, and I accepted at once. I told our baritone, Bégué, and his wife, who sang contralto roles under the name of Valdes, of my new engagement. They begged me to take them with me, as did Albertine, whom I had made a personal companion. She did not replace poor Betty, but she was most devoted and I had taken an interest in her.

One thing disturbed my plans a little, which was that Albertine had told me there was a young man who wished to follow her to New Orleans and marry her when they returned to France. I had already noticed this young Frenchman and his assiduous attention to Albertine; he was a planter in Costa Rica, Paul Bolo by name. Nevertheless, this was none of my concern. The French consul had warned me that Bolo was not to be recommended, but this I learned was spoken through pique and jealousy. So Bolo joined my little company, and that handsome and highly educated young gentleman became my private secretary, as some work was necessary to keep him out of mischief. He fulfilled his position splendidly. I would not have altered the arrangements even had I known the tragic role for which he was destined.

We all quitted Costa Rica on the same boat, in an atmosphere of mingled gaiety and sad regrets. Flowers, presents—it is unnecessary to say what lavish generosity the warmhearted inhabitants of that high and sunny land displayed. Rafael Iglesias and his family came down to Puerto Limón and smothered me in mountains of flowers, presenting me with a portrait of the whole family.

Bégué, his wife, Paul Bolo, Albertine, and I disembarked in New Orleans. Our colleagues went on to Le Havre. Costa Rica was another closed chapter, but what I learned there in practical experience about running an opera company stood me in good stead, and not long afterward.

$$\sim\!\!\Longrightarrow 21 \Longleftarrow\!\!\sim$$

THE FRENCH OPERA of New Orleans, in the Creole quarter of the city, was a charming house similar to the Opéra-Comique in Paris. Though larger, it retained a charming atmosphere of intimacy, without which so many operas fail in their effect. It was an added pleasure to sing there because the acoustics were as good as those of San José were poor.

I succeeded in obtaining engagements for Bégué and his wife, whom I represented as members of my own company, and we spent about six weeks in New Orleans. Added to the charm of the opera house and the Vieux Carré (the old quarter in which it was situated) was the famous *cuisine créole*, to which I cannot refrain from making a passing reference. Derived from the great French cookery of the eighteenth century—as interpreted by Negro cooks, geniuses in culinary art, and with an added exotic touch which crept in after the French ceded Louisiana to Spain— the native dishes of New Orleans are unique.

One of the most famous establishments of the Vieux Carré, however, was pure French: the house of Antoine. Here the old French cooking had survived untouched for over a hundred years, handed down from father to son. Though not a hotel, the house of Antoine included apartments on the floors above, and all the singers from the opera stayed there —including myself. The one drawback to New Orleans that I remember was the fierce mosquitoes. Every bed was furnished with a heavy *moustiquaire*, which kept the air out along with the pests, and large wooden electric fans were kept going, not to circulate the air but in the fond hope

226

that the mosquitoes would be frightened off or blown away, which they seldom if ever were.

I would read with regret several years after this that the lovely old opera house of New Orleans had gone up in smoke—another irreparable loss to my profession.

During my stay in Louisiana I fulfilled a number of private engagements, among them one to sing for the Hotel Men's convention which that year was held in New Orleans. It was a vast gathering, and we were photographed (with me appearing like a pigmy in white, lost in a sea of smoking jackets). The Hotel Men treated me royally and made me an honorary member of the association, which pleased me much. Since my engagement at the French Opera was over at this time, Mr. Hoffman, president of the association and proprietor of the famous old Hoffman House, invited me to return to New York with my entourage in his private Pullman. We had a delightful trip and felt ourselves, after the work and strain of the last months, "kings for a day."[53]

Spring was beautiful in New York that year, and I lingered in the city for some months. At last I booked passage on the *Bourgogne*. Surprisingly, however, I could summon no enthusiasm to return home just then. The day I was to sail, my trunks were all on board when at once a strange reluctance took hold of me. Without going up the gangplank I ordered all my luggage to be landed again. My insistence finally won, the last piece (I had nothing in the hold) coming down as the whistles blew. A few days later the *Bourgogne* disaster shocked the world. Passengers were lost, but casualties among the crew were light.[54]

A strange fate seems to watch over me. At a later time in New York I stopped at the Brevoort Hotel. Every morning at eleven o'clock I sat down for an hour of practice. From my position at the piano I could see through a window that looked out over a courtyard. One morning, after several months, I rose while singing and walked toward the door. At that instant a shot pierced the window and lodged in the wall, having passed across the piano stool at the height of my shoulder when seated. The story was hushed and nothing was ever discovered, but the trajectory of the bullet was traced by the police to the gentlemen's washroom across the court.

Shortly after my providential escape from the *Bourgogne*, a letter arrived from home bringing the news that my mother was seriously ill, and I sailed immediately for Rotterdam. Bégué obtained an engagement with the Metropolitan, where he would remain for a number of years, at the same time running a restaurant on East Thirty-eighth Street (and often cooking the main dishes!).

As we moved slowly into the docks at Rotterdam, a launch came down the river to meet us. Leaning over the rail, I caught sight of Angèle, Jeanne, and several other members of the family, all in deep mourning. Thus the news was broken. Added to the heavy strain I had undergone, a severe nervous attack forced me to a long rest.

When I had recovered well enough to sing again, it seemed unbearable to face yet another voyage into the unknown. I was ready for a little of the love and protection of home. As long as I actually lived at home I felt safe and secure, so I was glad to accept an offer to appear as guest at the Théâtre Royal de la Monnaie, appearing once more under my own name. These were the days when La Monnaie had an enormous reputation throughout Europe and appearances there carried great prestige. The celebrated singers who had made their debuts there were legion, both Melba and Calvé among the number, and *Faust* was the opera par excellence for such affairs.

The director of La Monnaie at this time was Ambroselli, a genial soul whose knowledge of the public pulse and astute management had raised the theater to the position La Scala enjoyed in Italy. The discriminating musical public of Brussels fostered the power of La Monnaie; it was largely on account of the aegis their critical approval bestowed that so many singers strove to debut there—with success. One would be made for all time.

Ambroselli put on several productions that were off the beaten track, because I was familiar with them. We made a great success with *Les noces de Jeannette*, and at the demand of the public repeated it many times. I also sang Saint-Saëns's opera *Le timbre d'argent*. The baritone in both of these works was Gabriel-Valentin Soulacroix, who occupied in Brussels the place Lucien Fugère enjoyed in Paris. He was a fine artist and an excellent actor. Likewise, Jeanne Maubourg was an addition to any cast. A mezzo-soprano, she was most successful in male roles such as Frédéric in

Mignon, Nicklausse in *The Tales of Hoffmann*, and Siébel. Her father was a conductor in the theater. Later she sang in *La fille de Madame Angot* at the Metropolitan.[55]

After leaving La Monnaie I sang in all the theaters in Brussels, including the Théâtre des Galeries St. Hubert (*Le voyage de Suzette*) and the Théâtre de l'Alhambra (*Ali Baba and the Forty Thieves* and *The Beggar Student*). The arrangement for royalties on these pieces was a peculiar one, for the percentage went up considerably at the hundredth performance, so for this reason we used to sing only ninety-nine and then close the house.

A new theater was erected opposite the Exchange, the Théâtre de la Bourse, which became the largest and most handsome theater in Brussels. For the opening attraction I was engaged to sing *Le grand mogol*. The composer, Edmond Audran, came from Paris, bringing with him a big, dramatic air full of pyrotechnics and high Cs which I was to introduce into the last act. Audran was an extraordinary, talented person. He was a frail little man with a small sharp face, but though scarcely taller than myself, he was a demon for work. When he had a production on foot he worked all night, and unlike other composers at that time he did all his own orchestrations. Also unlike other composers, he was always calm at rehearsals—calm, but sharp and demanding in his criticisms. And he could write not only delightful music of the lighter vein, with an inspiration and perfection that were truly enviable, but could also turn his hand with equal facility to splendid heavier compositions with the sure touch of a master.

One night, after I had been singing *Le grand mogol* for a month, I had just finished the big new aria and was all alone on the stage when two men suddenly appeared out of the wings. I was very much surprised at their unexpected appearance, and more so when they grabbed me and whispered, "Don't speak—come at once." I stood for a moment, irresolute, and they hustled me off the stage. A fire had been discovered in the costume store room. As the curtain came down, the régisseur appeared calmly before it to announce that I had been taken suddenly ill and the performance was over. After a few moments of disappointment the audience filed out. And subsequently the theater burned to the ground. Due to the régisseur's sangfroid no lives were lost, but of the men who had put their fortunes into it—a father and his two sons—one went mad and another died shortly afterward. The theater was never rebuilt. The Hôtel de La Bourse now occupies the site.

About this time I had a little adventure which did much to consolidate my point of view about the theater and arrange my future life.

It occurred during the run of Offenbach's *La fille du tambour-major*—another setting of *The Daughter of the Regiment*. I was appearing in this at the Théâtre Royal de l'Alcazar, another Brussels theater. The manager of this house was a popular young gentleman named Lucien Malpertuit, "Luc" among his friends. Under my contract with him I appeared in Antwerp, Liège, and other cities.

There was a rich old gentleman named Benjamin who owned a large palace at Middelkerke on the channel, about eight miles from Ostend. This old soul, who looked rather like the late John D. Rockefeller, fancied himself a great lady-killer. He was unmarried and had taken unto himself a little dancer from La Monnaie. Every time she had a child Benjamin proudly gave her a hundred thousand francs, and consequently she had children regularly, rain or shine.

Benjamin had a small theater built in the palace at Middelkerke, and one of his pleasures was to give private performances for large gatherings of guests. He engaged many of the biggest stars of the day to appear in his private theater, treating them royally and giving them jewels as well as large checks. But I had never fancied Monsieur Benjamin and had refused his invitations several times. It just did not suit me to be among the number receiving his bounty.

One day Malpertuit begged me to do him a favor, and I discovered that it consisted of appearing in a performance at Monsieur Benjamin's palace. At last, after much persuasion, I consented to be among his "scalps." I realized, however, that though Malpertuit had not couched his request in terms of command, I was under contract with him to go anywhere he willed and would have had to go to Monsieur Benjamin's if he had insisted. I rather suspect that Monsieur Benjamin gave Malpertuit money to help out with his theatrical ventures and to keep him in his debt.

I was staying with my brother Charles at Knokke, eighteen miles from Ostend in the opposite direction of Middelkerke, in a little villa of Angèle's which she had lent us for a vacation. Monsieur Benjamin sent his carriage for me, and at about eleven thirty in the morning I started out with my current maid, Louise, and a young boy named Louis, who was my groom. I promised Charles that I would not spend the night at Monsieur Benjamin's, but that come what may I would return by carriage or train after the performance; Charles would meet me at Ostend.

It was a four-hour drive to the palace at Middelkerke. When we arrived I was shown into the apartment prepared for me. I was furious. It was a nuptial chamber! Great bouquets of flowers embowered it, and white satin festooned it high and low.

"Louise," I said, "I am not going to spend the night in Monsieur Benjamin's nuptial chamber, so be sure to have everything packed and ready as soon as the performance is over."

She protested feebly that I could not do such a thing, and I went down to the theater. Malpertuit was hurrying about, making arrangements. I gave him a vivid account of my feelings. I had been engaged to sing, and nothing else. For two cents I would go off at once, but if he promised to have a carriage ready for me at the end of the performance I would stay. He tried to make me feel foolish, telling me what an insult it would be for me to leave before the supper, but he feared that I would not remain and soon promised me everything. I was determined to go because the whole thing was so obviously a trick to force me to stay the night. I had no fears for my *virtue*, be it understood—anyone could knock Monsieur Benjamin over with a feather if necessary; nevertheless, the situation had a moral significance to me. It was contrary to everything in my nature and to the reputation I had always enjoyed. And Charles had not wanted me to go at all.

After the performance I demanded the promised carriage. Malpertuit said he could not get one, and renewed his urgings for me to stay for supper. Monsieur Benjamin had a magnificent diamond spray to give me!

"Very well," I said. "If you can't get a carriage, I will get one."

Now it was Louise who refused to go. She was a large, heavy woman. She was comfortably fixed for the night and said she was too tired to go after any carriage at that hour. So Louis and I set out for home—I in my last-act costume, a satin evening gown, and, worst of all, small satin slippers. My other clothes were in the palace, and the theater was some distance on the grounds.

I thought I could find a carriage without much difficulty, but there was none to be had. It was nearing twelve o'clock, and in those days the towns along that coast were isolated and shut up tight. The early market trains did not stop at the wayside stations. And so we walked all night.

Toward dawn we passed a few roadside inns. Here we stopped to beg for a cart or some mode of conveyance, but not even money could buy one. Naturally we were a curious pair, a lady in an evening dress and a young boy. I told a tale, saying I had received a telegram about a sick relative and had to reach Ostend. One innkeeper suggested that if we waited there sooner or later some people would be passing to market with their vegetables and give us a ride to Ostend. But I was afraid that if I sat down now I would be unable to go on, so we started off anew.

Finally a cart, creeping along and full of turnips, overtook us. It was driven by a farmer and his wife. They were even more suspicious of us, as peasants generally are, but to them I told the same story and displayed a golden louis. This softened their hearts, and we climbed up among the turnips.

We had been walking for hours over dreadful cobblestones and now the cart, innocent of springs, jogged us nearly to death. It was agony. But at last we reached Ostend and the railroad station, and there was poor Charles waiting for me as had been arranged. I fell into his arms—and fainted. He had to carry me to a bench in the waiting room, where an astonished crowd gathered to see the disreputable lady, in tattered satin at that hour of the morning!

And now I am going to unburden myself about the theater.

As long as I was very young and innocent, these virtues were their own greatest protection. But as I grew older and observed more of what went on about me (my life in the theater was almost continual) I learned with horror and disgust that two distinct businesses were carried on simultaneously. Most theatrical managers were occupied not only with producing plays and operas but also with making contracts between the female members of their companies and the rich men who took a fancy to them across the footlights. One encountered it everywhere. An astute producer could increase his earnings with the handsome stipends slipped to him for arranging these meetings. Many girls went on the stage with the express purpose of thus meeting some wealthy protector, preferably old, who would leave a large legacy as soon as possible. In this way the atmosphere of intrigue and eager expectation was always present, going hand in hand with the actual business of playing roles. I don't believe any company can be free of it.

I had found that I was expected to make some concessions to the conventions of the theater. I had to at least sup with friends of my manager, meeting people who were in every way repugnant and uncongenial to me. I consistently refused to meet people whom I could not like. My private life and my chosen friends were my own and of no consequence to my business managers. I always hotly resented the notion that I was not free to choose my own circle without a battle.

After the affair at Monsieur Benjamin's, when my hand had been forced in this matter, I became more and more disgusted with such unwarranted interference in my private rights. I thought it would be an agreeable thing to be my own manager for a change—my own boss!

All this time I had been more or less in communication with the Russian ambassador, who kept assuring me that I would have my property and my legal rights if only I would hand over to him all papers in my possession which in any way proved I had been married to Sergei Peshkov, as well as my receipts for the valuables which had been deposited in the safety deposit vaults of Petersburg.

Still I could not see my way to do this.

At length, thoroughly wearied by the whole affair and determined to start out anew with my bridges burned behind me, free of it all, I went to Paris, called on Roberval again, and said bluntly, "What have you got for me? I want to be my own manager. And I don't care if I go to the Antipodes."

Well, Roberval said, there was one very good thing open if I did not fear to invest a little capital. There had been one good operatic company at Cairo for two years, and if I would take a company there I would be assured a great success. The big summer theater, Ezbekiya, was dark. Roberval suggested I go to Cairo myself with a letter to the owner, an Italian named Santine. If the ground looked promising I could lease the theater, cable him, and he would send out a complete company.

The proposition seemed a good one. I heard a few auditions by prospective members of my troupe, arranged a cablegram code with Roberval, and sailed for Egypt with Albertine and Bolo, who were now married and eager to join me again.

Egypt, from the first, delighted me, especially Cairo with its motley population. We went to Shepheard's Hotel and I lost no time in seeking out Santine. I found him most affable and gracious, though the same could not be said of his mother, who was part-owner of Ezbekiya. Still, Santine was genuinely delighted that I wanted to lease his theater. It was a lovely one, rather like the Arcadia in Petersburg, set in a summer park of great beauty, in which many national functions and celebrations took place. The Khedivial Opera House (for the opening of which Verdi had composed *Aida*) was of less interest and was usually closed. Ezbekiya suited me perfectly, not the least of its attributes being the very full collection of scenery its storerooms contained, enough for any production we might put on. I cabled Roberval to send out the company.

On my way to Cairo I had stopped for a week at Port Said, where the governor was an old Paris friend of mine. I told him of my Egyptian project and what I hoped to do if things turned out well, and he gave me a number of letters for various people of importance in the Egyptian capital. I made haste to present these letters, for I realized that the first thing I must do was to make myself known in Cairo.

One of these new friends was the personal doctor of the khedive, Comanos Pasha. He gave a reception in my honor, to which came all the people in the Egyptian colony. At this affair I met the wife of an aide-de-camp of Lord Kitchener. She had been a singer of sorts before her marriage, and we had much in common. She advised me that to be a success in Cairo I must be popular with the two elements, Egyptian and English. Through her I received an invitation to one of Lord Kitchener's receptions.

Now, I knew very well that she was right. Before leaving Paris, Roberval and I had settled on an English name for me to assume in Egypt. I was afraid to go under the name of Clara Lardinois when far from home, so nervous had the Russian ambassador made me. And what better name could be devised to appeal to an English public (so we thought) than one which would smack of their great hero Lord Nelson? It suggested victory too! So I had become "Ada Nelson," and as Ada Nelson I was presented to Lord Kitchener.

He was a tall man, and a typical Englishman in formal moments, though after most of the guests had left and supper was served to the few privileged people remaining (among whom I was proud to be counted), he thawed out amazingly with champagne, the problems of government forgotten.

This same Englishman, whose name I regret to be unable to recall, arranged for me to appear at several functions at various clubs, among them the well-known Club des Princes. This, I realized, was a valuable way of becoming known in Cairo.

But it was not the only way, and my days were full. I soon moved to an apartment (which was separated only by a narrow lane from Comanos Pasha's house, enabling us to gossip across to each other) and immediately set to work preparing the ground for our opening. Bolo and Albertine had their quarters in the rear section of my apartment, and we were busy night and day. One of the cleverest things I ever did was to give a reception there for the newspapermen of Cairo. Bolo and Albertine, however, had their own work. Bolo rose by quick degrees to be not only my secretary but also my general factotum, proving himself well able to fill any position. I had only to give him my orders and they would be fulfilled. We composed and arranged for posters to be sent to the printers, and then there was the business of having them placarded about the city. There were announcements to be sent to the press and general arrangements to be made for advertising. We had printed a leaflet setting forth the prospectus of the "Ada Nelson Company" with a plan of the theater, the result being that we had sold almost enough season subscriptions to fill the house before the troupe had arrived from France.

In the meantime Albertine plied her trade—truly, her art—of costume designing and making. With a force of twenty young girls from the French bazaar she designed and produced all my costumes for our repertory, for my old ones were worn and I intended to have a complete new wardrobe. We bought cloths, silks, and velvets by the bolt from the bazaar, and Albertine and her assistants turned out costumes, from the robes of La Grande-Duchesse to the Columbine skirts of Irma, the strolling snake charmer in *Le grand mogol.*

Finally the long-awaited ship carrying my company was due at Alexandria. One can imagine with what emotions I set out for that port! The verdict of success or failure for my bold adventure rested largely on these people. I had been rather reckless, I knew, but with the demand for seats at Ezbekiya beginning to outrun the supply, my confidence in my-self was not shaken. My company was a good and expensive one, suffi-ciently large to meet with contingencies such as illness. I had sent to Paris for a man named Saint-Martin, whom I knew to be invaluable in run-ning a company. He was a great expense but an equal necessity. He had come out at once and assumed his responsibilities so thoroughly that by the time the company was due every plan had been made for their arrival, including arranging suitable lodgings for them all.

Saint-Martin and I went to Alexandria to meet the ship, along with ten or a dozen of my new friends. It was customary to go down to Alexandria to welcome new arrivals. Members of the theatergoing com-munity liked to look over the choristers and dancers as they disembarked, in order to have first-hand knowledge of the new female charms coming among them.

Alexandria was very unlike Cairo. The Arab population was compara-tively small and the French colony large. All the important business houses were here, and the French language prevailed in the streets. We had to stay the night due to delays in unloading the luggage, for not only personal baggage but also trunkloads of costumes had come out with the company. This was an unexpected and added expense, but nevertheless I finally un-loaded the Ada Nelson Company in Cairo. Saint-Martin distributed them in their variously assigned lodgings, and our first rehearsal was called.

My scrapbooks tell me that we opened on 12 April 1901 with *Le grand mogol.* It should be evident by now that this was a role for which I was particularly suited. Truth to tell, it was one I particularly enjoyed singing. The music required real singers, and with the last-act aria Audran wrote for me for the Brussels premiere, *Le grand mogol* was a genuine opera. I should like to see it put on again!

My company contained two first sopranos, Mesdemoiselles Bouit and Giraud, and three second sopranos. I had an excellent tenor in Monsieur Gardon and a fine *comique* in Monsieur Wesphale—both famous names in France at that time. Our first baritone was Herault. I had sung in Paris and Brussels with several members of the company. Besides these I had two conductors, a first and second régisseur, and Saint-Martin, my secre-tary. There were twenty-four choristers and twenty-four musicians, as well as half a dozen professional beauties to stand about and add to the stage picture. For all these people I was responsible! But I was confident too, and enjoyed being my own manager so much that I never again signed up with anyone else.

We gave performances four times a week: Tuesdays, Thursdays, Saturdays, and Sundays. Monday was a poor day for the theater and Friday was the Arab Sabbath. There was one disadvantage in handling a company like mine. Because I had advertised myself as the star, it became fashionable to attend those performances in which I appeared personally. It was not "Are you going to Ezbekiya tonight?" but "Are you going to hear Nelson tonight?" And so I had to sing a great deal in order to keep the receipts as high as possible. Furthermore, Mademoiselle Bouit was a fine singer who deserved more appearances. She made a particular hit in *Le petit duc* and *Gillette de Narbonne*. But as the company was paid monthly and not by performance, their number of appearances was unimportant to them.

There was another difficulty in running a company in Egypt, and that was the delicate business of steering an even course between the Egyptians and the English. If seen too often in English company or at their functions, I would alienate the good will of the Khedivial faction. On one occasion I was invited to appear at a great hotel on the road to the pyramids for a large celebration of some English holiday (I forget which). I had received this invitation through Gallini Pasha, a man very prominent in politics and with the English. But my friend Comanos Pasha opened my eyes to the significance of accepting this invitation, and I refused it as politely as I could. This caused coolness on the part of my English friends. Later, when I wriggled out of appearing at a great water carnival on the Nile for the same reason, the coldness developed into something sub-zero, and the English were more or less through with me. I was sorry, but I was in Egypt after all. If I could not keep completely aloof from politics and factions, I would have to make my choice; and I chose the natives, perhaps wisely and perhaps not. Gallini Pasha, I never quite understood. He was the most friendly of all the Egyptians with the English, and I have often wondered if he was not some sort of—dare I say *spy*? At any rate *I* was not!

22

M Y GREATEST FRIEND and most helpful adviser continued to be Cominos Pasha. Through his influence at court I received a command to give a matinee for the ladies of the royal household. At this performance no member of the public was admitted. I chose *Le grand mogol,* and it was a good choice. The Indian setting and oriental music pleased the royal ladies—but most of all they were delighted by the character of the Englishman Crackson, a comic role well played by a member of my company who was very successful in portraying the English prototype, and the broad farce was not lost upon the Egyptians.

One evening when a performance of *Le voyage de Suzette* was billed I learned that Camille Saint-Saëns, who was in Egypt to conduct one of his own works, was to be in the audience.[56] To honor the composer I arranged a surprise. There is a scene in this *opéra comique* in which a group of students serenade Suzette with guitars and mandolins. To the four best musicians I gave the music of the serenade from *Le timbre d'argent,* and when the moment came I sang this instead of the couplets in the score. As I addressed myself to the stage box the audience quickly understood that the master was there, and an ovation ensued. He was so surprised and delighted by the affair that he leapt out of the box, down into the orchestra pit, over the head of the bass viol, and onto the stage to embrace me. The house was in an uproar, and the performance was stopped for several minutes.

The next day came a bouquet of flowers and the request for an hour at which I could receive the composer. We spent a wonderful afternoon. Saint-Saëns took possession of the piano and made me sing everything of his which I knew. Between the glorious music and his gaiety the hours fled, so I had just time to reach the theater. Before we parted I made him promise to accept my invitation to dinner at the apartment of my good friend Comanos Pasha, who had put his home at my disposal to honor the master. Saint-Saëns accepted with delight, knowing that he would meet some of the great people of Egyptian society.

Everyone who was invited accepted eagerly. At the dinner Saint-Saëns was the center of conversation and, being a celebrated raconteur, was very amusing. Alas, my memory does not go far enough back to recall his stories, but one thing occurred that night that I could not forget.

Comanos Pasha employed a celebrated chef of the Cordon Bleu, and together the pasha and I had consulted him about what dishes we should serve to honor Saint-Saëns on his visit to Egypt. We wanted to arrange an extraordinary menu. After much deliberation we settled upon *caneton á la Rouenaise*, the most difficult fowl to cook to the perfection demanded by a true gourmet, for the pièce de résistance. At the dinner everyone sat about the table eagerly waiting for the appearance of the pasha's famous silver charger, upon which the superb fowl was to be presented. At last the maître d'hôtel advanced with the footman, who presented the dish, as by custom, to the guest of honor. Saint-Saëns was right in the middle of one of his diverting tales. He turned his head and gazed upon the bird. It was cooked to perfection, the rich red juice oozing slightly upon the platter. Saint-Saëns made a sign to the maître d'hôtel and said confidentially, but loud enough to be heard by everyone, "But my friend, the duck is underdone. It is *saignant*. It must be cooked a little more." The guests looked at each other in despair. Everyone was impatient to taste that handsome duck, which, to be *á la Rouenaise*, absolutely *must* be *saignant*. Yet no one dared make a move. Comanos Pasha and I glanced at each other, but as Saint-Saëns noticed nothing and went on with his conversation there was nothing to do but turn our attention back to him. Time passed, and soon it was clear that our guests were growing very much worried over the fate of the cherished bird.

At last the maître d'hôtel and the footman returned with the dish. Poor duck! He had shrunk to half his former size and was black as coal. Saint-Saëns was happily laughing away and beginning another anecdote. The maître d'hôtel interrupted him and with a bland smile presented the dish for the second time. Saint-Saëns turned to him and with a start said, "Oh thank you, *mon ami*, but I never eat duck."

One day soon after, through Comanos Pasha's influence, I received an invitation to attend a party with the khedive's wife and her ladies of honor, to be followed by a reception given by the khedive.

These Egyptian ladies were an interesting contrast to the ladies of a Turkish seraglio. There used to be great rivalry between the two nationalities, but I must give the prize to the Arabs. They were a finer and more delicate physical type, more intelligent, better educated (most of them spoke French and English), and far more cosmopolitan in their outlook. One evidence of this was that they were dressed in an adaptation of European costume, though with fine muslin veils of native make, coquettish as Spanish women with their fans. They served tea instead of coffee—but they also had a magician entertain us by performing tricks, one thing surely unheard of at English tea parties.

After receiving their hospitality I went to the khedive's reception, and here again the contrast was equally marked. Abbas Hilmi walked about among his guests after the presentations were over, laughing and transforming what might have been a stiff and cheerless function (and surely would have been at the palace of Abdülhamid) into a pleasant hour of social intercourse.[57]

On the occasion of the tenth anniversary of the khedive's ascent to the throne, which took place, like all national fêtes, in the gardens of Ezbekiya, I was commanded to sing the national anthem. I sent to Paris for a dress to wear at this function, and the dress turned out to be as much of a success as anything in the celebration. Over a background of black satin hung a black lace net on which flowers of many colors were appliquéd, giving a rich and startling effect in artificial light. I kept that dress for years, and like many gowns that are works of art, it did not become unfashionable for a long time. Paquin designed it for me. Later in Australia it became famous in its own right, and my portrait was reproduced in the papers over the caption, "The seven-hundred-pound dress."

Comanos Pasha taught me the Arab words to the anthem, which I sang with the municipal orchestra of Cairo. The grounds and the theater were beautifully decorated, and the ceremony took place under the stars. The khedive bestowed on me the Order of the Medjedieh, the first time a woman was ever so honored.

After we had given twenty performances we received an offer of a week's engagement in Alexandria at the Alcazar. When we darkened Ezbekiya for those seven days the papers came out with tears and laments at being deprived of the Ada Nelson Company, and when we returned the demand for seats was greater than ever. We gave another series of twenty performances. A plan to take the troupe to Port Said fell through, for I was advised there was not a sufficiently large non-native population to fill the theater.

At length, after suitable celebrations, including a benefit for myself at which the company presented me with a makeup case in Egyptian silver and flowers and presents were received and bestowed in prodigious numbers, I saw my company off at Alexandria and was free once more.

But not for long. I assumed management of the Casino de la Plage at San Stefano, Ramieh, outside Alexandria.

This was truly a cosmopolitan place for gambling and amusement. Italians, English, French, many rich Greeks, and Egyptians frequented its rooms, restaurant, and theater, where I put on concerts three times a week with several other artists. At these concerts I seldom had my selections printed on the programs, so that I could sing whatever the mood dictated. The birds themselves are hardly freer in their will to sing than I was then.

Toward the autumn my continual work had its effect: I fell ill again, and my plans were uncertain once more. But soon the governor of Port Said appeared in Cairo and invited me to take a little trip up the Nile in his dahabeah. We went as far as Luxor, and the splendor of that trip, particularly of the Egyptian nights—better pens than mine have described it.

Once more in Cairo, I decided to remain the winter in comfort and peace. However, this did not prevent a number of appearances in concert, as well as guest appearances with an Italian opera troupe. It was not until the spring of 1902 that I finally tore myself away from Egypt, having been there for a year.

There are few places harder to leave than Egypt. It is not only an an-

cient world but also a most fascinating modern one. The habits and customs of Egyptians are at every turn surprising. When I was there the
whirling dervishes still existed, who in the height of religious frenzy
slashed each other cruelly with knives and rushed through the streets
bleeding, sometimes to death, though totally unconscious of any pain.
They were a horrible sight. Among the middle classes the marriage customs were also unattractive. The day after a wedding the bride and groom
rode proudly through the streets with a bloody napkin tied to the head of
the horse that pulled them. More comical were the delicate sensibilities
of the washerwomen who plied their trade along the banks of the Nile.
So modest were they that if they caught sight of any foreigners approaching they would hastily cover their heads with their long skirts,
with complete indifference to the rest of their anatomy. As in all places I
visited, I enjoyed as much of the local color as my often-limited time
would allow, but in Egypt that winter I spent many leisure hours.

Albertine and Bolo, who had been with me all this time, returned with
me to Europe. That last winter Albertine kept house, but poor Bolo had
no job to speak of except for taking Moushka for walks. We parted in
Paris, and I went home to Brussels. Albertine had been ailing for some
time. Now she went to the hospital for an operation, but it was too late;
she never came out of the anesthetic. Bolo went home to his family in
Lyons. I only saw him twice more.

Though nothing could have made me suspect the sad fate that was to
overtake Paul Bolo during the dark days of the war, I knew he was a curious man. I had noticed in Egypt that he had never wanted his name to
be connected in the papers or the playbills with his position as my secretary, and this I thought peculiar, if only a whim. Later it transpired that
he had a wife in Buenos Aires.

Bolo was a strikingly handsome man, and wherever he went women
followed. He was tall and well built, his hair of a dark ash blond that
many found attractive. He also wore a small clipped moustache. At his
trial, when pictures of him were in all the papers, that moustache was
enormous, so that I scarcely recognized him for the dashing young man
I had known.

He spoke Spanish like a native, and good English as well, and there
was something about him that proclaimed him a man sure to succeed. Yet

there was another, more mysterious quality in his personality that was almost alarming. One reads of people with a strange look in the eye, and Bolo was one of these. He had a sharp, volcanic temper. I remember saying to Albertine one day in Cairo, after some slight display of this temper, "Don't ever do anything that could give him cause to be really angry with you. I don't know about this husband of yours—sometimes he frightens me."

"Oh Madame!" Albertine had said. And more than once, after these warnings, she would add, "It's only that you are peculiar about men. You have your singing and your success, and these satisfy your nature!" The infatuated girl could not understand what I meant.

Once, while waiting for my company to arrive in Cairo, the dreaded desert wind had paid us a visit. At such times the windows of all the houses are boarded up, nailed shut so that an ignorant foreigner cannot be fool enough to open them. The blast lasts about a week, often longer. When the wind is expected, the houses and hotels stock up with food to last for this length of time, as it is virtual death to venture out when it is blowing, and the streets are even deserted of natives. The wind is like an actual blast of fire.

Albertine, Bolo, and I spent this week making designs for costumes and laying out our plans. On the day the wind died down Albertine opened the window and stepped out on the balcony for a breath of fresh air, having spent so many days in the house. Bolo went with her. It was still insufferably hot, and much cooler indoors than out. I called to them to shut the window behind them, but they were in no hurry to do so. As the room became hotter by the second, I jumped up to go and shut the window myself. At this moment Bolo kicked the window shut violently behind him. My left hand was caught in it, and my third finger was broken at the knuckle. For a long period after that I could not play the piano, and never since have I had the facility of the old days. I bear still the souvenir of Bolo's impetuosity.

The next time I saw him was not long after Albertine's death. I was en route to Marseilles for another long tour. Bolo met me at the station at Lyons, and we had luncheon in the buffet. At this time he had decided, or he wanted me to think he had decided, to settle down in Lyons. His uncle, who was a bell founder, had cast many fine church bells and carillons, and Bolo was planning to go into the family business. His brother was a monseigneur; in fact the whole family was deeply religious. He spoke feelingly of poor Albertine, and I considered that Bolo had at last found his place in the world.

Nine years later, after many vicissitudes, I was in Paris again. As I stood waiting for a friend in the lobby of the Grand Hôtel, a man carrying a large briefcase suddenly rushed by me. Looking up I saw Paul Bolo, and excitedly called his name. He turned, blushed crimson, and hurried forward, all smiles and delight, exclaiming, "You have not changed a bit!"

He told me he had married again, this time a widow from Bordeaux. He said he had two children. I congratulated him at this news, and he said a peculiar thing: "One never knows if they are one's own." This sort of remark was typical of Bolo. He gave me no information about his family in Lyons or how the bell foundry business was progressing, and in a few minutes excused himself, saying he had a very important engagement upstairs.

I had no further news of Paul Bolo until the Caillaux affair began to appear in the papers.[58]

Whether Bolo was an agent between Caillaux and the Germans, in his "defeatist" plans, I am sure I do not know. But Bolo alone paid with his life. At some period he had returned to Cairo and, using the connections he had made through me, became an important personage there, finally receiving the title of pasha from Abbas Hilmi.

At his trial in Paris his entire life was carefully delved into, though the episode of Albertine never came to light, which prevented the darkening of his character with the charge of bigamy. It was through the trial that I learned of his earlier marriage in Argentina. No account that I ever read, however, mentioned the two children about whose paternity he had such outspoken doubts, nor did my name ever appear. I felt it my duty to tell what I knew about the poor fellow, so I communicated with the French ambassador in Washington; but of course all I could do was to give an explanation of how he made his connections in Egypt. In those days he had already proven himself an unbalanced character. On one occasion Albertine came to me, white as a ghost, crying, "Madame, look what I have found among Paul's things!" She held in her hand a small vial marked "Prussic acid." I disposed of it where it could do no harm, but when Bolo discovered the loss he was in a fury. I reprimanded him sharply, and he said it had been enough poison to dispatch the whole British army. I demanded angrily to know what possible use that could be to him. He answered, "Oh, you never know when a little poison will come in handy."

After his arrest by the French authorities he was held prisoner in the Grand Hôtel, where I had last seen him. He expressed a great fear of being poisoned, begging the doctors in charge of him to perform an autopsy if he should be found dead.

Long after the war the Caillaux affair was made into a moving picture. The actor who played Caillaux looked much like him, but the Paul Bolo was not at all the type. Nevertheless, I witnessed with emotion the scene of the execution, which was drawn from an authentic account of the event. Bolo walked with arms folded across his chest, and when they blindfolded him at the end he nonchalantly said, "Must you pull it so tight?"[59]

I have always believed that he shielded others in that affair and was not the one who most deserved death.

Another visit to Roberval, on my return from Egypt, secured for me an engagement at the Colón in Buenos Aires, destined never to be fulfilled.[60] I was at Bordeaux ready to sail the following morning when I had a telegram from Roberval telling me to await a telephone call at a specified hour that evening (at that time a long-distance telephone call was an event and had to be arranged ahead of time by telegraph). The result of our short conversation was that I went back to Paris the next day, abandoning South America. My trunks were already in the hold, and it took all the offices of my old friend, the proprietor of the hotel, and his considerable influence to have them offloaded.

But it was worth the trouble. Between my leaving Paris and reaching Bordeaux, Roberval had secured me an appointment from the French government to head a company going to Hanoi, French Indochina, to play at the International Exposition of 1903. At this time the Colón at Buenos Aires did not have the worldwide fame it would later achieve, and so to sing under the auspices of the French government was a far greater opportunity. The company was already made up; it consisted of very good artists and was directed by a man named Nourrit. I was to be made virtual director, and this plan had its advantages, since I would not be personally responsible for a failure.

Nevertheless, the company was not sailing for another month, and it was a shattering thing to have a new adventure summarily halted on the eve of its beginning. I was in no mood to putter about Paris for a month, wasting time and spending money, when I had expected to be on the high seas bound for Argentina. And so at Roberval's suggestion I sailed at once for Saigon, French Cochinchina. Once there I intended to feel out the situation, learn a little of the customs and tastes of that part of the world, perhaps give a concert, join the company when their ship stopped, and continue with them to Hanoi.

The voyage to Saigon was one of the most delightful of all my many journeys. There was a group of young army officers bound for China and only a few members of the opposite sex—and I still felt young. We sang, we danced, we played games the entire trip. When we touched at Alexandria four of my friends came aboard and accompanied us to Port Said. We gave them a banquet and they left us disconsolately, thinking, I presume, that such gaieties and merrymaking were lifelong pursuits for the rest of us.

Saigon was one of the hellholes of the world then. The climate, a most dangerous one, was never intended for Europeans, as the heat requires a complete reversal of occidental ways. From six to nine in the morning the shops and offices were open. At nine the people went home and slept until three, when a light meal was eaten. Then the shops reopened. Dinner was at nine or ten o'clock, after which the whole world went out to ride in its carriages on the fashionable drives, as well as to pay calls.

In Saigon there were very few white women, the men who were stationed there living in single blessedness or taking Annamite mistresses. Whenever a white woman appeared at Saigon it signaled a rivalry among the important members of the colony to see who could first "land" her, as it were, and display her while driving in his carriage at the fashionable hour (I mean nothing more than this, only that the peculiar facts of life in Saigon rendered this struggle a proof of worldliness and unimpeachable social success).

But an artist—a theatrical artist—must be on her guard. She can have a thousand friends of the opposite sex, but she must not be more friendly with one than another. Otherwise it spells disaster. I, who know, would like to tell this to all girls who are ambitious to appear before the public. And you cannot tell me that times have changed, for human nature has not.

Consequently, I very carefully avoided invitations to go driving about, especially as I knew that in Saigon my appearance would only mean that so-and-so was the successful one who had driven with the singer from Paris in his carriage the evening before. I would not be a party to that triumph for anyone.

My circumspection prevented me from singing at a concert for charity that was arranged while I was at Saigon, for I had gained an influential enemy. However, my non-appearance worked in my favor, for the papers printed a long and mysterious account which darkly suggested that my failure to sing would be regretted at Saigon, especially if my real name should be learned. I had reverted to the name I was ever afterward to use professionally—Blanche Arral. After we opened in Hanoi this same friend of mine in Saigon took delight in writing fulsome accounts of the great success we were having at the Exposition, particularly because French Cochinchina and French Indochina were bitter rivals of long standing.

The foreign colony of Saigon was a strangely assorted group. Among the French, one met at every turn young men who bore the titles of some of the oldest families of France. *Le duc* of this, *le comte* of that, *le marquis* of the other: and they were all petty clerks in the custom house or telegraph operators. One knew they had all committed various offenses at home—forged Father's name to a check, robbed rich Auntie of her ruby bracelet to pay a debt, or some such—and through influence and position had succeeded in being sent out to Saigon instead of to prison. Nevertheless, it was a bitter disgrace and they resented their fate. To forget the failure they had made of their lives, they drank absinthe.

But the treacherous climate of Saigon is such that one must be circumspect in dietary matters and drink nothing but bottled mineral waters. The slightest deviation from this narrow path is apt to bring on all too quickly that most dreaded disease—called there *la cochin-chinette*, known to the rest of the world as cholera. One must have a deep respect for the tropics. Once ill you are hustled off to the pest house, and only leave it feet first.

And many of the scions of the great French families succumbed sooner or later to *la cochin-chinette*.

The more stable elements of the foreign colony were the Germans and Swiss who owned and ran large businesses and warehouses which supplied the interior of the country. They were a more serious people, living at Saigon for legitimate reasons; they knew how to take care of themselves and did not lose their heads or deteriorate like so many others. Absinthe was the great green devil of Saigon—and hashish. I remember vividly going to dinner with a French couple who lived in a magnificent villa. The man's family had owned a steamship line that sailed from Marseilles, but for various reasons he had come out to live at Saigon. The woman was not his legitimate wife but one of the few white women there. The luxury they had built about them was impressive, and likewise horrible. Although there was no guest besides myself, the table was set and the meal prepared and served as though for some great function in one of the most sumptuous *hôtels privés* of Paris. This reconstruction, in that lonely corner of the world, of the great life of a European capital, was to me infinitely tragic—entirely unreal, forced, and mysterious. These people lived under some curious shadow I could not fathom.

After dinner we wandered through the beautiful garden, and then the hashish pipes were brought out. They both urged me to try a pipe, but nothing could induce me. The tragedy of their lives was explained, the heartbreaking deterioration of white people. They had probably come to Saigon in a burst of independence from the disapproval of the world. Regret and boredom had led them to the hashish pipe.

Sometime later I was on a ship that touched at Saigon and stayed in port overnight to load a cargo. A young couple on the boat urged me to come ashore with them to see the sights, but I had been through enough and felt more at ease on board. Before they left me I said, "Take my advice. Saigon is a wicked place, and if you are wise you will drink nothing and smoke nothing." They thought me a foolish calamity-seeker and went gaily ashore. The next night as we sailed into the China Sea I heard the most horrible screams coming from their cabin, which was next to mine. I went to offer help. The ship's doctor met me in the passageway. "My God, child, go away—get away from here!" he cried. I was not afraid and wanted to nurse the woman but was not allowed to. Before morning she died in agony, of cholera. All I could do was attend her burial, which took place at once. Even then the passengers were allowed no nearer the coffin than the captain's bridge. *La cochin-chinette* had worked quickly.

Saigon was a strange, strange place, unnatural and unhealthy in every way. Just outside town began the great jungles, full of curious creatures of the animal world, who from time to time paid a visit to the city. But one soon got used to anything. There was no glass in the windows of the houses, only screens and lattices and mosquito-net curtains. As one sat in the hotel during the evening, at any moment a small ice-cold lizard might leap with a *plop* from the ceiling onto one's shoulder. Likewise, a stray mongoose wandering through the rooms at night was thought no more of than we think of a cat.

Another French couple, originally from Marseilles, once stopped at the hotel. They owned large plantations in Siam and had come down to Saigon because the wife suffered from asthma and was being treated by a Saigon doctor. Because of her asthma she used to leave the lattices up at night in order to get more air. One late night I was awakened by horrible screams and the husband knocking frantically at my door, across the hall. I ran into the room and found the poor woman covered with blood. We both thought she had been murdered, but we soon discovered that except for a small cut on her breast she was sound and whole. A mongoose had crept into the room while she slept. In a day or two she was perfectly well.

There was a strange bird I never heard tell of anywhere else, around which the natives had built a complicated superstition. This bird sat in the tallest trees and in the stillness would begin a curious cry. Beginning high up on the scale it would emit short cries, not unlike a cuckoo, descending by half-notes for almost three octaves. If the number of cries was even, the luck was good, and if uneven, bad. Many other omens were read in the quality and length of the notes. At the first note the natives would cease their occupation to listen and count the uncanny sounds.

The asthmatic lady and her husband returned shortly to Siam, after making me promise to pay them a visit, and I followed them to Bangkok in a few days. It was a short voyage to Bangkok, across a gulf of the China Sea and up the Mekong River, and I had ample time for this before the company was due in Saigon. I was met at the dock and driven to their house in elaborate state, for they were great people in Siam due to their enormous plantations.

On the day after my arrival the king's chamberlain called with a command to the Royal Palace. The next morning at ten the coach arrived with coachmen and outriders in long, brightly colored robes. We were ready for them, in full evening toilette. As we drove through the city the curtains of the coach were drawn to conceal us from the gaze of the natives—why, I don't know. The grounds of the Royal Palace were immense. We finally reached the women's quarters and were conducted into a long, cool room. About eight ladies in native costume were standing some distance away. We bowed low but were not permitted to approach closer until we had engaged in some little conversation with the aid of an interpreter. After this I was conducted to a piano. It was the old-fashioned square sort, and I seated myself with trepidation, though to my surprise it was perfectly in tune. The Siamese have acute musical ears, and before I had sung more than a few bars they each took up a small instrument, a sort of Siamese lyre, and began to accompany me as I sang. After we were served the usual tiny cakes and refreshments and entertained with a dance by the attendants, we took our leave and were conducted to the throne room.

Unlike his womenfolk, King Chulalongkorn spoke a little French and English.[61] He did us the honor of rising and coming forward to shake our hands.

When we returned, the chamberlain conducted us through the royal gardens, and there for the first time in my life I saw Siamese cats. They lived in a large sort of greenhouse on the palace grounds and though free to come and go, we were told, never strayed far. They were royal Siamese cats, as the natives never owned any but a rather ordinary Maltese sort. Tremendously struck by the beauty of these curious creatures, I said unthinkingly that I would love to have one.

A day or two later, when my host accompanied me to the ship which was to take me to Saigon, a palace functionary was waiting at the dock. He presented me with a purse of one hundred golden louis and, wonder of wonders, a beautiful wooden cage containing a pair of Siamese cats.

These royal cats followed me wherever I went. Wiki-Wiki and Mou-Moute were their names. And after the manner of cats and kings, they had many children. Wiki-Wiki and Mou-Moute were, I think, the first Siamese cats to be imported to the United States, and their last descendant died in 1937.

Clara Lardinois as Lakmé, with cat. Courtesy William R. Moran.

Some Siamese cats have a kink in the tail and arguments rage among cat fanciers as to whether this is a defect or a virtue.

In Siam I heard a legend: an ancient king owned a magic ring, which, as we all would do under the circumstances, he prized highly. One day while hunting he discovered that the ring was lost. Great rewards were offered and everyone in the kingdom went searching for the magic ring, but nobody found it. One day a cat appeared with the ring on his tail. So fearful had he been that the ring might slip off that he had grown a permanent crook in his tail to keep it on. And though not all Siamese cats have a kink in the tail, they are all royal nevertheless and demand the deference due to their rank.

I was in Saigon again in time to meet the ship bringing the company from France, and I joined them with my two new cats and my new little Saigonese maid, Tinan, for the voyage to Haiphong. Fortunately Haiphong was a far cry from Saigon. The climate was better and the people more serious. They attended to their work and made no attempt to drink themselves to death. Besides this, there was a beautiful little theater there. Like so many theaters in remote places, it was a small-scale model of the Paris Opéra, new and with all the latest equipment for theatrical productions. It was our plan to give performances in Haiphong until such time as the International Exposition at Hanoi opened, and then to alternate between the two cities. Hanoi was the official residence of the governor-general of French Indochina, as well as the resident superior of Tongking, but the former also had a palace at Haiphong, which is a day's train trip into the flat interior. Haiphong was given over to commerce, while Hanoi was mostly governmental, with many troops garrisoned there and all the show of diplomatic and governmental life.

We sang the usual repertory at Haiphong and were splendidly supported by the public. Not often did so good a company penetrate to so remote a place. It was the occasion for a fine flowering of society, and we were naturally fêted and welcomed in grand style. I shall never forget one gentleman in particular, who sent me many bouquets and attended many of my appearances—always, of course, with his wife. One gala performance came along with all the great world of Haiphong in attendance, and I was receiving, I must say, a great deal of applause and encouragement. Between the acts there was much visiting from box to box, and the good lady in question heard a little too much about me—how fine an actress I was, what a lovely voice I had. I presume this bored her, for finally when someone made a flattering remark about my teeth she said, "Yes, they look lovely. What a pity they are false!" This was repeated to me as a good joke, but I was furious. The woman had no cause to be jealous of me or do any backbiting, for I had been as correct and polite to her and her husband as to everyone else. Later, when the husband came up to me and raised my hand to his lips, in a sudden moment of rage I leaned down and gave his hand a good bite! Everyone who was near saw this cannibalistic action, and I explained, "You can show your hand to your wife and tell her my teeth are my own."

I would not wish it to be believed that I was without temperament.

23

SHORTLY BEFORE we were scheduled to leave for Hanoi and the opening of the Exposition, we put on *Carmen*. All went well until the final moment. When Don José stabbed me the audience saw me fall, with great reality, to the ground. My frenzied lover, a fine tenor named Eternod, had turned his dagger in the wrong direction and it had entered my neck, nearly piercing the carotid. I lay unconscious for I know not how long, and was bandaged and done up for weeks afterward. As a result I was unable to sing in operatic performances for some time, though I soon managed some numbers in concert form in which I was not called upon to make movements or gestures.

We were disappointed by the small, ugly, unattractive theater at Hanoi, and I did not much regret being unable to sing in it. After the fine house at Haiphong it was a painful contrast to see this dirty and miserable little edifice in which we were supposed to uphold the glory of French culture—though I presume if the performance is good the audience soon forgets the surroundings (and I have sung in some extraordinary places in my time).

Through the kind aid of an intimate old friend of Madame Imberton who was living in Hanoi, where he had large interests, I succeeded in renting a charming villa which he had formerly occupied. At that time, tropical cities such as this were built almost entirely of wood; in fact this villa was the only stone edifice in Hanoi. I already had a little villa in Haiphong, and now as we alternated between the two cities I had two homes always open and ready to receive me. Tinan did not acclimate herself well, so I sent her back to her native city (which she was welcome to) and acquired a little Annamite named Tika, who stayed with me for some time. In my villa at Hanoi I now had a small staff of domestics, and as is wisest in these cases, I made sure they were brothers and sisters. No fine shades of difference in caste, thought, or religion, which often mar concord in pagan (as well as Christian) households, could trouble my little kingdom. It was a delightful spot in which to rest and relax after work. A flight of steps led up to a veranda in front, though because the house was built on a sharp acclivity, the rear of the grounds was level with my bedroom at the back. A short distance behind the house lay a small lake.

About a five minutes' walk away stood another villa, occupied by four young Frenchmen stationed at Hanoi. We had many good times together, and I soon found myself in a small, congenial circle which included Madame Imberton's friend, who had been so helpful to me, and several other charming people—wives and husbands. Fortunately there were more women (aside from natives) in Hanoi than in Saigon, which made social life more natural and agreeable. In fact, with my little villa, my Annamite domestic staff, my work and my friends, my strange new cats, carriage, pony, and basket wagon, I was so peaceful and content in Hanoi that I had no wish to leave when our season was over and the company was preparing to return to Paris.

My problem was solved when some officials and leading citizens of Hanoi called to ask if I would not stay in their city and organize a company of my own for the summer months. Though the Exposition was more or less over, the aftermath still lingered, and many people were expected to visit Hanoi for a long time to come. In fact a number of exhibits and traveling performers, peddlers and so forth, intended to stay on to catch these latecomers.

The proposition sounded excellent to me. I accepted it on several conditions, all of which were acceded. One was that we should build a new summer theater, for I was set against the scrubby little building we had utilized heretofore and felt that for a successful summer season such as I wished, a more agreeable gala house would be indispensable. I offered to put up the building myself if I would be given the right to raise it on the site of my choice. There was a large public garden in the center of the city, with many beautiful trees and flowering shrubs, and a little ornamental lake.

I proposed to erect our little theater beside the water. The most influential members of the colony offered to band together and dispose of season subscriptions to the extent of guaranteeing the salaries of my company. I would have to assume the responsibility of paying their passage home when I closed the theater, since they had forfeited their own passages by remaining with me. All the rest of the venture was to be my responsibility.

When these things had been arranged to my satisfaction, I set to work with mounting excitement to organize my project. I selected the best of the singers and musicians with me, augmenting the latter with several excellent musicians who had been attached to other exhibits and concessions. I also sent for all the architects available in the city, giving them an idea of what I wanted for a theater and asking them to submit sketches and plans.

The winning plans were immediately carried out, and the little theater in the gardens rose with magic speed. Those Annamite workmen were quick and clever with wood. The finished building drew praise from everyone and was a source of delight to contemplate. It was a summer theater in the Arabic style, with pilasters and rounded arches reminiscent of the Alhambra in Granada, all worked in wood and gaily painted in scarlet, green, yellow, and blue. The scenery and seats from the old theater (and whatever else was possible to salvage from the dilapidated building) were utilized. The cost of the building, completed and installed for theatrical performances, was about 80,000 francs. I christened it Le Casino du Petit Lac.

Our performances were simple but effective, for though my company was small it comprised the cream of the larger one, and the orchestra was excellent. The cool summer nights at Hanoi were beautiful, and our house proved very popular. Between the acts the audience drank beer in the buffet (I had sold the buffet concession) or wandered in the gardens. The lake, though small, tempered the breezes. I felt I had been wise in building this theater, for the ratty old barn would never have attracted as much of the public.

Our rather limited company and lack of chorus prevented anything elaborate. However, we opened with *Les noces de Jeannette*, which was always popular, though it demands only three principals. Often we gave separate scenes in costume, interpolating concert selections. I also engaged a well-known magician named Grossi, who appeared three times with great success and to the delight of the papers, which complimented me on my astuteness in giving the public what it wanted.

During the day I rode about in my pony carriage, went over our accounts, planned the next week's performances, and enjoyed a smooth and pleasant existence, with enough leisure and enough work to make me happy.

That is how it was, anyway, until about the middle of August, when we had been running for a little more than two months. It began during a performance of *Les noces de Jeannette*. The wind came up rather more violently than was desirable, and as it became increasingly evident that we were in for a storm, we hastily finished the performance with as many cuts as we could manage. The musicians packed their instruments, the orchestrations were left upon the music stands, and we all went home in a rush.

By the time I reached the villa the wind was blowing a gale, great clouds of dry dust darkening the sky and the landscape. My domestics were busy locking doors, boarding up windows, making all as tight as possible. I collected my cats and dogs about me and called for Tika, but she was folded up into the smallest possible space in a corner of the salon and no coaxing on my part could budge her. The high, excited voices of the little staff grew more and more alarming. They knew what they were in for, and their always-limited command of French forsook them immediately in this contingency.

In the history of Hanoi, the great typhoon of 1903 is well remembered yet.

The wind continued to rise and roar, with increasing fury, and soon the sky was as black as deepest night. Trees groaned and creaked, and above the roar from time to time we could hear them crashing all about us. Every window in the house broke, splinters of glass flying in all directions, but still the boarded-up screens held fast. By now Tika had ceased praying to her native gods and was in the grip of hysteria. Adding to our troubles, the lake in the rear of the house began to invade us. The wind blew it first in flying drops and then in heavy sheets into my bedroom, through the cracks in the boards over the windows, and from there it poured into the salon.

The horror of a typhoon, the invincible strength of nature lashed into fury, dwarfs every emotion. We climbed onto chairs—even Tika pulling herself together when the water oozed about her—but soon we had to forsake the chairs and climb upon tables. The two cats stood where I placed them, immovable and trembling in the general peril. Before long I had to forsake even the table and hoist myself up onto the high marble mantelpiece, which was fortunately large enough to accommodate the animals and myself.

About this time I became aware of faint sounds on the veranda. My four young friends had come to my rescue from their villa five minutes' distance. By holding hands, lying on the ground between gusts, and running three steps forward after being blown two steps back, they covered the distance between their house and mine in a little over an hour.

Now came the problem of letting them in, opening the door and being able to shut it afterward against the wind and swirling waters. But the impossible was accomplished, and my four exhausted rescuers, who might so easily have been killed, finally reached shelter, such as it was, and found me on the mantel with my livestock.

By now the wind had died down somewhat, but we spent a horrible night. When the water leaked out of the rooms we dragged some mattresses to the floor of the salon, and as our fear and horror subsided a great appetite and thirst took their place. Luckily we found something in the pantry which had not been too much ruined by lake water and rain.

The nervous strain under which we had labored for so many hours was not easily overcome. But finally my young friends, seeing that the typhoon was over and that all was as well as could be expected, left me in my desolated villa to look out for their own affairs. Naturally we were much worried over the fate of all our friends in Hanoi and Haiphong, and likewise over the fate of Le Casino du Petit Lac, in which they too had an interest. All the telegraph wires were down and Hanoi completely cut off from the rest of the world.

The house, though somewhat *déshabillé* after the storm, was still whole. As the water receded we set to work with mops. My bedroom, being closest to the lake, had been hardest hit. Water plants and all kinds of things were found in it. And there were countless little dazed green frogs in the bed, in the corners, and even in my high riding boots standing on a shelf.

The next day was gray and gloomy. Water dripped, slower and slower, out of the thick clouds. We went out to reconnoiter and see what damage had been done. Half the city was in ruins, but the greatest loss of life had been in the native quarters, where the little flimsy structures were wiped away like crumbs. Many Annamites, hysterical and uncontrollable in the face of the storm, had attempted to flee with their pitiful valuables. Many had been killed, while luckier ones escaped with broken arms and legs.

The path of the wind had been peculiar and, as is often the case, played some curious pranks in its deadly passage. Certain sections of the city had been completely overlooked, while others were laid waste. I remember the largest bazaar and hardware store in the city. The wind had pounced upon the storeroom, which occupied a center court, swooping up all the stock-in-trade and flinging it high in the air so that the telephone poles along the street were hung with an odd collection of merchandise: garbage pails, brushes, mops, tongs, *pots de chambre*, and bathmats, caught securely in the glass insulators and along wires.

And Le Casino du Petit Lac! Nothing was left of my charming little theater but a few pieces of broken wood and splintered sticks of furniture. All the rest had found haven in the lake. The scenery belonging to the old theater, my costumes and those of the company—everything, in fact, including a serious loss, the orchestrations for all our productions, which had been rented from the Paris publishers. Ironically enough the old theater I had taken such a dislike to had not been in the path of the storm and stood untouched.

Martial law had been declared at once, and the soldiers from the barracks began the long business of clearing and rebuilding the city. The loss of property had been dreadful, particularly among those who could least afford losses—the poor. A series of concerts was organized in the old theater, at which I was glad to appear, but the effects of the typhoon were long felt.

As for myself, I was in a particularly bad position, for not only had I lost the theater and my 80,000 francs, but I still had the company on my hands and was responsible for getting them back to France. However, most things work themselves out in time, and I received able assistance from the government. The typhoon had been a public calamity, an act of God, in which suffering and loss were general, so the French government consented to return my troupe to Paris. I was offered, in compensation for my personal losses, the concession of the casino at Boson for the following summer.

Boson is a watering place not far from Haiphong, much frequented in the summer months, and this concession from the government could have been a great piece of business for me. It meant that I could run the gambling rooms for my own profit. However, I was doubtful of being able to undertake so ambitious a venture and felt that my only hope would be to return to Paris to find someone who would take over my concession and run the bank. That meant finding someone who was not only experienced in such things, a good businessman, but who was also honest, and I rather despaired of finding anyone in the six months left me who could fill the requirements. It might well take a lifetime to stumble upon such a person: Diogenes never did.

However, it was better to accept the concession at Boson than go away with nothing but losses, so the papers were signed, witnessed by everyone in sight and stamped with many impressive governmental seals. I still have the document. Much good it did me!

But though my losses were heavy, I was not ruined. And I could take comfort in the realization that things might have been worse had I not owned the only stone house in Hanoi, for I had been in the direct path of the wind.

My interests in Hanoi were now terminated, and I decided to leave for a holiday. Because so many people I had met at Hanoi had assured me I must not miss Hong Kong and Shanghai, Tika and I, and the cats and the dogs, set out for China. When we reached Shanghai I was willing to stay there indefinitely. I felt it would be impossible to see too much of that fascinating city. An old Frenchman to whom I had a letter of introduction from the Belgian consul at Hong Kong entertained in great fashion. Knowing me by my reputation in Paris from the old days, he could not do enough to make my visit successful. He was one of the most prominent citizens of Shanghai, the agent for the French mail ships, and gradually had grown more and more indispensable to the French government and the French colony; he was in those days very necessary indeed to Shanghai.

He finally suggested I give a concert, and I was very willing to do so, though it would have been impossible without him. Problems vary in different cities, and the problem at Shanghai was a special one. The

French colony was too small to draw a large audience, but there was an active musical group made up of society people of various nationalities. I hit upon the plan of inviting several of the most outstanding among them to be "assisting artists" at a Blanche Arral concert, and they all eagerly accepted. One knows the type—Miss Teahouse, who sings so charmingly "My Mother Bids Me Bind My Hair," and the young violinist who interprets a trifle of Bach, as well as Mrs. Supplefoot, whose mission is to sing Tosti's "Good-bye." Thus I drew a really "brilliant" audience of all their friends—as well as brilliant receipts. (I had not been in the business in vain.) The ruse worked beautifully and everyone was delighted. And the assisting amateurs were surprisingly good.

As I had been in other strange places, I was soon thoroughly at home in Shanghai. I had a personal rickshaw man who could take me wherever I wanted to go (unlike the public rickshaw men, who had a habit of stopping just before reaching the section of the city you wanted to visit with the information that some other rickshaw company owned the concession to operate in that particular district). Through the Chinese poet Li Hung-chang, reputed to be the richest man in the world and the right hand of the emperor, and whom I had known since my Opéra-Comique days, I also had the rare pleasure of witnessing an aristocratic Chinese wedding.[62] In those days the Chinese women of the upper classes still bound their feet. I watched as the mother and sisters hobbled around on their horrible little pegs, painting the bride's face until it was as thick as a mask, loading upon her one elaborate embroidered cloak after another, and placing in her hair so many gold and silver ornaments it was miraculous that she could hold up her head at all. It was practically unknown for a foreigner to be admitted to a Chinese wedding, especially in that exalted station of society.

One day I received a letter which began, "My dear little cousin: how surprised and pleased I was to learn that you are in Shanghai. Before you leave China you must certainly come to Hankow and pay me a visit." This was a complete mystery to me, and I searched my mind for some time before the signature meant anything. I seemed to remember a distant cousin from long ago in my childhood who had departed for China. As it turned out, there was a colony of Belgians at Hankow connected with the building of the railway to Peking. This cousin of mine was not only engaged in that work but was also the doctor, chemist, and general factotum for the colony.

I was perfectly ready and indeed delighted with the opportunity to travel into the interior of China, even after I discovered that Hankow was eight days' journey by ship up the great Yangtze Kiang. Tika, the cats, and I boarded a German cargo ship and set out.

My presence in Hankow was the signal for gala days, at which I could not wonder. The little colony of Belgian expatriates was far from home and had been so for a long while, whereas I, though away a year, still brought a breath of their old homes and of the great world with me. I gave them a concert and we sang together the songs of home, everyone contributing whatever his talents permitted to the general entertainment. The celebrations came to an end only when the ship started back at the end of two weeks.

The Yangtze Kiang is an extremely wide, leisurely river; at times both banks are beyond the horizon and one might think oneself on a calm, muddy sea. There was some traffic on it, but our ship—a German cargo boat on which Tika and I were the only passengers—was as big as any that went up to Hankow.

We had been progressing for four or five days when one morning I noticed that we were no longer moving. It took some time to learn the cause of our sudden halt, but when the truth came out it appeared we were stuck in the mud. In such cases there are two options: wait patiently until the ship floats off herself, or run up a signal of distress. In this latter alternative, of course, by the laws of the sea the rescue ship enjoys the right of salvage; and no captain of a ship in distress likes to lose for his company the value of the cargo he is carrying.

I was assured that there was no danger, and I knew perfectly well that this was the truth insofar as sinking was concerned. It was merely a question of sitting there until we floated off—a sufficiently distressing and boresome wait. Every possible thing was done to dislodge us, but the mud held fast. All that day and night we remained stationary, and all the next day and night. In the meantime several ships steamed serenely past us, ignorant of our plight.

By the third day matters became a little more unpleasant, and grumbling among the crew began. Though the officers were most kind and pleasant people, the old captain was a brute, a Prussian if ever there was one, and still he refused to run up the signal.

By now I was less calm than I had been heretofore. If there was no danger of sinking, starving would not be an agreeable death either. For two whole days we had lived upon nothing but rice, and now the water supply gave out and there was nothing to drink. Nonetheless, that insufferable captain still refused to send for help, and the discontent of the crew became more active. Every time we sighted another ship heaving in sight, it added fresh fuel to our rage. By the afternoon of the fourth day, when I was frantic with despair, the crew took matters into their own hands and mutinied. The captain found himself locked into a cabin and the distress signal was hoisted. Shortly after, we were rescued. We were hauled off the mud bank and proceeded on our way to Shanghai, under the command of the first officer: the captain was seen no more!

Shanghai looked good to me. I went for a meal of victuals in which rice would have no place, while the cats, feeling much the same, had an enjoyable meal of fish.

My good friends welcomed me back. The story of my adventure on the Yangtze Kiang had gone about, and I was treated as one returning from the dead. At any rate, I had returned, and that was enough to be thankful for.

Having returned, I had no desire to disappear, and I lingered in Shanghai as the weeks slipped by. After that first concert, I was asked to give several more, this time without the assistance of amateurs.

The facts of the case being understood, I was rather taken aback at this time. It was announced that the great Hungarian-American magician, Harry Houdini, was to give a performance in Shanghai, and so of course there I was in a seat in the front row.[63] I was enthralled by the great Houdini, as much by the charm, grace, and perfect coordination of his movements and his wonderful stage presence as by the inexplicable things he did before one's eyes. At a certain place in the performance he paused and looked down at me.

"I see Madame Arral in the audience," he said, pointing with a graceful wave of the hand in my direction. "And I hope she will be so kind as to come up here beside me on the stage to let me make her vanish!"

Awful moment! The audience began to applaud and Houdini continued to smile, but the proposition chilled me to the bone! I stood up on my chair, waved my arms, and cried, "But I don't *want* to disappear!" The audience continued to applaud, and I called out, "Which do you choose—that I disappear, or that I stay here to sing for you again?" And they let me stay.

But the next day Houdini called at my hotel and seriously proposed that we go into partnership and make a tour. "Why wouldn't you come up on the stage last night? You know nothing would happen to you!" It was an amusing thought, and I had done a good many things in my life, but I decided that my career lay primarily in music and that I had no desire whatsoever to disappear yet, either temporarily or permanently!

The chief interest of Singapore, as all visitors to that city can testify, is the rich mixture of nationalities that lend its streets the air of a fairytale. Hindus, Chinese, English, Germans, Javanese—all sorts of people jostle each other in the marketplace. I was charmed by the international and ever-varied aspect of Singapore; it was a great change from anything I had seen for a long time. I put up at the old Raffles Hotel and, in a moment of revolt from the things that had frightened and haunted me, signed the register with the name of Peshkov.

In Singapore, life was arranged in a peculiar manner, as in all Eastern cities inhabited by many westerners. Everyone soon became acquainted, learning more or less of each other's story; and some were strange stories indeed, as Singapore attracted all sorts of people who wished to live far from their native lands. Surely I must have given rise to some speculations, with my Russian name, my curious cats, and my little Annamite attendant in her native costume who slept outside my door (or doorway, rather, for in Singapore there were no doors, only bamboo curtains, and everyone had a servant who slept on the threshold).

In fact everything was open and aboveboard in a rather naïve and delightful way. The bathing facilities, for instance, which occupied a back section of one's rooms in the hotel, consisted of a barrel with a little ladder against it, which one mounted and jumped into, standing there like a schoolboy swimmer whose clothes have been stolen.

I had a piano in my little living room, and naturally I practiced daily. Due to the open domestic architecture of Singapore, however, I was unable to shut myself up. Consequently my exercises and arias were heard all over the hotel and even in adjacent streets, which added to the gossip about me and made me more than ever a woman of mystery.

Before long an article, or rather a news item, appeared in the *Straits Times* and served to rouse more general curiosity. It convinced me of what I had long believed, which is that for singers to be surrounded with a little harmless mystery is almost a necessity, as it does much to build the glamour and romance with which they have from time immemorial been associated.

> For the last few days the residents and visitors to Raffles Hotel have been charmed while listening to the strains of a soprano voice which for beauty, range, and flexibility is the most wonderful that anybody can remember ever having heard in this part of the world.

The article went on to describe this voice more thoroughly, mentioning my name at the end and hoping I would be prevailed upon to give a concert.

> Even heard from behind the screen of a private suite—for Madame Arral has never yet appeared in public here—the effect of this combination of qualities is a revelation to music lovers in the Straits.

Could better advertising have been devised than this? And yet I had nothing whatever to do with it.

My first acquaintance was the Russian consul. He had learned my name from the hotel register and called upon me, introducing himself as an old university friend of Sergei's. Even as far away from Russia as the Straits Settlements, I still found contact with happier days. I was anxious, of course, to give a concert in Singapore, and through the consul one was arranged in the beautiful concert hall of the Teutonia Club, taking place on 25 February 1904.

Among the guests at the hotel were several Americans with whom I had a bowing acquaintance. One of these was a young man of twenty-eight or twenty-nine named Hamilton Bassett, who seemed much impressed by my singing.[64] But the Russian consul assured me that I must have as little to do with these people as possible, warning me especially against Mr. Bassett. The reason, though he did not explain it, was that the Americans belonged to a different group from the Russians and Germans; and I realized that Sergei's old friend rather considered that he had prior claims on me and that I should identify myself with his group. Foreign colonies are riddled with cliques and social pitfalls.

I am *un drôle de coco*, as I have often been assured, and I became increasingly cordial to the Americans at once, finding them excessively kind and charming, and refreshingly free of the qualities which mar goodwill among so many foreign residents. Mr. Bassett was in Singapore on insurance business, a traveling agent for some American company. When the man he was associated with moved to Shanghai to take over the field there, he had been left with all the territory outside China for his own. We became well acquainted, and soon Mr. Bassett pestered me to make him my manager for a good long tour. He knew Austalasia well and believed we could make a great success.

Though I was anxious to go on singing, I was rather doubtful of Mr. Bassett, for his activities had never been in the managerial field, and I knew well that the theatrical business required experience. Still, we went on discussing and laying out plans, and Bassett mapped out an ambitious tour. He was full of confidence. As I grew to know him better I saw that he had truly great business acumen and might well prove a find.

As I had been living long enough in a hotel, I took a villa outside the city, not far from the racetracks, and installed myself comfortably where I could gratify my love of animals. I bought a wonderful horse, Coeur d'Or, and every day went riding on the bridle paths and avenues around the villa. Bassett, who was a fine horseman, often joined me on these canters, full of talk about the projected tour and big ideas for launching me into the musical life of Asia and Australia. Some of his conceits were truly novel and interesting at that, and I finally knew that he was the man to be my manager—a manager after my own heart, ready to brave something untried, and with a good sense of drama and advertising. In short, he could handle just the sort of tour I would be delighted to make.

My villa, as it turned out, had one drawback, which was the sad fact that it stood on the road that led to the native cemetery. Funerals took place at dusk and went right by my door. The corpse was carried on an open stretcher covered with a bright cloth, preceded by dancers with cymbals and followed by hired mourners, wailing and shouting. The combination of joyous mirth and wild despair (both paid for) created a truly strange bedlam, and I never got used to these performances. Worst of all, at the cemetery the corpses were cremated. When the wind came from that direction, the smoke from the pyre and the smell of roasting Malayan was far from agreeable.

⇥ 24 ⇤

B Y NOW I had succumbed to the wanderlust. I took Tika with me and went to the place I had long wished to visit: Java. We would remain there until plans were more fully made and the opportune moment to begin a tour presented itself.

If Saigon was hot, Java was hotter, and the long native costume absolutely indispensable. These garments were made of thin opaque cotton which repelled the rays of the sun but did not require anything much beneath them, and they were worn universally. Batavia was so hot indeed that everyone spent as much time as possible outside the city. In spite of it being a Dutch colony, a great many English subjects as well as other foreigners made Java their home.

The Belgian consul gave a fête in my honor at his beautiful estate at Surabaya, during which I had of course to sing. I chose Berger's "Pourquoi ne pas m'aimer," better known as the "Valse bleue," which I had introduced into that first production at the Casino de Paris, *Cocher, au Casino!* It was at night. Lanterns hung between the trees, Javanese music sounded, and Javanese girls appeared among the trees to perform a native dance. While the girls moved in unison, one among their number detached herself from the others and began to dance alone. She was easily the star of the occasion and all eyes were turned in her direction, but she was so heavily veiled and enveloped in floating draperies that it was impossible to see her face or anything particular about her.

Javanese dancers had been seen from time to time in Paris, but this girl possessed a personality of her own which riveted attention. Afterward at the supper she was the only one of the dancers present, and I thought myself correct in assuming her to be something out of the ordinary.

The next day her story was on every tongue. She had fled Java on an English ship which sailed an hour after the fête in my honor was over. It appears she was a vestal connected with a temple nearby and was breaking her vows to dance in any secular affair. A young English officer had fallen in love with her and persuaded her to flee to England, where he promised shortly to join her. Her reason for appearing at the fête was a good one, for only there on the estate of a foreign consul was she safe from arrest and imprisonment by the outraged priests of her strict sect. At least, that was the story I heard that day.

At any rate, this romantic dancer made a deep impression on me, for though I was fascinated by Javanese dancers as a whole, by the exotic music and the distinction of the slightest movement of their graceful figures, even the uninitiated could see that she was outstanding among her colleagues. From then on, whenever I sang the "Valse bleue" my mind would go back to the wonderful Javanese fête at Surabaya.

Java, however, is no more the white man's country than Cochinchina, and the inevitable miscegenation which occurs in all such countries brings its aftermath of tragedy. Javanese women who have the misfortune to live with white men also have the pleasure of taking their revenge on those who abandon them and their children.

There is a reed that grows in marshy lands in Java, the soft inner fiber of which, when chopped fine and served in food, hardens through some chemical reaction into splinters as sharp and brittle as bits of glass, perforating the stomach and intestines after a passage of months.

Years later in New York I answered an advertisement to sublet an apartment and found the tenants to be a young Frenchman and his wife. The man was dreadfully ill. His unhappy wife told me that no American doctor seemed able to help him, and they were returning to France in search of medical aid. I looked at the man. He was lying on a couch, pale, thin, and feverish, with a wracking cough. "The man is a consumptive!" I thought. "I cannot take this flat."

The poor wife went out of the room for a moment. When she was gone the young husband looked at me and, reading my thoughts, said,

"You needn't be afraid—I am not consumptive. I know what is the matter with me."

At this moment my eye lighted on a little figurine of a Javanese dancing girl on the mantelpiece. In horror I exclaimed, "You have been in Java!" Our eyes met, and each read understanding in the other's.

"Yes, I deserve it," the doomed man said. And he added in a whisper, "She had a child."

If the man deserved it, his poor wife did not, and neither for that matter did the unfortunate woman and child in Java. I was long haunted by that terrible tragedy, but somehow I had no desire to take the apartment.

I returned to Singapore, and though I visited Java professionally not long after, the fleeing dancer was already forgotten.

About eight years later I was in Paris once more and went with my dear old friends the Imbertons and several other people to see the review at the Casino de Paris. During the performance the orchestra played the "Valse bleue," which I had so many times sung, and all at once I was again at that beautiful fête in Java.

A little while later in the performance the curtains rose and a girl stood alone on the big darkened stage. It was evident at once that she held the audience, for that sensation of complete attention, which anyone who has ever been on the stage can recognize, stirred in my mind. "Why, I know that girl!" I said half aloud.

When the curtain fell and the tremendous applause was over I learned who she was.

"That is Mata Hari!" the Imbertons told me. And had I not been so long away from France, their tone suggested, it would have been impossible for me to be ignorant of her identity. She was the toast of the town.

At the first *entr'acte* I could not wait to hurry backstage. The good old Casino de Paris—I was in the inaugural production there and, strange indeed, had at that time also sung the "Valse bleue." It was like a homecoming to go through the stage entrance again. I enquired for Madame Mata Hari's dressing room and was conducted to the very dressing room I had been the first to occupy. In response to my knock one of those very superior serving-persons came out. I explained to her that I would like to see her mistress for a moment, but it was evident that this was an old story by now. The woman looked doubtful, so I said that I had known her mistress some years before. She disappeared into the room and in a minute I was admitted. Mata Hari stood in the middle of the room, calm and dignified, with a faint look of inquiry. She was really a fascinating creature. Coming forward, she took my outstretched hand and peered into my face.

"But I know you, Madame," she said in slow, perfect French, with a charming little accent. "You were the guest of honor the last time I ever danced in Java!"

I begged her to join us for supper after the performance and she accepted. We then had a little opportunity to talk, and I learned something of her subsequent history. Of the young Englishman for whom she had left her native land, she did not have much to say. "We did not stay together long," was her only comment about him. Her French was easy and correct, her manner that of a woman of the world, tempered with that enchanting poise and cool self-possession of the East. Her dignity was inborn. She told me that as soon as her engagement at the Casino de Paris was over she had one in Brussels, and that in fact she had more offers than she could possibly accept.

Everyone was charmed by her simple and dignified manner, and my exclamation during her dance had been substantiated, so it was a successful evening. After this time I would hear of Mata Hari from time to time and of the sensation she produced everywhere, but I never saw her again. Many years later I had the melancholy interest of seeing her fate depicted on the screen by that great artist Greta Garbo. And Mata Hari has remained a mysterious and romantic figure. That her beauty and her brains betrayed her no one can doubt, but as in the case of poor Paul Bolo, I am convinced that her true story is not yet known. I have been told that she was really a Dutch girl who learned her Javanese dance in Europe and never saw the East. She may well have had Dutch blood in her veins, as many do in Batavia, but I can attest, if my word is of any weight, that she certainly danced in Java before she was famous in Europe.[65]

The more I saw of the world the more I wanted to see, and after this I took time off to go through the Malay Peninsula and into India, visiting Rangoon, Bombay, Madras, and going as far as Delhi to gratify my curiosity about the temple there of which I had so often sung in *Le grand mogol*. Once I returned to my villa at Singapore, Bassett came to me and renewed his arguments that I should make him my manager, and I decided that I would. I knew him well enough now to realize that he had splendid qualifications for the position.

My great problem now was to find homes for my considerable menagerie. Wiki-Wiki and Mou-Moute had produced a handsome *quintette* of offspring, and there were the two dogs, several horses and ponies, and my devoted baboons, Baron and Baronne (Baron had had the misfortune to break a front tooth and now proudly displayed a gold one when he smiled). It seemed more than one could expect of me to part with any of these children of mine. But I finally met an Australian whose interest was the breeding of racehorses on a large ranch in Australia, and as I had fully made up my mind to visit that continent, professionally if possible, this seemed a good solution to my difficulty. Alas, poor Coeur d'Or died of pneumonia, his head in my arms, after he had been left out in a rainstorm by the groom; otherwise I should never have been able to leave Singapore. The Australian took the baboons and a pair of my kittens, which finally paved the way for my new project.

For this long tour I had no desire to appear, like other singers, in an elegant gown and with a pianist, singing through a program of songs and arias. The prospect of doing that in the long series of cities Bassett and I had mapped out, after days with our heads buried in atlases and steamship folders, chilled and depressed me. I do not believe operatic singers enjoy concert appearances half as much as they may pretend to. I have always detested them. For one like myself, long used to the stage, including a story, scenery, costumes, and above all an orchestra, there is something dull and disheartening in the removal of all these at once, in being left nothing but the thin support of a piano with which to sing the big arias, and the latest fashion in which to sing them. Singing was the great joy of my life, and now I believed I had a plan which would make a financial success as well as satisfy the needs of my nature.

I called upon the musical director of the Teutonia Club, where I had first sung in Singapore, to see what he could do for me. And he did very well, for he told me of a Dutch violinist named George Paanz, who was in Singapore at the time and intended to go on to Java to give concerts. "That is where I am going!" I thought.

I listened in astonishment to Paanz play. He was a superb musician, his mastery over his instrument complete, and what is more, he played with fire and feeling and magnificent tone. I have never heard finer playing, not even excepting my good old Ysaÿe; however, to play his best Paanz had to be drunk.

The second person the manager of the Teutonia Club brought to my attention became an equally important necessity to my little company. He was a small, middle-aged, and rather formal Englishman, to whom music was the breath of life. His name was Allpress. His conducting was just the sort I could best work with, and I signed him up at once.

The last thing I did in Singapore was to go to a clever French *couturière* I had discovered there and cause to be made an inordinate number of elaborate gowns—startling gowns, simple gowns, hats, and ensembles, for these were necessary too. With trunkloads of these, Paanz, Allpress, Bassett, Tika, the cats, and I sailed for Java.

In Batavia there were, as I knew from experience, a good number of fine musicians, and Allpress engaged eleven of them for the concert I intended to give. My idea was to put on a kind of entertainment which no one had ever before attempted, and for this I required not only a small orchestra but also scenery and costumes. Besides offering a new kind of entertainment, I intended to preserve to some degree the atmosphere of the operatic stage, as opera was a thing the people of Batavia had small chance to enjoy. I hoped to give, in short, a truly operatic concert. First I planned to sing several airs from various works, changing my gown for these so that the female members of my audience might have something to interest them if they were not fond of music; then, as the pièce de résistance, I intended to present a series of selections comprising popular soprano numbers from a single opera, and in costume. The first opera I chose to make the experiment with was, of course, my dear *Mignon*, which had always been so lucky for me. For this I had two costumes made from my sketches in Batavia, and Allpress set to work with the score, demonstrating his indispensability by orchestrating it for our twelve musicians.

As I was to sing in costume, a theater where something in the way of scenery was available, as well as correct stage lighting, was another prime necessity. This was the kind of concert we wanted to give, and this is what we did give.

I opened the program in a concert gown and sang the great air from Gounod's *La reine de Saba*. This I found was a fine warming-up number; it had the requisite wide range and flowing emotional crescendo to rouse an audience. While I changed my dress, either Herr Paanz or the orchestra played. Then I came forward again and sang the Mad Scene from *Hamlet* or something from *Paul et Virginie, Les noces de Jeannette,* the "Cours-la-reine" scene from *Manon,* or some aria of that nature, invariably using gay boleros or old waltzes for encores. After the intermission the curtain would rise on the first act of *Mignon.* The score Mr. Allpress had devised was truly the meat of the starring role. In those days, before radio, and in those remote countries, few people had ever had any opportunity to hear operatic music except in small individual selections. My innovation may be truly said to have in some slight measure filled a long-felt want. The "Cameo Mignon" took three quarters of an hour.

I began with "Connais-tu le pays?", Mignon's first number, going through all the stage business, and then sang the Swallow Duet, which unfortunately had to be treated as a solo, the orchestra filling in with the bass part. Next came that dramatic scene I have always been so fond of, and of which so little seems to be made in most performances of *Mignon.* It is the scene of jealousy, in which Mignon, beginning "Elle est là, près de lui" and torn by despair, first contemplates suicide in the ornamental lake. But she hears the crowd applauding Philine in her role as Titania in *A Midsummer Night's Dream* at the castle theater, the echo of it wafting to her through the trees. All thoughts of death leave her, consumed in her raging heart—poor little wanderer!—and she calls down a curse on the castle and everyone in it, with the hope that raging floods of fire will fall from heaven and destroy all beneath them. It is the most dramatic number in Thomas's opera, and the audience was invariably roused to genuine excitement by it. I would rush off the stage at the end of the Cantabile, "Et l'engloutir sous des torrents de feu!" leaving the audience in a pitch of dramatic fever, while the orchestra broke into the charming Gavotte "Me voici dans son boudoir," sung in the opera by Frédéric. The merry lilt of this gay music was a thrilling contrast to the heavy scene just finished. Few people know that this Gavotte was originally part of the Overture and was only added as a song for the great French contralto Zélia Trebelli when she consented to assume the minor role of Frédéric.

While this little eighteenth-century Gavotte was played, I would have a quick change. At the end of it I appeared as Philine, complete in costume and powdered wig, and finished up the performance by singing the Polonaise. No better device could be imagined. Not only was the correct sequence of arias preserved, but the brilliant Polonaise made its best effect in this place, the last number on the program.

We were all delighted by the success of our undertaking, which was even greater than we had hoped for. And it was more of an undertaking, perhaps, than I had first bargained for as well. In the *Mignon* act, for instance, I had four minutes in which to change from my simple Mignon costume, a white blouse and brown skirt, into the elaborate costume of Philine, which meant shoes and stockings as well as the wig. I devised a costume which opened up at the back with a special arrangement of whalebones so that, once on, it snapped shut of its own accord; and a long train hanging from the shoulders would hide any gap that should appear. Tika stood on the stage with the theater dresser, to whom she handed these things, in correct sequence, for me to put on. As the last notes of the Gavotte died away I was always ready, staff in hand, for my entrance. My appearance, so wide a contrast to the simple, long-haired, barefoot Mignon of four minutes previous, invariably provoked wild and long applause. Thank God it did! As I stood waiting, serene and smiling, I was regaining my breath. The first words of Philine are recitative and come without any more introduction from the orchestra than a chord, and I had to begin at once: "Oui, pour ce soir je suis reine!" How many times I did that—and there was never a contretemps!

We gave several performances in Batavia, and the great success was not only encouraging but also gratifying, as the people of Batavia were particularly musical. A considerable number of musicians came out to Batavia, but they were all either Dutch or German, so that my French concerts were entirely new for that part of the world. It was in Batavia that the great and beautiful American artist Lillian Nordica died under tragic circumstances in 1914.[66]

From here we sailed for Australia, making Perth our first stop. We repeated our programs of Batavia, augmenting our orchestra by three or four members, for whom Allpress had to create additional orchestral parts.[67] The people of Perth were so wrought up by our performances that the news was learned in Adelaide and Albany before we had reached there. It was Bassett's habit to go ahead and make contact with a local manager, hiring the theater and putting out the placards and other advertising. In Adelaide we found the public eager to hear me, and I was given a great reception on the very day of our arrival. This was particularly curious, for aside from having read the press reports reprinted from the Perth papers, all these welcoming people—the mayor and the council—had no idea who in the world this Blanche Arral was who they were fêting.

In Adelaide we augmented our orchestra until it numbered forty musicians, and so Allpress's work became more severe than ever. I added *Faust* to our repertory, which had not been feasible with a smaller orchestra. It proved one of my most popular cameo operas. We were lucky enough to find a theater with the requisite scenery, and for *Faust* we needed two sets. First there was the Garden Scene. I came out in the traditional Marguerite dress to sing the beautiful spinning song, the Ballad of the King of Thulé. As in the opera, this was followed at once by the Jewel Song, that brilliant and eternally popular aria, which I not only sang but also enacted. Kneeling before the casket of jewels, which had been hidden on the stage beforehand, I put on the diamond earrings of tradition and rose in the middle of the song, ending with the mirror in my hand, bowing to my own reflection so as to make the jewels glitter with all the excitement of a lightheaded young girl. The curtain fell, rising again on a darkened prison scene, for which I had only to loosen my hair, letting it fall disheveled about my shoulders, over a long white gown that hid my other costume.

I do not know what people will think of my next move, unless they take into consideration the lack of opera in the Antipodes: I sang the entire prison scene all alone! In my opinion it is the finest music in the opera, for here Gounod really rises to dramatic heights. I sang the scene of the fair, in which the demented Marguerite imagines herself back at the *kermesse* the day she met Faust; and I sang Faust's music too, changing my voice to a darker tone to contrast with Marguerite herself. When the final trio began, the orchestra rose to fortissimo and I sang Marguerite's wild pleading to the angels to save her, with all the power and passion in me. Even now, when I think of it my eyes fill with involuntary tears! No other music has the power to move me like that. On my knees

I invoked the angels, arms outstretched, palms toward me, as though to summon the audience to rise with me to the heavens.

"Anges purs! Anges radieux!"

As my voice rose by half tones at the repetitions of the motif, I gradually rose with it, clasping my hands together only at the last repetition. Never did this fail to stir the hearers, and as I fell to the ground at the last note and the curtain descended, the applause was truly thunderous. People stood up on their seats, crying, waving their handkerchiefs, wrought to a pitch of enthusiasm I had never believed possible. No matter how many times the curtain rose and fell to their response, I lay inert on the stage, for I could not break the effect I had produced. And the emotion of the audience was never greater than mine! How anyone could ever sing that scene and remain unmoved, I confess I do not understand. Alas, it was beyond the scope of the Blanche Arral Opera Company to present the apotheosis.

I may add that in this part of the world French was very little spoken or understood, so that in the arrangements I was forced to make to carry the music without obvious breaks, when I sang words in the character of someone else, few were wiser. For *Carmen* we began with the third-act prelude by the orchestra, and then I appeared as Micaëla and sang the first-act duet with Don José, "Un baiser de ma mère!", singing most of both parts. The stage was plunged in darkness as I delivered Micaëla's grand air from the third act. This long aria (which whether sung well or poorly always delights an audience) requires a passionate, convincing, and prayerful delivery, or fails of its particular message. Coming directly after the simple, sentimental music of the duet with Don José, the aria benefited by the contrast in moods, and upon the fateful notes of "Protégez moi Seigneur!" the curtain fell. At once the orchestra took up the introduction to *Carmen*, so eternally young and thrilling, while I changed into my Carmen costume. With the stage brilliantly lighted, Carmen appeared and sang the Habanera and the Séguidilla, as well as the dance "Dragon d'Alcala." I remember one critic found fault with the fact that I did not wear a Spanish shawl like Calvé, but mine was the traditional costume of the Opéra-Comique. Mérimée's story takes place in 1820; Bizet set it to music in 1875, before shawls were worn in Spain. Therefore, though it may be correct to wear a shawl (and Elena Sanz, a Spaniard, did so before Calvé), I had authority to wear the bolero jacket of the original Carmen, Galli-Marié.

One problem that confronted us in Adelaide was that though there were many theaters, all were occupied with either legitimate attractions or vaudeville. And where were we without a theater? If this could happen in Adelaide it could happen in other places. Through our local manager I got hold of the name of a little Italian scenepainter and sent for him.

"How long will it take you to paint six backdrops?" I said. I told him what we needed: two gardens (for a change), a square in Seville, a tropical forest (for Lakmé), a prison (for Marguerite), and a palace room. The little Italian set to work with his assistants and painted my drops in a few days. They were constructed on solid screens with rollers so they could be put up in town halls, assembly rooms, barns, or any other place we could rent to perform in that might not have a bridge or any facilities for suspending scenery from above as was usual. One scene was painted on each side of these screens to save space and hauling charges, and with a few moveable pieces—trees, fountains, statuary—to vary the monotony from time to time, wonders could be accomplished. When delivered, the finished sets were a trifle of a shock, so utterly Italian were they. The grass was too green, the sky was too blue, and the clouds were too white, like great puff pastes floating in bluing, all in the familiar style of frescoes in small Italian restaurants. Nevertheless, they worked; the vivid colors were gay and theatrical in their effect. I have even seen sets at the Metropolitan that I suspected of coming from Adelaide.

Then there was the question of a curtain, for where there was no scenery there would be no curtain either, and how then could the changes be made? My Italian devised for me a complete proscenium arch, and we went shopping and bought yards of rich red plush—what color more suggests a theater? My curtains, when finished, were rich and simple, their only decoration being great gold tassels; they were theatrical and at the same time dignified, no "Blanche Arral" in tinsel embroidery stretching across them. Two men traveled with us to work all these things—as did a man for lighting, for I likewise provided myself with electrical equipment.

Thus, all complete and ready to give our performances, we were haughtily independent of theaters—and that was a good, good thing.

Until now I had been limited by the lack of a good harpist, but I found one in Melbourne in the person of a little Italian named Torzillo, who played in the orchestra in one of the theaters. After one audition I engaged him to join our troupe as soloist, for he was well worthy of that station. Heretofore Paanz had been obliged to supply harp obbligatos with his violin, such as the important one in the Swallow Duet in *Mignon*. The harpist proved a real find. Later an Australian named Conway, who played the French horn, also became a member of the company. The French horn was unknown everywhere we went, but for rendering French scores it was a prime necessity.

We moved on to Melbourne, and here I was much helped by Elise Wiedermann, who conducted a school of singing there.[68] She was the first to sing Carmen in Germany and had authored a very good treatise on the technique of singing. She at once became my champion, taking me under her wing, as it were, leaving no stone unturned in giving me advice regarding local conditions and supporting my desire to be recognized amongst the musical people of Melbourne. She also arranged for my appearance at a symphony concert, at which I sang several selections. This served as a splendid public introduction, and when we announced the first "operatic concert" at the Princess Theater, booking was heavy— so heavy in fact that three performances sold out in rapid succession, at the last of which the very walls were thick with people. I forebear from quoting at length any of the reviews I received, but they were quite frenzied. The lights had to be turned out before we could induce the people to leave at the end of every performance, and they blocked the streets to cheer as I drove away. What days those were! And how Bassett and I congratulated ourselves on the unprecedented frenzy! My operatic concerts were hard work, but worth it in every way. Singing to me is like drinking absinthe to some—once begun I cannot stop. Anything that makes me sing a *lot* is so much the better.

Melbourne was really wrought up over the whole affair, and people naturally began to ask each other, "Who the devil *is* Blanche Arral? Why have we never heard of her?" It soon became apparent that my name must be a *nom de guerre*, and then all sorts of entertaining stories were devised as to the reasons for my incognito. "Blanche Arral—has she a double?" queried one paper when we reached New Zealand, printing a picture of me and one of Calvé as Santuzza, which had a superficial similarity. But even more diverting was my portrait coupled with that of "Princess Alexandra von Ysenburg Dudingen." The portrait of this mysterious lady bore a legend beneath as follows: "It is alleged that it was the princess's fad to buy old castles and furnish them on credit, which has led to her imprisonment for debt at Arbon. She was liberated on the intervention of her relatives, *and has now disappeared.*" Could I be this princess whose unfortunate extravagances had brought grief to her and embarrassment to her relatives? Was I now singing in order to pay up on all those old castles in Europe? I almost wondered myself!

25

Now launched upon our Grand Tour, we proceeded to Sydney and opened there in the Town Hall on 14 September 1906. Here the scenery and proscenium came into good use, Bassett having heralded in advance the fact of the Town Hall's transformation into a theater. What is more, the fact that all our décors had been made in Australia, as well as all the posters and photographs we used in advertising, was commented upon in the papers as a noteworthy piece of information, and this prejudiced the Australians in my favor. An artist must not forget when visiting a foreign country professionally that he is taking money out of it, and in a place like Australia (in the early 1900s) this was not altogether a popular thing to do.

While in Sydney I lost no time in visiting the zoo, which, with Antwerp, is the most famous in the world in the business of raising, exchanging, and selling animals to all countries. As I was walking among the monkey cages, a baboon suddenly began to raise a clamor, stretching out his hand and trying to grab me by the dress. When I observed him more carefully, what should I see but a gleaming gold tooth! My own Baron—in a zoo! I was horrified. Rushing to the keeper's house, the first thing I saw was a Siamese cat sleeping on a chair. Yes, my suspicions were confirmed. The horse-breeding Australian had sold my baboons and cats to the zoo the moment he reached Australia. The best I could do was call upon Baron every day I was in Sydney.

We gave five performances in Sydney between the fourteenth of September and the first of October. On the thirteenth we were back at the Princess Theater in Melbourne, where we gave four full-length performances in seven days, with the theater full at each performance and crowds turned away. If my name suggested no past, by now it suggested a present, and from all over Australia and New Zealand we were receiving offers and requests to appear. The next engagement we filled was a return to Adelaide. Here we were forced to give six performances, after which we gave one performance each in Ballart, on the way to the gold mines, and in Bendigo. From there we sailed for Dunedin, New Zealand, where we gave three full performances in five days.

For the sake of the record, then, we performed twice in Christchurch, four times in Wellington over ten days, and four times in Auckland over a week. At Wellington it was somewhat difficult to get a full house, as the public did not seem to be impressed with the notices from Melbourne. But those who did come came again, bringing more with them. Frankly, I must say I do not know how I accomplished such work—or rather, I do, and it was because I had Alfred Cabel to place my voice and Mathilde Marchesi to finish its training. Without these two teachers my voice could never have stood the strain of those performances. Bassett timed the productions and found that often I was on the stage two hours and forty-two minutes in an evening. This meant I was not only singing all that time but also carrying the whole performance on my shoulders without a moment's rest or relaxation. The *New Zealand Graphic* observed, "Her versatility is nothing less than amazing, and her 'staying power,' if one may so put it, is beyond conception. Numbers of the most intricate difficulty succeed each other till it seems as if no mortal voice could stand so terrific a strain, and tiring is not in her vocabulary. It is an absolute fact that after a program including some dozen world-famous operatic solos and concluding with the Polacca from *Mignon,* Madame seems if anything in finer voice than at the beginning of the program. . . . She worked the audience into a passion of enthusiasm such as in thirty years of theatergoing in all parts of the world the writer has seldom seen excelled."

From Auckland we returned by request to Wellington and gave three performances in six days. This time it was a very different story. The mayor welcomed us to the city at a large reception, where less than a month before half the house had been empty. The enthusiasm of the audiences was as great as any we had experienced.

Then on to Christchurch, with three performances in a week.

Our work kept us hurrying from town to town. In some towns musicians were plentiful, in others scarce. At several places special trains were put on to accommodate the public from as far as two hours away, and almost everywhere the houses were packed. Then we returned, playing Dunedin again twice, Nelson, Napier, and other towns—in all, more than forty-five concerts.

But let it not be supposed that all was roses, roses. Though Bassett was my manager, he was young, and sometimes our relations were more like those of mother and child. As for poor Paanz, that talented violinist, drink was his curse. Every possible device was tried to keep him sober, and before a concert I used to pay someone to watch outside his door all night. Refusing to give him his money, I would tell him that I was depositing it in a Melbourne bank. At these times he would weep like a child and blame himself for his weakness. Yet he was always able to find the money for a bottle, somewhere and somehow. Had I ever realized what trouble, anxiety, and despair that violinist was to cause me I never would have engaged him. Once engaged, however, I could not very well let him go, and so I had to put up with the worst to avoid talk, scandal, or other unpleasantness.

Though I had a manager, I felt that at the last I was really responsible for the whole company. One never can tell what men will do! Naïve and charming as children, they are off when most needed and usually return with some beautiful tale. At one place Bassett and Paanz went off into the town while our ship stopped to load coal. Frantically I waited, watch in hand. The ship was to sail at noon. Noon came and no Bassett, no Paanz. I begged the captain to wait but he said it was impossible. He sounded the ship siren, but as far as we could see up the long road there was not a living soul. With what I had on my mind, and with the long programs I had to sing or rehearse every day, it's a wonder I kept my reason! Arguing and disputing with the captain, the wretched vagrants finally appeared, smiles and charm, with a pearl brooch for me, which, so they declared, they had been having set by a native jeweler all morning!

Then there was a good deal of trouble here and there with managers and theaters.

On one of my return seasons in Melbourne an amusing situation developed. I had engaged the Town Hall long in advance, and the placards had long been up in the streets. On these placards were printed the complete programs I was to offer at the various performances. At this moment, the great Melba appeared on the scene. She too wanted the Town Hall for her concert, but it was booked, and had been long in advance, by the little girl whom she had advised to eat soup to grow up and to learn not to be impertinent. So Melba had to sing in another hall. But that was not all. Her program too was announced, and it was a coincidence to say the least when everyone observed that she was singing much the same program that I had announced months before. I was down to sing the "Cours-la-reine" scene from *Manon*, the Mad Scene from *Hamlet*, and "Ah fors' è lui" from *La traviata*. And these same three numbers Melba elected to sing too, that night.

But Melba blundered here badly. Since my program had been announced so long in advance, everyone saw at once what was occurring and it developed into a sort of holy war. Evidently Melba had been known to do other things of the sort before, for everyone crowded to my concert and Melba had a half-empty house. The next day the papers (they too were aware of the comedy) gave my concert a long review at the top of the page. Underneath it a news item began, "The enthusiasm expressed inside the Town Hall last night developed outside into a notable display of friendly fervor," continuing for twelve more lines to describe the ovation in the streets, the flowers that were hung on my horse's harness, and so forth. Under this was a short line, and then came the interesting caption: "Madame Melba's Concert." For so great an artist as Melba, for a woman with such worldwide position in music, to stoop to such undignified and petty behavior was a curious thing. It seems she was well known for such little games.[69]

As it turned out, Melba thought she owned the continent. Still, others came out from time to time, and during the two years I was singing there a Frenchwoman who went under the name of Dolores enjoyed a vogue. Though she had an unimportant voice which she did not use with any particular skill, she had succeeded in building up a following and, what is most important, a "press." She sang ballads and light songs, but her tour de force was "L'éclat de rire" from *Manon Lescaut*; though not her sort of music at all (surely a paradox for anyone such as Dolores to attempt), she had great success with the hysterical little song from Auber's opera. It was Dolores this and Dolores that in all the music chatter. She traveled with a woman companion from whom she was inseparable, and she had launched herself through the medium of the clergy in a clever manner. The most interesting thing about her was that she was the daughter of Zélia Trebelli, whose name will surely always live in the annals of song. Dolores had been estranged from her illustrious mother. Later she bought some long-haired Australian sheep and took them back to France, hoping, as I understood, to raise them commercially. But I doubt if the sheep enjoyed the French climate.[70]

In 1907 a truly great soprano toured Australia, the Canadian Emma Albani. Unfortunately, Madame Albani should have arrived a few years earlier, when her great abilities as a vocalist would have been appreciated to the degree their merits deserved. Albani was one of the most finished singers of her time, her legato and her portamento effects remarkable and unique. Indeed, I never heard anyone who could so leave a note floating in midair, an echo of itself, spinning it out like a spider's silver thread to the point of incredulity. And she preserved this gift over a long period, even after her voice was far past its prime.[71]

Melba's manager wanted to become mine as well and offered me another tour for the next year, but he said I would have to cut down on expenses. Though I felt it politic to be on the best terms possible with such people, I shrewdly suspected what was afoot with this proposition. While I was touring Australia other singers were at a great disadvantage—I say this though it sounds dreadfully self-satisfied, but I certainly was the only one who put on a *real show*, in the language of the theater. I usually had a good orchestra, but others only a piano. I had scenery and costumes, and I acted as well as sang, so that my audiences would have a good impression of the selected numbers as they would appear in the authentic context—rather than treating operatic selections as though disconnected songs, complete in themselves, and designed for the parlor or the concert platform. As Marguerite I had the jewels and went through all the business, and my critics became so educated to my point of view that the lack of a spinning wheel for the Ballad of the King of Thulé was regretted! Give them an inch and they want a yard. But in truth the absence of the spinning wheel was due to the exigencies of the day: spinning wheels were not available in the nearest shop. In fact we went hunting for some time before the sight of a spinning wheel in a curiosity shop in Melbourne gladdened our eyes and rewarded our search. It promptly joined the company.

Melba's manager, I believe, wanted to get me under his thumb and then break me. But having once given my audience so much more than other singers, how could I go back on my established precedent and become stingy? Besides, I hated to sing—I *couldn't* sing—without acting. One critic observed that when I sang the Shadow Song from *Dinorah* at a symphony concert it seemed almost more than I could do to not give the dance as well! And so I said no to the proposal. Thus an enemy was made.

Early in 1908 we went to Tasmania, performing in Hobart, Launceston, and other places, and returned for a final season in Melbourne, Sydney, and Adelaide. I had traveled enough, having been away from home for six years, and wanted to return to Belgium. Instead of the two months we had planned for Australia and New Zealand, we had been touring, retracing our steps and setting out again, for eighteen before I finally left the continent.

In the cities the crowds now had to be kept in check by the police. In Melbourne over five thousand people were crowded into the Town Hall, while many more blocked the streets, hung onto telegraph poles, and climbed over the building itself in order to catch some of the strains of music that floated out on the still Australian air. The peculiar tenacity of those with English blood was evidenced by the crowds which would wait even in the rain outside the stage entrance, no matter how long it was before I came out, to offer their small bouquets of wildflowers, their applause and cheers. Those small bouquets were surely the most touching of any I received. The more hearty and unrestrained elements in these crowds used to purloin, I regret to say, bouquets out of the two carriages that followed mine, usually sending me by mail the next day the cards they found in them.

Finally, in May 1908, the time to leave Australia arrived. As the ship steamed slowly out of lovely Sydney Harbor, my thoughts were mixed indeed. In no other country of the many I had visited had I been more cordially received by the public, and now I was leaving, perhaps forever. It had been a busy and successful two years since we began the operatic concerts, and six years since I had left home, but as I left Sydney I suffered from acute homesickness. People laugh when singers tell them of a wish for a home and family, not believing a word of it. But I was genuinely lonely, and Belgium was still half a world away. It is fine to be successful, admired, and applauded, but surely this cannot satisfy forever when one is a wanderer on the face of the earth.

It was my plan to give a concert in San Francisco and perhaps New York, and then to rejoin my family in Brussels. However, between San Francisco and Australia there are interesting places to visit, and we stopped first at Suva in the Fiji Islands. My arrival had been announced in advance, and the official people of Suva were at the dock as our ship came in. Among others present, we met a young American. He was tall and good looking, of a type often associated with Americans but not so frequently seen. His whole manner breathed the outdoors—in fact, the wide forests. Bassett, I could see, was delighted at the acquaintance, for the man was Jack London, then at the pinnacle of his fame and the *beau idéale* of many young Americans. He and his wife were equally charming. An event shortly after ripened our acquaintance into real friendship.

I gave a concert at the Town Hall, and there was a reception by the governor-general. Almost best of all, there were no mosquitoes! Another concert was announced, but at the second one I was not destined to sing.

I was still very tired from my protracted work, and one afternoon I went to my room intending to have a good rest before dinner. My eyes ached. As I lay on the bed I told my maid, now an Englishwoman of *incertain âge* whom I had acquired in Australia, to bring me the small bottle of eyedrops from the dressing table. Beside the bottle stood another one, containing creosote for inhalation against colds in the head. The bottles looked something alike, though they were well marked. As I lay on the bed with the eyedropper poised and my eye open, I suddenly caught the familiar smell of creosote—too late. The drop fell. How can I describe the result? I shot up from the bed as though a bomb had burst below me. My shrieks echoed all over the little wooden hotel, and the first of the many people who crowded into my room were Jack London and his wife. To Jack London I owe the saving of my left eye. While others remained helpless and the poor maid threatened suicide (which served no purpose at all), he seized a bottle of castor oil and poured it over my eye, which was already swollen to the size and color of a hard-boiled egg and almost entirely out of its socket. I cannot paint the agony of such an accident to the eye, though one may imagine it. However, the castor oil began at once to reduce the swelling and ease the pain. My eye was covered for weeks, and I left Suva without knowing whether I was half blind or not.

But out of ill comes good, and I developed a warm friendship with that talented man and his altogether lovely wife. I could not accept their invitation to proceed with them on their yacht for a voyage of exploration in the Pacific—though how I regretted the fact! Jack London died not long afterward at the height of his success as a writer. He had wanted to write the story of my life. What a book he would have made of it![72]

By the time I reached Honolulu I found my eye was sound and whole, and the benediction on that discovery was the beauty of that island of flowers. It was a month before I could face the dismal thought of leaving. I abandoned my carriage for the open electric trams, which were a novelty then, and spent the days driving through the avenues of flowers— one entirely pink, one white, one yellow, one rose. Not one green leaf, just trees covered with blossoms. And I had two eyes to see all this with.

The Hawaiians, as everyone knows, are musicians, and it was pure joy to sing with the natives, accompanied by their fascinating guitars. An American theatrical company was in Honolulu. I gave two concerts at the Hawaiian Opera House, with an orchestra augmented by native musicians, before I could summon the courage to leave this garden of the Pacific.

We reached San Francisco in the autumn, and of course I was more than ever determined to sing there too. Bassett searched about and found a local manager, Will Greenbaum, who was at this time the theatrical czar of the city. Greenbaum offered me a concert engagement. I stipulated a full orchestra and a first-class theater instead of a concert hall, impressing upon him that my appearance could not be termed a recital or even a concert: it was an operatic performance in miniature. He finally consented to this novel departure, though like many he found it difficult to accept something new; and other singers had been content to sing two arias and a few songs. I made my debut in my own way at the Van Ness Theater on 11 October 1908. Steindorff conducted; Allpress, Paanz, and Torzillo were no longer with me.[73]

Perhaps because San Francisco so delighted me and I was so happy to be singing there, I pleased the San Franciscans in return. From the first, something electric sprang up between the audience and myself: we were friends at once. What warmhearted, generous people filled the Van Ness Theater to hear a completely unknown singer! And how they welcomed me, privately as well as publicly, to San Francisco! Nowhere in all my wanderings have I ever been so kindly treated and taken into people's homes with such warm affection, not as a visiting professional performer but as a personal friend. In particular I shall never forget Mr. and Mrs. Meyerfield and all they did for me, a stranger. They took me not only to receptions, teas, and dinners but also on long drives along the scenic coast and around the Golden Gate, on excursions into the mountains, through the city, and into Chinatown. Here on one occasion I was recognized by a Chinese tong dining in a restaurant, and the demand was raised in chorus: "A song! A song!" Good heavens, what could I sing them, with not even a piano? I never cared to sing on the spur of the moment, unprepared, and they finally let me go.

Luisa Tetrazzini had made her debut in San Francisco the year before. Arriving with a small and insignificant Italian company from the wilds of South America, she took San Francisco by storm, and her name has been known throughout the world ever since.[74] It was known that while in San Francisco she delighted in going to little Italian restaurants and singing there, eating the good Italian food, and being surrounded by her adoring compatriots, even if of humble station. Seeing this, her manager arranged a very clever publicity stunt. He had her dress like a peasant and go into the Italian market with a cart of oranges and lemons, where she would sing with that wonderful ease and simplicity of vocalization which is innate among the Italians, and which she possessed in so superlative a degree.

It had been my habit ever since I began my Australian tours to take a house or villa wherever possible rather than go to a hotel. One is far from free in hotels, where people spy and pry. Worse still, I could not practice there without being heard, and nobody likes to listen to vocalises. Besides this, I liked to have my manager and soloists under my thumb. They could not so easily go off when most needed, and we could rehearse quietly and untroubled whenever necessary. People do not understand artists or musicians, and have no idea at all of the tremendous work of presenting such programs as what we gave. For them all that counts is the concert, the singing, the playing, the flowers, and applause. What do they know of the daily practice, the long rehearsals with and without the orchestra, the arranging and planning of new music and new programs, the changing of costumes and makeup, the continual business details that filled my life to the exclusion of pleasure, rest, and recreation?

The San Francisco earthquake was only two years in the past, and though the city had been rebuilt with wonderful speed there was still a housing problem. I took an apartment overlooking the city, while Bassett had rooms on the floor above. After I got home from a concert I used to send the maid away, and this was my favorite hour of the day. Coming home after a performance, gloriously alone, it had long been a habit of mine to take a good bath and then, enveloped in a long and heavy peignoir, to let my hair down my back comfortably, sit there in the stillness, and live over again the performance just finished. At such times I was too wrought up to sleep, my mind especially clear and alert. I would think through the performance, its defects as well as its virtues—I must remember to tell the conductor not to play that section too loudly, I can find a better way of phrasing that passage, I can be more effective in acting that scene. These silent communions often lasted until two or three o'clock in the morning.

It grew bitterly cold at night in San Francisco at that time of the year. The apartment house had not yet been completely finished, though there were already a number of tenants, and the heat and the hot water were turned off early. I had a small alcohol stove which traveled with me everywhere, and that night I lit it and sat cross-legged like an Indian in front of it on the floor, my hair down my back, comfortably going over the finished performance.

Suddenly, without reason or warning, the stove exploded. Burning alcohol was dashed in my face, on my head, and over my robe. With a scream I leapt to my feet, flung open the door, cried for help, and then had presence of mind enough to fling myself down on the bed and bury myself in the heavy blanket upon it.

People soon came rushing from various apartments nearby. And the last thing I heard before fainting was the cry, "Lard! Lard!"

When the doctor finally arrived he said he could have treated me no better himself, but he called for flour and covered my face, neck, and shoulders with it as well. Though my peignoir had fortunately prevented further burns, I had had a narrow escape. The first rescuers on the scene had not only to tend to me but also to put out the fire, which was already spreading to the rugs and curtains.

The next morning I sent for Mrs. Meyerfield, as I knew that kind-hearted woman would want me to do so. When news of the accident was published in the papers, people whom I did not know, people who had merely heard me sing, began coming in such large numbers to the house that the police had to be summoned to keep them in check. And Mrs. Meyerfield did everything humanly possible for me. She held a consultation with all the specialists in San Francisco, though no more could be done than had been done already. The lard and the flour had entered the raw, burned flesh on my face, and heavy scabs formed that only little by little fell away. All my hair, of which I had been proud, was gone, burned away, as were my eyebrows and lashes. And my next concert was two weeks off.

When Greenbaum heard the news he came raging and bursting through the door. He was ruined and I was ruined—a full house was waiting to hear me sing! With a long delay the impetus of my first appearance would be lost. My misfortune was completely forgotten in his own, and as his stampedes were only making me more ill, the doctors turned him bodily out of the room and forbade his return.

But I thought to myself: two weeks off—surely I can sing in two weeks.

Worse than my burns, worse than the injury to my scalp above the forehead where my hair would never grow again, seemed the fact that I could not open my mouth more than half an inch. The burns on my lips, at the corners of my mouth, were so severe that I could hardly even drink. How could I hope to sing?

As I lay in bed an idea came to me. Finally, against all advice, I declared that I would go to a rehearsal. I had a mask made of thin muslin, with holes for my eyes, nose, and mouth. On the inside of this I would spread a salve made with cocaine, so that my face would be insensible and I could open my mouth without feeling pain.

I drove to the theater and walked out on the stage in that ludicrous mask. My voice was there; if only I could manage to open my mouth, I knew I could sing.

But no music came from the orchestra, and I saw that the musicians had put down their instruments. Many of them were in tears. They believed that Greenbaum had forced me to sing, and at the risk of their jobs these men refused to play. "My good friends," I said, so touched I could hardly find the few necessary English words, "I am here because I *want* to sing. Please play for me!"

The night of the concert every seat was sold and the standees were as thick as the law allowed. I had two doctors backstage, and just before I went on they painted my entire face with cocaine. I walked onto the same stage where a few weeks before I thought I had received an unprecedented welcome, but tonight men stood on their chairs shouting my name, women waved their handkerchiefs, and the whole house was in a state of hysteria. Ah, what a wonderful thing, what a great consolation for my misfortune, to see a city, a foreign city where I had been unheard of a few weeks before, show me, a stranger, its wonderful warm sympathetic heart! It was worth anything.

I stood there and let my hands fall to my sides. How could I sing? How can anyone sing when she is weeping?

For fifteen minutes that noise continued. If ever I make an effort in my life, I thought, I will make one now. At last I signaled Steindorff, and the orchestra began Gounod's majestic air, "Plus grand dans son obscurité!" Music exerted its ever-powerful magic almost at once. When I heard my voice pour out, I knew I was saved. I never sang in my life as I sang that night.

⟿ 26 ⟾

ALTHOUGH I did not realize it then, America was destined to be my home, a permanent home after years of wandering in far places. Yet I yearned to see my family in Belgium after such a long absence. After four more recitals on the Pacific coast in quick succession, I entrained for New York to take ship for Europe and repose. The loss of a trunk containing many of my most valued possessions (important documents and souvenirs of my triumphs, for the most part) delayed me in New York.

During this interval (March 1909) I was approached by a representative of the Victor Talking Machine Company and offered a contract to make Red Seal records of some of my most successful arias.

This was not my first experience in recording, however. Several years before (in 1898), when passing through New York on my return from the season with the ill-fated opera company in Costa Rica, I had met Lieutenant Gianni Bettini, a pioneer in the development of the phonograph, and made for him a series of about fifty cylinder records under my family name of Clara Lardinois. Not long afterward he became involved in patent lawsuits and closed his business. He was to have sent me a set of the records, but I never received them, and so far as I know no copies exist today. I had completely forgotten these recordings until some forty years later when I was shown one of the very rare existing catalogues of the Bettini Records.[75]

I also worked with Mr. Thomas A. Edison in his private laboratory while he was making a study of voices in which he could find organic perfection. I never understood fully the nature of his studies, but Mr.

Meadowcroft, his intimate friend and secretary, explained exactly what was expected of me. Though Edison was very deaf and seemed unable to hear voices even when raised, he could understand Mr. Meadowcroft, who spoke in a low natural tone.[76]

I sang scales of sustained tones, sometimes chromatic scales, or short arpeggios of one or two octaves. Mr. Edison had a small apparatus in his ear and kept in front of him a book in which were written the exercises I sang. Under each, as I sang it, he made a pencil mark. He had evidently made these experiments with other singers, for one day he showed me pages similarly marked and laughed as he pointed to a line.

Mr. Meadowcroft told me that Mr. Edison found my voice almost without fault, a very rare phenomenon.

When we began our seances Mr. Edison had before him the records I had previously made for his company. I told him these were not my first Edison records. He seemed surprised, and I explained that when I was a little girl my family took me to the Brussels Fair, and in a certain booth we discovered a curious machine into which one spoke and sang a few words, after which a sort of tin foil came out with scratches engraved upon it. When put back in the machine and the crank turned, out came one's voice—strangely distorted, but still one's voice. The man in charge snipped off the tin foil with a large pair of sheers and handed it to the speaker, though I cannot imagine for what purpose except to wrap around chocolates. Mr. Edison was delighted with this story and said I had spoken into the first machine he patented.

Our work halted abruptly when the laboratory was destroyed by fire. I was in Orange at the time, so close to the fire that we were forced to flee the heat of the flames. It was a great scientific disaster. I never saw Mr. Edison again, but Mr. Meadowcroft told me he had been so affected by the loss of his studies that he had wept, and for a long time he could not bring himself to take up his experiments with the phonograph again. Mr. Edison was as simple a man as he was a great genius. The cylinders I made for his company were a miracle of recording, with a limpidity altogether exceptional. I was told that he personally used them for demonstrations, particularly the Polonaise from *Mignon* and the Couplets du Mysoli from *The Pearl of Brazil*. Later I made flat disc records for another company and was thus able to judge the difference. In the Edison cylinders there was a three-dimensional quality which gave a feeling of air and space, and an admirable balance throughout the scale, even the highest notes being as pure and untinny as the lowest. Since the invention of the microphone, of course, the science of recording has undergone immense changes. However, Edison not only discovered the secret of imprisoning sound on wax but also raised it to a high degree of excellence. Sometimes he sat and played my records for me, and it was wonderful to note the double point of view in his admiration for his invention. He moved his hand, and often his arm and head as well, to illustrate his pleasure with cadenzas that were successfully recorded. Where some blast or blur might have been occasioned, his scientific interest was uppermost, but then some phrase in the music would particularly delight him and he would forget for a moment everything but the music. Still, the scientist always triumphed!

I had been delayed in New York for some time. Finally giving up hope of recovering my lost trunk, I sailed for Antwerp and home, looking forward to a long rest.

How hard it is to repose after a life of activity! I was urged to give a recital in the city of my birth and childhood, Liège, and of course I was proud to do so. Who has ever gone out into the world and won fame and glory without wishing for the acclaim and applause of the folks back home? This was the crown of my career, for the Liègeois are proud of their own.

A month later I was in England, invited by Colonel Mapleson, the famous impresario, to give two concerts under royal patronage at London's Steinway Hall. But I returned quickly to Belgium, for the years of travel, irregular diet, and nervous strain were taking their toll and I found myself on the verge of a breakdown. The following summer and fall I spent with my family at Ostend and Brussels, and then felt the call to America. I returned to New York and sang at Carnegie and Aeolian Halls, followed by a tour that included St. Louis, Memphis, Jacksonville, and New Orleans, after which I returned to Brussels.

A summons to Paris brought me the proud news that the French government had recognized my work in Paris and French Indochina by decorating me with the Palms of the Académie Française. This was my third decoration, the two previous having been the Order of Oldenburg presented to me by Nicholas, czar of Russia, and the Order of the Medjedieh from the khedive of Egypt. Later I was to receive the decoration of which I am proudest of all, the Order of Elizabeth of Belgium, proving that I have been "not without honor in my own country." I was able to express my gratitude for the French decoration within a month after I received it, for President Fallières of France was given an official reception by the king of the Belgians at Brussels and I was chosen as soloist on that occasion.

On my return to New York I resumed my musical connections. Plans were being developed for another American tour when suddenly I found myself in the midst of a commercial enterprise. It was the business of a Java tea which had had its beginnings in the East Indies years before.

When I had need of a maid, I liked, if possible, to find a native one wherever I happened to be, and while in Java I sought and finally engaged a native Javanese girl. Though these experiments were not always successful, they were at least interesting; and this time I had good cause to be thankful for my choice. The girl's father was some sort of medicine man or priest. As things are conducted there, one had to go to the father and pay him for the services of his daughter, undertaking to guard and care for her and to return her, when she was no longer needed, in the same condition as that in which she had been delivered. It was like hiring a piano.

The girl was faithful, pleasant, and a good worker. One day she said she wanted to go home for a visit. I was suffering from headaches and indigestion, as is little wonder in those hot climates, and I let the girl go, thinking that was the end of her. Much to my surprise, however, she came back, bringing with her a box of herbs from her father with the message that if I would brew myself a tea from them every day I would soon be cured. Of course, I tried a cup at once. It was pleasant and I tried it again. Within a few days, to my amazement, I felt perfectly well.

When I went to Brussels with a bad breakdown after my first New York recitals, the doctors had a hard time building me up. Finally, with their consent, I began taking the old priest's tea, of which I still had a small store. Three months later, when I returned to sing at the Aeolian Hall in New York, I was thirty-four pounds lighter and had never felt better in my life. The papers commented on this strange and miraculous change, printing my portrait "before" and "after." What had happened? I needed a second secretary to answer all the inquiries I received asking what I had done. And my New York manager said, quite sensibly, "You have a good business there!"

Well, I never intended to go into business, but I did. A contractor put my tea on the market and I supplied the herbs, which I imported from Java. The contractor paid me for the use of my name as well. Madame Nordica had gone into the bath-salt reducing business, so I knew my venture was not *lèse-majesté*. But soon the contractor died and the business fell into my own hands.

By the time the United States entered the First World War, I was married to an American, a new contractor had taken over my tea business, and I was able to give much of my time to singing at Liberty Loan drives and army camps.

The years have passed. Now I live in retirement in my home in New Jersey, enjoying the mellow glow of the setting sun. Occasionally over the radio my ears are struck by the lively notes of the overture I most often used to open my concerts with, the vivacious *Merry Wives of Windsor*, or I hear the opening bars of the Polonaise from *Mignon*. Like a flash I am back in my dressing room, nervous and tense, eager to step out onto the stage to hear the initial burst of applause and once again mark a bravura step in my passage through this life.

Singing Then and Now

Often when listening to young girls with good voices it is all I can do not to rush up on the stage in my usual impulsive way and say, "Dear girl, stop! You have a good voice, you have great possibilities, but please, please listen to me! I can show you how to produce those notes that are now ruining your voice. If you go on like this, in five years you will be worse instead of better."

It is a sad fact that rising singers seem to be too content with themselves as they are, and do not suspect they could be better. They lack true ambition for the achievement of perfection, which can keep us working eagerly for a lifetime. One reason for this may be that approbation is more easily won now. A coast-to-coast hook-up on the radio does not have to depend on the things that count. And how can one opera appearance a year ever lead to greatness in a role? It is only constant repetition through the years, constant study and improvement, that can make one outstanding in any art, and make one realize the possibilities not only in one's work but also in one's self.

I had the great fortune in my formative years to listen to truly great singers daily. It is an interesting thing to compare the art of song as it was practiced then with singing as it exists today. The main thing that has changed, I think, is the method of emission taught now. Madame Marchesi, García, and other great teachers of the past began with the voice as it naturally existed. Every voice is different, which is the wonderful and glorious fact in song. Everyone except a mute has a voice, but only a few are suitable for singing. If the scale is built on what is already there, the beautiful, personal quality of the individual voice is retained. Those teachers found the natural quality of each voice and preserved it, so that what nature had begun was developed, polished, and equalized, not changed. That is why such voices lasted.

The pupils, finding art securely built on nature, grew confident as one never can be with artificiality. They gained authority because they were manifestly singing the right way. They felt at ease and were able to express their individuality in song. Authority is the great thing in singing. After all, one sings with one's mind. When that high B-flat comes you will be able to get it if you attack it with joy and authority—not if you are dreading its arrival throughout the passages that come before, and not if you stop, with eyes shut, to plunge into it like a swimmer who hates the icy water.

Madame Marie Miolan-Carvalho was a wonderful example for me. Her voice was so even, so clear. It floated out onto the air in one perfect phrase after another, till the listener only wanted to lie back with eyes shut and float off with those pure, soft, ravishing equal notes. And I only heard her in her decline.

Emma Nevada and Marie Van Zandt were other examples of art built on nature. Van Zandt's light, merry voice, with its curious trace of the exotic and its enchanting little accent, was saved from being too thin by sheer charm and naturalness. Nevada's voice was rounder, but her American accent did not have the charm of Van Zandt's, the perfect Lakmé.

I heard Christine Nilsson, the second Swedish Nightingale, at the Trocadéro in 1885—a tall, majestic woman with coils of blond hair and piercing cold blue eyes. No one ever sang the Mad Scene from *Hamlet* like Nilsson. The role was written for her. When in that long aria the haunting Danish folk melody, plaintive and solemn, sounded in Ophelia's brain, Nilsson sang those few bars with an authority, a tragic languor, beyond any power of words to describe. Will anyone ever equal her in that music?

In short, all must be built on nature. This would seem to be a truism, but in singing it seems frequently to be forgotten now.

Art such as poured from the throats of singers in my childhood and youth is seldom heard now, and what a tragic thing that it has vanished. Composers, writers, painters: their art is immortal; but a singer leaves only a name at best, a name and descriptions—how inadequate!—written by some who once heard him sing. The best singers are gone forever, for the phonographic record is but a poor semblance.

Adelina Patti ruled supreme through my early years, and as I was supposed to look like her, I was honored by the sobriquet of "the little Patti." Therefore, when I heard her in Brussels and Paris it was with a double interest. The memory of her incomparable voice still lingers with many. I lately met a colored woman whose great reminiscence was that she had paid two dollars and stood to hear Patti sing in St. Louis nearly forty years ago. Those were the best two dollars she had ever spent, for the pleasure they gave her lived vividly into the present. And the legend of Patti never will die. Hers was the epitome of effortless natural singing, the tone of her voice so exquisite and warm that no other singer ever approached it. She was the born singer par excellence, and it is said she never had a teacher.

A finer personality, however, was her unhappy sister, Carlotta. I heard Carlotta Patti sing in Paris when I was still a child. Except for some opera appearances in America at the beginning of her career, Carlotta, due to her lameness, confined herself to concerts. I still remember her sweet and heartwarming smile as she limped onto the stage to acknowledge the applause of the audience. What she sang, I cannot tell now, but something about her voice touched me strangely. Hers was a true coloratura voice, and she shone in very brilliant and intricate dazzling vocal feats. Any singer today with the voice and talent of Carlotta Patti would be a worldwide sensation, but in her time she was only another fine singer, the sister of Adelina Patti. Her life was made very hard for her by Adelina, the darling of her generation and several following ones, and Carlotta had to fight hard to achieve her position. She was a fine vocalist, however, and her later years were happy. She taught singing in Paris and died in 1889. Adelina never taught.

None of these singers was famous for anything but pure voice. Now operatic stars are expected to act, and most of them do. But lest it be said that one cannot expect both acting and singing, there is always the example of Pauline Lucca, the Viennese for whom Meyerbeer wrote the role of Sélika in *L'Africaine*. At one time Lucca was Patti's rival, and if Patti was uninteresting histrionically, Lucca is acknowledged to have been one of the finest of actresses. She was most famous as Sélika, Carmen, and in such elemental roles which require acting of a high order. Most singers feebly suggest by their actions the course of the plot. I remember my surprise when Madame Miolan-Carvalho, as the countess in *The Marriage of Figaro*, stepped straight out of her part when her big aria "Porgi amor" arrived, and then smilingly stepped back as if nothing had happened!

Each of these famous voices had a color which was peculiar to it. One voice might be said to be golden, another silver, one a brilliant vermilion, one a rich dark purple. There was a wide variety in texture, color, and tone, and I attribute all this to the method of emission of which I have spoken. This is not the place to become technical, but to my ears most of the young singers I hear now possess what we would have called in my youth *la voix blanche*. This means, as well as I can describe it, a voice lacking in musical ring, lacking overtones, as they are called now, in fact having very little true tone of any sort—colorless, flat, artificial, and far from the genuine article, the true natural quality, for few voices are naturally white.

For the honor of belonging to the Opéra-Comique, *pensionnaires* had to have a repertory of twenty-four roles. No tobacco company paid us sums to explain how, by smoking a certain brand of cigarette, we gained tremendous vigor and thereby preserved our voices from the strain of singing four times a year. Nobody thought we were under a strain if we sang four times a week and on the other days rehearsed. No newspaper reporter interviewed us on any subject at all. We worked hard because we enjoyed it. Applause and more work were our reward, and we knew that hisses would be the immediate reward of failure. Singers thrived on that life.

And now most people will probably express wonder when I write that, having begun my matrimonial ventures married to a Russian nobleman, I am ending them married to a man with intellectual tastes, one who possesses the stoical calm characteristic of New Englanders. This is the key of the mystery. I have seen many, indeed *most*, professional women begin their attempts at married life with members of their own profession, or else with cavemen—in either case a disaster. If they stay married they lose all interest in their art (if they ever had any) during the alarms and dramas of a too-turbulent domestic life. Or, if they are "lucky" enough to marry a title or something of the sort most desirable in the evening of their successes, their hard-won fortunes are soon dissipated, they are left with their eyes to cry with, and the tale ends there.

I think of the past with joy, and it is a matter of amazement to realize the wonderful life my voice has given me. In all the vicissitudes of the past it has preserved one continuity. My father opposed my singing, but I sang. I married and tried to give up my career, but widowhood forced me back to my earliest master: music. Companies were stranded, my theater destroyed, but singing mattered most.

Now I sing with my pupils, and illustrating my lessons has done much to preserve my voice. In these young voices I find a charm that leads from my earliest years in the garden at Liège, where I first awakened to the power of music through my sister Mélanie's singing, to the Opéra-Comique, to Russia, to all the places I have seen and, better yet, worked in, to the many fine and splendid people it has been my privilege to know, and to the happiness that comes to those who devote themselves to their art—be it painting, writing, composing, or the one art which brings the hush at the front of the house, the invigorating sound of the orchestra, and the bright, sudden glare of the footlights.

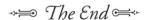 *The End*

Editor's Notes

1. Born 25 July 1889, George Wheeler was twenty-five years Arral's junior and would have been about forty-three at the time of Glackens's first visit. He died 9 October 1961.

2. Usually billed as Madame Pilar-Morin, Spanish actress and pantomimist Pilar Morin (dates not found) was internationally known for her performances in such "wordless plays" as *L'enfant prodigue* and *Pierrot the Prodigal*. She also appeared in vaudeville and silent films, including a 1910 version of *Carmen* called *The Cigarette Maker of Seville*.

3. A notation in the Edison files states that Victor paid her three hundred dollars per title.

4. Famed violinist Eugène Ysaÿe (1858–1931) was indeed a native of Liège, but his father and first teacher, Nicolas Ysaÿe (1826–1905), was a theater conductor, not a locksmith. Eugène Ysaÿe studied on scholarship at the Brussels Conservatory 1874–76, and it was undoubtedly during this period that he participated in the Lardinois family musicales.

5. At the Brussels Conservatory, Arral is said to have studied harmony with Belgian composer Auguste Dupont (1827–1890) and solfeggio with a Mademoiselle Tordeus.

6. Arral was misinformed about her teacher. He had been neither a "celebrated baritone"—that was Louis Cabel (1819–1884)—nor the husband of the still-living Marie Cabel (1827–1885)—that was Louis's brother, Georges Cabel (1822–1881). In fact, we have no proof Alfred Cabel was even related to that famous family of Belgian musicians.

7. During her lifetime, it was widely believed that Marie Van Zandt (1858–1919) had been born and raised on a Texas ranch. It would appear, however, in light of more recent investigation, that, rather less romantically, she probably entered the world via Willoughby Street in that much-abused borough of Brooklyn, New York.

8. Jennie Van Zandt (dates not found), *née* Blitz, made her New York debut in 1864 as Gilda in *Rigoletto*. When she reappeared there in 1871 it was as Madame Vanzini, the name under which, in the interim, she had sung abroad, including an 1867 engagement at La Scala.

9. During the period of which Arral writes, the Opéra-Comique was housed in the second of three theaters, all called the Salle Favart. It burned in 1887, by which time her brief career with the company was behind her.

10. Jules Danbé (1840–1905) was principal conductor at the Opéra-Comique 1877–98, where he led the premieres of *Manon* and *Lakmé*, among others, but not *Mignon*.

11. Whatever its origins, the Van Zandt affair occurred in late 1884. The singer withdrew for three months, only to provoke the riot of which Arral writes upon her reappearance in early 1885. Thereafter she pursued her career elsewhere, returning briefly to the Opéra-Comique in 1896. Two years later she married a Russian aristocrat (as had Arral in the interim) and retired.

12. German-born Mathilde Marchesi (1821–1913) had been a concert singer before turning to teaching in 1854. In 1881 she established a Paris studio where her many pupils eventually included Emma Calvé, Nellie Melba, Emma Eames, and Frances Alda. Her daughter, Blanche Marchesi (1863–1940), was also a singer and teacher. If Arral did indeed begin working with the elder Marchesi "nearly a year" before her debut, she would have come to her in early 1882. Arral is not mentioned in the memoirs of either mother or daughter.

13. Legendary Australian soprano Nellie Melba (1861–1931) was three years and five months Arral's senior. If in fact the incident occurred at a time when Melba "had but lately made her enormously successful debut in Brussels," we have problems. That debut was 13 October 1887, by which time Arral had long since abandoned the Opéra-Comique for the operetta stage. As for having heard Melba in *Hamlet* and *Faust* in Brussels, Melba did indeed sing Ophélie at La Monnaie in 1888, but she seems not to have sung Marguerite there or anywhere else prior to Paris in 1890. On the other hand, Arral would have had ample opportunity to sample the Marguerite of famed French soprano Emma

Calvé (1858–1942), who made her operatic debut in that role at La Monnaie 22 September 1881.

14. Exactly eight years Melba's junior and long (1892–1919) a pillar of the Paris Opéra, soprano Lucienne Bréval (1869–1935) was born Berthe Schilling in the Swiss village of Mannendorf, near Zürich. She and Melba did indeed sing, respectively, Chimène and the Infanta in two Metropolitan Opera performances of *Le Cid* in 1901, but Arral's memory is faulty regarding the *Salome* production. Bréval seems never to have sung Strauss's work, but she did portray the character in the one-act opera of the same name (also based on Oscar Wilde's play) by Antoine Mariotte, singing in both the Paris premiere (Théâtre de la Gaîté, 22 April 1910) and the Opéra premiere (2 July 1919). Surely it is one of these performances Arral is recalling.

15. It's easy to forgive Arral for wanting the world to think she began her career with an important part in a new work, but in fact her Opéra-Comique debut (8 December 1882) was as one of the three young Israelite girls in a revival of Etienne-Nicolas Méhul's *Joseph*, with Jules Danbé conducting a cast headed by Juliette Bilbaut-Vauchelet, Jean-Alexandre Talazac, and Arthur Cobalet. This was followed (13 March 1883) by a revival of Mozart's *Die Zauberflöte* in which she sang one of the three ladies. It was not until 18 June 1883 that she undertook the ingénue role of Anita in the premiere of *Le portrait*, a two-act *opéra comique* by Théodore de Lajarte (1826–1890), whose dozen or so stage works, mostly one-act curtain-raisers, seldom survived more than a few performances (this one reached twenty-eight). The libretto was by "Monsieur Laurencin" (Paul Aimé Chapelle) and Jules Adenis, with other roles entrusted to mezzo Esther Chevalier (the original Mercédès in *Carmen* and Javotte in *Manon*) and famed baritone Lucien Fugère.

16. Paris-born Cécile Merguillier (1861–1938), at the Opéra-Comique 1881–88, later made a number of recordings for Pathé and Edison, fifteen of which may be heard on Marston CD 52013-2, a 1998 issue shared with Emma Calvé.

17. A native of Marseilles, Marie Caroline Miolan-Carvalho (1827–1895) made her debut in 1849, married Léon Carvalho in 1853, and was Gounod's first Baucis, Mireille, and Juliette, as well as Marguerite, the role in which she bade farewell to the stage in 1885.

18. Belgian soprano Marie Heilbronn (1851–1886) sang *Manon* nearly ninety times at the Opéra-Comique in the two years between its premiere and her death at thirty-five. Perhaps it was because Arral was still a teenager that the older singer, then barely past thirty, struck her as "no longer in her youth."

19. Léon Carvalho (1825–1897) was approaching sixty at the time of the *Manon* premiere. After running the Théâtre Lyrique 1856–68, he served two terms as director of the Opéra-Comique, 1876–87 and 1891–97. Held responsible for the fire that destroyed the second Salle Favart in 1887, he was sentenced to prison but acquitted on appeal.

20. Fabled French actress Sarah Bernhardt (1844–1923) leased the Théâtre de la Porte Saint-Martin 1883–93, introducing Sardou's *La Tosca* and other plays on its stage. In 1912–13 she made a twenty-two-week Orpheum tour of the United States, ending with a May engagement at New York's Palace Theater, to which she returned for an additional three weeks in December 1917, playing (at age seventy-three) the eighteen-year-old Joan of Arc.

21. "Lardinois" does indeed appear on the original program in the small spoken role of the Maidservant, although the confused compiler of *Opera Premieres M–Z*, volume 14 of *The Mellen Opera Reference Index* (Lampeter, Wales: Edwin Mellen Press, 1992) inadvertently lists her twice, as Lardinois ("A Servant") and as Blanche Arral ("A Maid").

22. Jean-Henri-Arthur Cobalet (1855–1901) was born in the village of St. Cyprien and raised in nearby Bordeaux where he studied at the local conservatory and made his debut. At the Opéra-Comique 1881–91, he was in the premieres of *Lakmé* (Nilakantha), *Manon* (Count des Grieux), and *Le roi d'Ys* (title role), all with Bordeaux-born Jean-Alexandre Talazac (1851–1896) in the tenor leads. In 1890 he sang Alphonse in *La favorite* at Covent Garden (Shaw found the evening "terribly dreary") and later took the title roles in the French premieres of *Der fliegende Holländer* (Lille, 1893) and *Eugene Onegin* (Nice, 1895) before turning to teaching at the Paris Conservatory. In a quirk of fate, he and his great friend Talazac both died at forty-five.

23. Perhaps because she hadn't sung the work in fifty years, Arral's recollections of who's who in Hérold's *Le Pré aux Clercs* are confused. The story concerns two young couples—Nicette and Girot, Isabelle and Mergy—whose paths to the altar are smoothed by Queen Marguerite de Valois. The roles Arral claims to have alternated are Nicette and Isabelle, who is a lady of the court but not a princess. Fugère's part, Girot, is Nicette's betrothed, not her father, and the two do indeed share one of the most popular numbers in the score, the delightful first-act duet "Les rendez-vous de noble compagnie." On occasion Fugère also sang the supporting tenor role of Italian nobleman Cantarelli.

24. Paris-born baritone Lucien Fugère (1848–1935), a fabled name in vocal history, progressed from cabarets to a long reign (1877–1911) at the Opéra-Comique,

where he last sang in 1932. The two dozen extraordinary recordings he made 1928–30, when past eighty, are collectors' favorites. Brother Paul Fugère (1851–1920) was a popular figure on the Paris operetta stage from the 1880s until his death.

25. Emma Nevada (1859–1940) was born Emma Wixom in Alpha, California. Her father, Dr. William Wallace Wixom, lost his wife when Emma was a child. A Marchesi pupil, she made her debut in 1880, arriving at the Opéra-Comique in *La perle du Brésil* in May 1883.

26. Sacramento-born Sibyl Sanderson (1865–1903) made her Opéra-Comique debut in the premiere of Massenet's *Esclarmonde* 14 May 1889, fully five years after Arral had departed the company.

27. Arral errs in ascribing the "Chanson de Barberine" to Terry's impecunious Spanish friend Mario Costa (dates not found). The 1884 song, with words by Alfred de Musset, is from the prolific pen of Italy's P(asquale) Mario Costa (1858–1933), purveyor of such popular Neapolitan staples as "Napulitanata" and "Sei morta ne la vita mia."

28. Alas, Arral has seriously fudged facts here: the Théâtre de la Gaîté revival of Léon Vasseur's 1878 operetta *Le droit du seigneur*, in which she sang the leading role of Lucinette, opened 23 April 1884, just sixteen months after her Opéra-Comique debut. Far from running "more than one hundred nights," it reached only thirty-nine performances.

29. Enrique Granados (1867–1916) studied privately in Paris 1887–89 with Charles Wilfride de Bériot, son of famed violinist Charles Auguste de Bériot and legendary singer María Malibran. He may have lived "in poverty," but, according to one source, he still managed to enjoy the city's musical life and even "indulged in a bit of hell raising."

30. Though "improved" here, the story is more than mere legend. On 2 June 1875 Célestine Galli-Marié (1840–1905) arrived at the Opéra-Comique for the thirty-third performance of *Carmen* in a high state of inexplicable nervous excitement which culminated in her fainting following the Card Scene. She recovered and finished the performance, only to learn next day that Bizet had died shortly after the final curtain, in the early morning hours of 3 June.

31. See discography note 61 for the probable provenance of this song.

32. Isabella II (1830–1904) inherited the Spanish throne at age three and was forced into exile in 1868. According to John D. Bergamini, in *The Spanish*

Bourbons: The History of a Tenacious Dynasty (New York: Putnam, 1974), "Her life was outrageous, her rule was tumultuous, and she was deposed for being a nymphomaniac."

33. Arral's account of the life of Spanish contralto Elena Sanz (1849–1898) is essentially correct, although she was neither Spain's first Carmen (it was Galli-Marié) nor France's first Dalila (the Rouen premiere was sung by a certain Bossy, the Paris premiere by Rosine Bloch). Her liaison with young Alfonso XII (1857–1885), who was at least eight years her junior, began soon after the tragic death of his first wife (barely eighteen, she had been wed to her twenty-year-old cousin only five months) and lasted some sixteen months, until his responsibilities obliged him to marry Maria Cristina (1858–1929?), by whom he had three children. Their last child, Alfonso XIII (grandfather of the present King Juan Carlos), was born six months after his father's death from tuberculosis. His sons by Sanz, Alfonso and Fernando, remained with their mother, whom Spanish novelist Benito Pérez Galdós described as "a woman as good as bread, all passion, generosity, tenderness."

34. Arral's history of the "little dancer from Brussels" is suspect. Born in Lyons, Blanche Deschamps-Jehin (1857–1923) studied singing there and in Paris before going to Brussels, where she was heard in Lecocq's *Giroflé-Girofla* as early as 1874. Her debut at La Monnaie was as Mignon in 1879. She married conductor Léon Jehin in 1889.

35. Wherever Arral had her brush with Illinois-born Loïe Fuller (1862–1928), it can't have been at the 1885 Antwerp concert. Fuller began as an actress and in 1885 was still employed as such in New York. After creating her Serpentine dance in 1891, she took it to Paris, becoming an icon of the Art Nouveau movement. In later years she produced ballets, including *Le lys de la vie* (Paris Opéra, 1920) with a scenario by Queen Marie of Romania. A hand-colored film of her famous Fire dance was made by Edison in 1901.

36. Audran's three-act "opéra-comique fantastique" *Le puits qui parle* had its premiere at Paris's Théâtre des Nouveautés 15 March 1888 with a cast that included Clara Lardinois (Églantine), Mademoiselle Debriège (La Vérité), and father and son Jules and Albert Brasseur, then comanagers of the theater.

37. Arral states that her costars in *Cocher, au Casino!* (31 December 1890) were Marie Grisier-Montbazon (1861–1922)—by far the most famous of the three at the time—and Juliette Méaly (1867–?), who was just beginning a career that would continue into the 1920s. The show's poster, however, identifies the

trio as Lardinois, Montbazon, and a certain Lantelme, suggesting that either Arral's memory played her false or Méaly replaced Lantelme at some point after the poster was printed.

38. On 30 September 1891 the unfortunate General Georges Boulanger (b. 1837), forced to flee Paris in April 1889, did indeed commit suicide at the Brussels grave of his mistress, Marguerite, vicomtesse de Bonnemain (b. 1856), who had died in July.

39. American naturalist Raymond Lee Ditmars (1876–1942), long curator of reptiles at the New York Zoo, was an internationally recognized authority on snakes.

40. Arral's biographical "facts" regarding Bucharest-born Raoul Gunsbourg (1859–1955) are almost as fanciful as those found in his own posthumously published memoirs. In truth he studied medicine and briefly acted before drifting to Russia, where for some years he produced annual seasons of French opera and operetta in Moscow (from 1881) and St. Petersburg (from 1882). His fame now rests on the six decades (1893–1951) he spent as director of the Monte Carlo Opera. By his first wife, soprano Emma d'Alba (dates not found), he had two daughters (not sons, as Arral remembers). Madame d'Alba may have "never studied singing seriously," but that didn't prevent her partnering Jean de Reszke (1850–1925) in the stage premiere of Berlioz's *La damnation de Faust* at Monte Carlo in 1893.

41. See discography notes for numbers 32, 60, and 80 for the provenance of the "Bird Waltz."

42. Italian-born, London-based Tito Mattei (1841–1914) is now remembered solely for this 1875 song, for which he also wrote the words, recorded in its original Italian version ("Non è ver") by John McCormack, John Charles Thomas, and others.

43. Arral claims she met Siberian-born Grigory Rasputin (1871?–1916) at St. Petersburg's French Church in 1891, yet no evidence exists that he ever visited the city prior to 1903. On the other hand, Joseph T. Fuhrmann's *Rasputin: A Life* (New York: Praeger, 1990) states, "It is impossible to establish an exact chronology of Rasputin's life from the late 1880s to 1902."

44. Kurt Gänzl's *The Encyclopedia of the Musical Theatre* (New York: Schirmer, 1994) describes the heroine of Audran's 1890 operetta as "a pubescent little American Salvation Army lass" who, falling off a cliff, "is left hanging upside

down from a branch with her skirts over her head" until rescued by a stranger whom she sets out to wed solely on the basis of his having seen "a portion of her anatomy that only a husband should see"—rather a naughty little dish, one would think, to set before the czar and his court.

45. Arral errs in believing she "created" Millöcker's *Der Bettelstudent* for Russia. It had already been heard, in German, in both St. Petersburg (19 December 1883) and Moscow (29 April 1884). She did, however, sing Laura in the unsuccessful Paris premiere (twenty-two performances) of *L'étudiant pauvre* at the Théâtre des Menus-Plaisirs, 18 January 1889.

46. Bisected by the Golden Horn, an inlet of the strait of Bosporus, Constantinople became Istanbul in 1930. In Arral's time the southern or Asiatic section of the city was called Istanbul, the northern or European section Pera (properly Galata-Pera). These areas are now known as Stamboul and Beyoğlu, respectively.

47. Abdülhamid II (1842–1918) became sultan in 1876 on the deposition of his mentally deranged brother Murad V (1840–1904). Strongly opposed to Western intervention in Ottoman affairs, he suspended the constitution in 1878 and, secluded at Yildiz Palace, ruled ruthlessly as an absolute monarch until his own deposition by the Young Turks in 1909.

48. Audran's *La fiancée des verts-poteaux*, a three-act *opéra comique*, had its premiere at Paris's Théâtre des Menus-Plaisirs 8 November 1887. In addition to Clara Lardinois and Monsieur Bartel the cast included Messieurs Jacquin and Darman, both of whom also appear to have turned up in Costa Rica, suggesting that Aubry's company was geared more to the presentation of light opera than of grand opera.

49. Born in Toulouse in 1860, baritone Bernard Bégué studied at the Paris Conservatory, making his debut in the provinces in 1885. Later, in fifteen seasons (1902–17) at the Metropolitan Opera, he would sing more than seven hundred performances of forty-eight small roles, including Marullo in Caruso's debut in *Rigoletto*, Gregorio in Farrar's debut in *Roméo et Juliette*, and Jim Larkens in the world premiere of *La fanciulla del West*.

50. A century later the Teatro Nacional is still considered the jewel of San José, if not of all Central America. It is described in the third edition of *The New World Guides to the Latin American Republics*, edited by Earl Parker Hanson (New York: Duell, Sloan, and Pearce, 1950), as a "lavish million-dollar Renaissance building with solid marble stairways and balconies, decorations of

beaten gold and bronze, and fine murals. Its salon, decorated in the grand manner with mirrors, red velvet, and gold, is really one of the truly splendid rooms of Central America; when performances are given, it is the gathering place of San José's elite."

51. Today's traveler will still find the rail journey from Limón to San José one of the most spectacular in the world. Construction of the line was begun in 1871 by Brooklyn-born entrepreneur Minor C. Keith (related by marriage to Costa Rican president Rafael Iglesias, who welcomed Arral's party to San José), whose problems, topographical, political, and financial, were immense. The first through train arrived in the capital 7 December 1890, just seven years before Arral's visit. Even today the line is frequently closed for repairs and relocation, and passengers can see multiple generations of track and even whole tunnels that have been carried away by massive landslides over the past century.

52. The Teatro Nacional did indeed open with a performance of Gounod's *Faust* by "la compañia francesca Aubry" 21 October 1897. One hundred years later to the day, the occasion was commemorated with a gala concert.

53. Arral claims to have sung two months in Costa Rica, which would have brought her to New Orleans in late 1897 or early 1898 to join the French Opera House troupe for "the balance of their season." Alas, local opera historian Jack Belsom reports that, apart from a short visit by the touring Jules Grau Light Opera Company, the theater was dark that winter and he can find no trace of Arral, Bégué, or Madame Bégué ("who sang contralto roles under the name of Valdes") performing anywhere in the city. Curiously, however, French Opera House records for 1899–1900 show a baritone named "Beguer" or "Beguin" on the roster, as well as a single performance (19 December) of *Il trovatore* featuring one Valdès as Azucena. As for Arral's "private engagements," *Musical America* for 27 November 1909 carried a photograph of the elaborate badge presented to her "by the Hotel Men's Mutual Benevolent Association in the time of its general conclave at the national convention in New Orleans. During the entertainment which had been arranged for the families of those attending . . . Madame Arral arrived . . . from Costa Rica . . . and arranged a unique performance for the exclusive enjoyment of the visiting members. The principal members of her company gave excerpts from a number of operas, and so pleased were the officers of the association that they voted her an honorary life member."

54. The French passenger liner *La Bourgogne* and the British ship *Cromartyshire* collided near Sable Island off Nova Scotia, 4 July 1898, with a loss of 650 lives.

55. Arral tells us she returned to Belgium "shortly after" the *Bourgogne* disaster of July 1898 and, following a "long rest," sang *Les noces de Jeannette* and *Le timbre d'argent* for Ambroselli at Brussels's famed La Monnaie, her colleagues including contralto Jeanne Maubourg (dates not found) and baritone Gabriel Soulacroix (1853–1905). Jules Salès's *Théâtre Royal de la Monnaie: 1856–1970* (Nivelles, Belgium: Imprimerie Havaux, 1971), which does not mention Arral or Lardinois, cites at least one performance (28 November 1898) of *Les noces de Jeannette* (no cast given) on a triple bill with the ballet *Milenka* and Adolphe Blanc's operetta *Les deux billets*, in which Maubourg is known to have sung. But Soulacroix was not there that season, nor is there any sign of *Le timbre d'argent*. More perplexing is the absence of Ambroselli from the roll of La Monnaie directors, who during 1889–1900 were Edouard Calabresi and Oscar Stoumon. Dates of some of Arral's other Brussels appearances may be found in the chronology.

56. Inveterate traveler Camille Saint-Saëns (1835–1921) visited Egypt more than once, including an extended stay during the winter of 1901–02.

57. Egypt's last khedive, Abbas II (1874–1944), called Abbas Hilmi Pasha, ruled from 1892 until deposed by the British in 1914.

58. Joseph-Marie-Auguste Caillaux (1863–1944), controversial premier of France during 1911 negotiations with Germany, was charged with treason during World War I and spent two years (1918–20) in prison awaiting trial. Found innocent of treason but guilty of committing "damage to the external security of the state," he was deprived of his civil rights until 1924 when his credibility was restored and he returned to politics.

59. Presumably the film to which Arral alludes was *The Caillaux Case*, an American silent feature released by Fox in 1918 with a cast that included Henry Warwick as Caillaux and Australian-born George Majeroni as "Bolo Pasha."

60. Arral's purported 1902 Buenos Aires engagement cannot have been with the Teatro Colón. The first theater of that name ceased operations in 1887; the second (and present) didn't open until 1908. There were, however, at least three or four other local theaters offering opera at the time, and perhaps her engagement was with one of those.

61. In fact, Chulalongkorn (1853–1910) spoke and wrote perfect English, having been educated in part by Anna Leonowens (1831–1915) of *Anna and the King of Siam* fame. He appears as the crown prince in the films based on that book and in the musical *The King and I*.

62. The only Li Hung-chang (1823–1901) found in standard reference works was a statesman, not a poet, and already dead when Arral visited China. At that time, too, all power was in the hands of the notorious Empress Dowager Tz'u-hsi (1835–1908), who kept the rightful ruler, Emperor Tsai-T'ien (1871–1908), under virtual house arrest from 1898 until his death.

63. Kim Louagie, curator of the Houdini Historical Center, Appleton, Wisconsin, states that, to the best of her knowledge, master illusionist Harry Houdini (1874–1926) never visited China.

64. Although sometimes called Hérold Bassett in contemporary press stories (perhaps a passing affectation born of too-long proximity to the multi-aliased Arral) Hamilton Dwight Bassett (dates not found)—the name is emblazoned on a 1909 letterhead preserved in the Edison files—is identified in one 1914 clipping as "a former newspaperman of Cincinnati."

65. Herself responsible for many of the myths that surrounded her, including claims to have been a temple dancer, Mata Hari (1876–1917), *née* Margaretha Zelle in Leeuwarden, Holland, married a Dutch colonial army officer in 1895 and lived with him in Java and Sumatra from May 1897 to March 1902, during which time she's known to have danced at private functions. Obviously Arral could not have seen her there in 1904 as her memoir suggests, but one source insists the singer first visited Java in the course of an 1898–99 Asian tour unmentioned in her book—a fascinating claim, impossible to confirm.

66. Lillian Nordica (b. 1857) died in Batavia 10 May 1914, the victim of exposure and pneumonia contracted during a shipwreck in the Torres Strait following a concert tour of Australia.

67. William Arundel Orchard was for many years director of the New South Wales Conservatorium of Music. In *Music in Australia: More than 150 Years of Development* (Melbourne: Georgian House, 1953) he wrote, "[In 1906] the gifted Blanche Arral was another welcome singer who gave opera excerpts in costume, accompanied by an efficient orchestra conducted by Rivers Allpress, a gifted violinist and pianist of some ability [who] was born [in Bendigo, Victoria,] but lived chiefly in Sydney as an orchestra leader and chamber music player." There are many references to Allpress (1864–?) in the Australian musical press of the period.

68. Vienna-born soprano Elise Wiedermann (1854–?) had a successful European career before settling in Australia as the wife of Carl L. Pinschof, Austrian consul in Melbourne. It was she who gave Nellie Melba a letter of introduc-

tion to Mathilde Marchesi, the presentation of which furnished the oft-told story that began Melba's career. As Carmen Pascova, daughter Carmen Pinschof sang with the Chicago Opera 1920–21.

69. Melba is known to have sung at least one Melbourne concert in November 1907.

70. Viola Tait's *A Family of Brothers: The Taits and J. C. Williamson* (Melbourne: Heinemann, 1971) preserves a different view of Antonia Dolores (1864–?): "Madame Antoinette Trebelli, daughter of the famous French mezzo-soprano Zélia Trebelli, made her Australian debut in 1896. She returned to Europe after her mother died and changed her name to Madam Antonia Dolores. She was a great favourite with Australian audiences and returned three times on concert tours. . . . *The Argus* wrote: 'The charm of Madame Dolores's singing is the result of a combination of many elements. Her voice is singularly pure and every note in it affords an exquisite sensuous pleasure like that given by pure colour quite apart from the picture in which it is found.'"

71. Famed soprano Emma Albani (1847–1930) began her career in 1870 and was well past her prime when she visited Australia in 1898 and again in June–October 1907.

72. See "Blanche Arral and Jack London."

73. Twice postponed due to illness, first from 11 October and then from 18 October, Arral's San Francisco debut actually occurred 25 October. Paul Steindorff (1865–1927), who conducted all three of her local concerts, was a German-born operetta veteran who had been employed by both Lillian Russell and Alice Nielsen (for the latter he led the premieres of Victor Herbert's *The Fortune Teller* and *The Singing Girl*) before settling in the Bay area around 1902, where he remained a familiar musical figure for the rest of his life.

74. It was actually three years before. Luisa Tetrazzini (1871–1940) made her sensational United States debut in San Francisco 11 January 1905, as Gilda in *Rigoletto*, with a company that had come not from South America but from Mexico.

75. For more on Gianni Bettini (1860–1938), see "Blanche Arral and the Phonograph."

76. William Henry Meadowcroft (1853–1937), in Edison's employ 1881–1931 and his secretary from 1908, was the author of *The Boys' Life of Edison* (New York: Harper & Brothers, 1911) and other works.

Afterword

by Jim McPherson

> For singers to be surrounded with a little harmless mystery is almost a necessity, as it does much to build the glamour and romance with which they have from time immemorial been associated.
>
> —BLANCHE ARRAL

AND HEAVEN KNOWS our enchanting subject was a past mistress at surrounding herself with little harmless mysteries. Did she really have those extraordinary encounters with Rasputin in Russia, Mata Hari in Java, and Harry Houdini in a Shanghai variety theater? Who can say? Yet even after her arrival in America, from which point many of her activities are corroborated by contemporary press accounts, the mysteries continue. In the last chapter of her irresistible memoir, for instance, she skims over the thirty years from 1908 to 1937 in just a few pages—pages, like many of those preceding them, notable for their jumbled chronology, errors of omission (artful or artless?), and general tendency to raise more questions than they answer. As the lady is conspicuous by her absence from almost all reference books and has never been honored with a full-length biography—a consummation as devoutly to be wished as it is unlikely to be realized—let's at least take this opportunity to set down in some detail what is known of her later life and let the many little harmless mysteries that accrue fall where they may.

315

Blanche Arral's modest contention that the audience was "pleased" with what it heard at her first San Francisco concert on 25 October 1908 is something of an understatement. In fact those present at the Van Ness Theater that Sunday afternoon promptly elevated the newcomer to equal footing with some of the world's most famous singers. The *Musical Review* proclaimed her "by far the greatest coloratura soprano that has visited San Francisco since the early days of Patti and Sembrich." *Musical America* found her "an easy comparison with Tetrazzini," who had taken the city by storm three years before: "Her voice has the same sweetness . . . and the same effortless brilliance of execution." The *Call*, while agreeing that "her flexibility is marvelous," thought her "primarily a musician" whose simple rendering of "Voi che sapete" from *Le nozze di Figaro* was noteworthy for "its rare and exquisite beauty." The *Chronicle* declared her an artist "whose claims have not been exaggerated, whose voice is beautiful, whose musicianship is exquisite, and whose spirit and magnetism are absolutely irresistible." And the *Examiner* pronounced "the little prima donna from Belgium" quite simply "one of the greatest singers ever heard in America. . . . More like Sembrich in appearance and voice than any one else I know, [she] seemed to me even greater." After her masterful *Hamlet* Mad Scene, "women dried their eyes with their handkerchiefs and men stood up to applaud and shout bravas."

The debutante's other offerings included an aria from Adam's *Si j'étais roi* (probably the lilting "De vos nobles aïeux," exhumed and recorded in 1993 by Sumi Jo), the "Chanson napolitaine" (actually a baritone pleasantry filched from Saint-Saëns's forgotten opera *Le timbre d'argent*), the *Mignon* "Polonaise," Bishop's "Lo! here the gentle lark," and songs by Offenbach, Ivanov, and Denza (the last self-accompanied on the piano), with the inevitable "Bird Waltz" as the coup de grâce. Those who returned to hear her a second time the following Sunday were rewarded with an entirely different program, embracing her oft-sung arias from Gounod's *La reine de Saba* and Massé's *Les noces de Jeannette*, the "Bolero" from Verdi's *Les vêpres siciliennes*, the closing scene from act one of *La traviata*, Aliab'ev's "The Nightingale" (a popular Russian showpiece much favored by coloratura sopranos of the time), Braga's "La serenata" (better known in America as the familiar "Angel's Serenade"), and Bemberg's "Aime-moi."

Nearly three weeks passed before Arral's third and final San Francisco concert, but they were certainly not without incident. On 4 November she visited the state capital to sing under the auspices of the Saturday Club ("The rarest musical treat ever offered to a Sacramento audience," opined *The Union*), and ten days later came the terrible episode with the alcohol lamp. Although she tells us that only two weeks remained before her next appearance, contemporary reports suggest that in fact a mere five days separated the catastrophe from her emotional farewell on 19 November. Oddly, too, she neglects to mention that Hamilton Bassett spent that memorable evening in St. Mary's Hospital, receiving treatment for a leg wound suffered some days earlier when an unknown assailant shot at him in the street. Convinced he was the target of Russian thugs in the pay of the Peshkov family, Bassett's first act upon arriving in New York soon after was to apply for and receive permission to carry a gun of his own.

The two were not slow to turn that prolonged New York stopover— occasioned, she claims, by the loss of a trunk—to their advantage. By the end of March they had been in negotiation with all three of the leading phonograph companies of the day (who approached who, one wonders?) and she had recorded successfully for two of them. Columbia's files reveal that an Arral test record of an unknown number was "Rejected March 24 1909"—possibly because management discovered that, since cutting it on 29 January, the singer had been busy in the studios of both its major competitors. On 3 February she made four cylinders for Edison (at a flat fee of seventy-five dollars each—even a company executive later admitted the paltry sum was "ridiculous"), and over two days in mid-March she made her eight Victor Red Seal records (at a considerably more gratifying three hundred dollars apiece, plus royalties).

Between these two sessions, she trekked all the way to St. Louis, Missouri, for a solitary Apollo Club concert on 9 February, to which she contributed her arias from *Hamlet, Mignon,* and *La perle du Brésil* (plus the *de rigueur* "Bird Waltz") under the baton of local musical factotum Charles Henry Galloway. The *Star*, apparently oblivious to events any farther west of the Mississippi than itself, declared that, "in this, her American debut, Mme Blanche Arrall [sic] quite won the hearts of her audience, not more by her musical abilities than by her charming manner." Curiously, although *Musical America* reported (3 February) that the singer was also booked for appearances in Cincinnati and Louisville, these seem not to have taken place.

A mystery far more perplexing arises three months later when, following the Liège homecoming concert she called "the crown of my career," the lady journeyed to England in May, invited, as she tells us, "by Colonel Mapleson, the famous impresario, to give two concerts under royal patronage at London's Steinway Hall." In fact this was not the legendary Colonel James Mapleson (1830–1901), whose colorful adventures with Patti and other nineteenth-century luminaries provided fodder for a famous memoir, but his titleless son, Henry Mapleson (1851–1927), then active as a concert manager. The great puzzle here, however, is that despite a later publicity brochure boasting dated extracts from purported *New York Times* reviews, no trace of these concerts, neither announcements nor notices, can be found in an examination of the actual issues in question.

Casting doubt, too, on her claims to have returned to Belgium from England "on the verge of a breakdown" and to have spent the summer "with my family at Ostend and Brussels," the 17 July 1909 issue of *Musical America* informed readers that "Mme Blanche Arrral [sic], fresh from the triumph of her London concerts, arrived [in New York] on the *Oceanic* last week and was the first passenger to flit down the gangway as the big liner came into the dock." It seems she had also managed to fit in a sentimental visit to Paris, where "I renewed all of my old acquaintances and saw my friends," among them André Messager, Lucien Fugère, Albert Carré, Eugène Ysaÿe, Raoul Pugno, and Mathilde Marchesi, now eighty-eight and only recently retired from teaching ("She is very old, and failing, but I was glad to know she remembered me"). It was further reported that compatriot Ivan Caryll—born Félix Tilkin in Liège, the hugely successful musical comedy composer had long lived in England—was writing an opera for her in which she would star at the 1910 Brussels Exhibition. As with so many of the singer's announced plans, it didn't happen.

Two weeks following her forty-fifth birthday, our lady made her New York debut at Carnegie Hall on 24 October 1909, as guest soloist with the Volpe Symphony Orchestra, a youthful aggregation cobbled together five years earlier by Lithuanian-born conductor Arnold Volpe (1869–

1940). The program, vintage Arral, included the usual excerpts from *Hamlet*, *Le nozze di Figaro*, and *La reine de Saba*, the "Cours-la-reine" aria ("Je marche sur tous les chemins") from Massenet's *Manon*, and, to provide what the fledgling show business newspaper *Variety* would term "a boffo finish," her unique *Mignon* potpourri consisting of Overture, Romance (the Swallow Duet without benefit of partner), "Connais-tu le pays?", Cantabile (the dramatic second-act passage beginning "Elle est là, près de lui"), Gavotte (instrumental version), and the dazzling "Polonaise," the orchestra filling out the afternoon with selections by Cherubini, Saint-Saëns, and Grieg.

Alas, the hard-nosed New York critics were not as easily won as their West Coast counterparts. The *Times*'s Richard Aldrich, for example, after raising an eyebrow over the fact that "concerts made up in this manner have become somewhat out of date and out of fashion," coolly assessed the newcomer as "evidently a singer of experience and routine. . . . Her voice is powerful and well under her command, and she has a certain amount of skill in the delivery of the florid passages." It was not, however, "a voice in the first freshness of youth," nor did it possess many of the "refinements" one expects in "a musically gifted singer." Mozart's little aria in particular, in her hands, "was not a thing of beauty" (*pace* San Francisco). In conclusion, frowned this Harvard-educated product of Providence, Rhode Island, "The disagreeable purist might also find fault with her treatment of certain of the vowel sounds in both French and Italian." One hopes that Arral, whose English was always limited, had someone translate this last concern for her, that she might profit from the critic's superior knowledge of her native tongue.

The leading journals were much more welcoming, *Musical America* noting that this singer "of great attainments" was "the recipient of much applause, enthusiastic and prolonged, and was called out many times during the concert, as well as at the close," while *Musical Courier* decreed that the newcomer, "gracious in manner and serious in purpose," created "a most favorable impression" and easily proved herself "a decided addition to the ranks of high class vocalists." In a separate piece, reading almost like a deliberate rebuke to Aldrich and company, the magazine addressed the "considerable comment both pro and con" engendered by her style of program and the fact that some had censured her for infusing her offerings with "the same spirit as she would were she singing in opera," thereby flouting the widely held view that a concert artist "must stand like a block of wood." Pointing out that "the general public took very kindly to these innovations, and as the public is what the artist primarily endeavors to please, she should be well content," the writer concluded that any singer "who can meet with the enthusiastic reception which was accorded Arral must be credited with a genuine success . . . a genuine triumph . . . won solely on her merits as an artist."

Six weeks later, on 5 December, the soprano was again soloist at a Volpe concert in Carnegie Hall, although on this occasion she seems to have sung only two selections, "Divinités du Styx" from Gluck's *Alceste* and (in French) "Leise, leise, fromme Weise" from Weber's *Der Freischütz*, both quite devoid of any opportunities for coloratura display. Nonetheless, "Hardly a seat in the great auditorium was vacant, and it was an unusual sight to see all of the boxes in two balconies filled by appreciative listeners," reported *Musical America*, assigning full credit for this phenomenon to the popularity of the guest artist, who at afternoon's end "was recalled fully a dozen times to acknowledge the applause and floral tributes." For its part, *Musical Courier* was convinced that "Madame Arral is a representative of a great school of singing which is gradually disappearing and which has faded from our concert platforms and from the operatic stage. What a tremendous acquisition she would be to one of the opera houses here."

Of that there was no question the winter of 1909–10. At the Metropolitan, from which the mighty Sembrich had retired the previous February, the coloratura banner was being upheld respectably if unexcitingly by America's Bernice De Pasquali, Spain's Elvira De Hidalgo, and Russia's Lydia Lipkovska. At the Manhattan, Oscar Hammerstein had the hugely popular Tetrazzini for the standard warhorses, but his productions of such frothy French *opéras comiques* as *La fille de Madame Angot* and *Les cloches de Corneville*—naturals for Arral—were seriously compromised by largely mediocre casts. This dearth of star performers for the florid soprano repertory would continue until the arrival on the American scene of Frieda Hempel in 1912 and Amelita Galli-Curci in 1916.

Shortly after the second Volpe concert, negotiations between Bassett and Edison resulted in a one-year contract, effective 1 January 1910, calling for eight new four-minute cylinders at three hundred dollars apiece, plus a ten percent royalty, with selections to be chosen mainly from the "comic opera" repertory. Yet, as far as is known, what were to be Arral's last commercial recordings were made in the closing days of December 1909 and numbered only six.

And now we come to the greatest puzzle of all. What happened to the promising American career so well begun in San Francisco and New York? She embarked on that hopeful season of 1909–10 under the aegis of Illinois-born Loudon Charlton, a respected concert manager whose client list included such distinguished names as soprano Johanna Gadski, pianist Harold Bauer, violinist Jan Kubelik, and the Flonzaley String Quartet. Presumably it was he who produced a nine-page publicity brochure touting Arral as the "Prima Donna of Four Continents" (by some mathematical legerdemain, the count would later rise to five), quoting liberally from her international press notices (including those elusive London reviews), and generally paving the way for what was advertised as the singer's "First American Tour," which, after New York, was to have taken her to Boston, Chicago, St. Louis, Cincinnati, Washington, and possibly other major centers. Yet it would appear that none of this happened. Indeed, as far as can be determined, following her second Volpe concert and that final recording session in December 1909, she returned to Europe and, barring one brief private visit in 1911, was absent from the United States for well over two years. And when at last she returned, in March 1912, it was to undertake yet another "extended concert tour" that also failed to materialize.

Little harmless mysteries indeed!

To untangle the skein of Blanche Arral's public and private activities in the last half dozen years of her professional life is impossible. Too many pieces of the puzzle are missing, and the lady herself is of little help, the last few pages of her reminiscences being as hopelessly skewed in their ordering of events as they are uninformative. When she writes, for example, that America's 1917 entry into World War I found her "married to an American," does she mean Hamilton Bassett or George Wheeler? Did she in fact *ever* marry Bassett? And if so, was it in China as per one report, or in New Orleans as per another? They were certainly intimately associated for the ten years or so following their 1904 meeting in Singapore, and press reports of the period repeatedly and routinely identify him as her husband. Yet she tells us that, upon arrival in San Francisco in 1908, "I took an apartment overlooking the city, while Bassett had rooms on the floor above," scarcely an arrangement conducive to connubial bliss (or perhaps it was).

Rather than engage in the unprofitable pursuit of questions to which we have no answers, let's scan this perplexing period via a brief chronological review of those few activities for which confirmation can be found in the contemporary press.

Reporting from the Belgian village of Spa, whose popular mineral springs had made its name a synonym for all such resorts, the 23 November 1910 *Musical Courier* announced that Blanche Arral had taken charge of the community's "artistic destinies" as a result of the local "concession" for entertaining visitors having been awarded to "a company of which Herold [sic] Bassett of New York is at the head." Although the agreement was to remain in force for twenty-four years (!), we hear no more about it.

A year later, on 21 October 1911, a clipping from an unidentified American paper records that Blanche Arral "returned to her home in Brussels a few weeks ago, after a very pleasant visit with her husband here. Mr. Bassett had planned to return with her, but at the last moment the call of the business in which he is engaged proved too formidable to be overlooked and he remained. He may visit her in Europe later in the winter."

On 16 March 1912 *Musical America* noted that Arral had arrived in New York the previous week to begin an "extended concert tour" which she hoped to combine with appearances "in opera and possibly in light opera" while also "filling engagements with one of the talking-machine companies." But the only confirmed activities we have for the next eight months are a private musicale "under the auspices of Mr. and Mrs. Benjamin Van Dyke" at the Oriental Hotel in Brooklyn's Manhattan Beach and, on 14 July, a Bastille Day celebration, location unknown, to which she contributed "La Marseillaise" and "The Star-Spangled Banner." By August she appears to have set up house, complete with "her remarkable collection of Siamese cats and dogs" but apparently *sans* Bassett, in a "pretty little cottage" or a "fine suburban home" (take your pick) in Orange, New Jersey.

At the new Aeolian Hall on 4 November, an afternoon recital with

Maurice Lafarge at the piano marked the soprano's first New York appearance in three years. In *Musical America*'s opinion, "She sang with much brilliancy—more, in fact, than she exhibited when last heard here," while *Musical Courier* recorded that "a large audience" was stirred "to many demonstrations of enthusiasm" by a program that included arias from Verdi's *Jérusalem*, Gomes's *Il Guarany*, Massenet's *Hérodiade*, the *Mignon* "Polonaise," and songs by Bemberg, Bishop, Bizet, Chaminade, Costa, Gregori, Grieg, and Hollmann. A return to the same venue 25 January 1913 found the soprano sharing honors with two Czech musicians—neither pianist Betty Askenasy nor cellist Bedrich Vaska appear to have achieved sufficient celebrity to earn a niche in the reference books—with Lafarge again supplying her accompaniments. On this occasion her performance of an excerpt from Massé's comic opera *Galathée* evoked demands for an encore, which she satisfied by singing, of all things, "Annie Laurie"—oh, to have a recording of that!

Despite the fact that she was once more under the management of the capable Loudon Charlton and these New York appearances were intended as mere prelude to "a tour through the United States and Canada," we next meet her as an unlikely adjunct to a New Assembly musicale at the Hotel Plaza on 8 May, essentially a showcase for American works played by their composers (among them John Adam Hugo, whose opera *The Temple Dancer* would reach the Metropolitan in 1919). *Musical America* is our witness that "A most delightful feature of the evening was the group of songs delivered in costume by Mme Blanche Arral, her brilliant soprano being happily displayed in an aria from *Mignon* and 'The Songs of the Birds'"—presumably the ubiquitous "Bird Waltz."

On 20 September the same journal reported a visit to the soprano's New Jersey home, which found her busily engaged in "a limited amount of teaching" while also "preparing for another tour," helping Edison with his "experimental work," tending a garden rich in "fruits and vegetables of every description," and importing Javanese herbs for her recently marketed weight-reduction tea (this short article is illustrated with the striking "before" and "after" portraits mentioned in her book).

Before "a moderately filled house" at the Casino on 18 November, a five-hour benefit matinee for the Professional Women's League found her "charming, vivacious, and in excellent voice" as part of a decidedly motley grab bag of performers ranging from star vaudevillian Nora Bayes to drama queen Fannie Ward, who would achieve screen immortality two years later when Sessue Hayakawa branded her naked shoulder in Cecil B. DeMille's sensational melodrama *The Cheat*. A month later a benefit for the *New York American-Evening Journal* Christmas Fund found the singer sharing top billing with twelve-year-old Spanish pianist Manolito Funes, "the sensation of the century in musical circles."

On 4 August 1914 Germany invaded Arral's beloved homeland, thereby igniting World War I. At virtually the same moment, while attending to the tea business in her office at Fifth Avenue and Forty-second Street, she was attacked and choked by an intruder who made off with a cashbox containing over two hundred dollars. Press reports of the incident identified her as "the wife of Hamilton Bassett, a former newspaper man of Cincinnati." Adding to these misfortunes, Edison's West Orange laboratory was destroyed by fire on 9 December, writing *finis* to their purported collaboration.

Three months later, on 24 March 1915, she wrote to the great man from her home at 144 Cleveland Street in Orange, advising him that she was to be "leading lady in a series of French *opérettes* to be given in New York" beginning in April and asking if he would care to have her record some of the principal numbers. "Should you see your way clear to accede to my request," she concluded, "you will not only help me as an artist . . . but also aid me to overcome the loss that I have incurred through the war, for you know that I am a Belgian and most of my money was invested there." Across the top of this poignant appeal, preserved in the Edison files, someone has written, "Might try if she can sing a couple of good songs from the operas she speaks of," but as far as is known nothing further transpired. At the bottom of the letter, incidentally, are the initials "BA/W," the unknown amanuensis presumably being responsible for the singer's smooth-flowing English. Could this perhaps have been George Wheeler, the man destined to become (if Bassett was indeed number two) her third husband? A full quarter-century younger, Wheeler was only twenty-five at the time, Arral fifty.

Alas, the "series of French *opérettes*" began and ended with a single performance of Hervé's *Mam'zelle Nitouche* in the "sweltering heat" of the Century Theater's rooftop auditorium, 26 April 1915. Billing herself once more as Clara Lardinois—perhaps in sentimental homage to the days, now thirty years since, when she had charmed Paris in such parts— Arral "showed herself an excellent comedienne and sang lustily" in the leading role of saucy schoolgirl (!) Denise de Flavigny. Her leading man, young Belgian baritone Désiré Defrère (1888–1964), came to the "picturesquely crude" production fresh from his first Metropolitan Opera season and a dozen appearances as Moralès in the famous Toscanini revival of *Carmen* with Geraldine Farrar and Enrico Caruso. In later years "Dee-Dee" would long serve the Met as a beloved stage director. The "hybrid orchestra" was led by Russian-born Alexander Smallens (1889– 1972), whose eventful career would include conducting the 1935 world premiere of *Porgy and Bess*; and, as an added attraction, a beautiful twentysomething immigrant made her American debut singing songs of Russia and her native Poland between the acts. Although her dreams of operatic glory were never to be realized, Ganna Walska (1892?–1984) consoled herself by marrying six times and becoming an early example of that now familiar phenomenon, the celebrity famous mostly for being famous. Why the operetta, presented by the French Drama Society, was given only once, and why there were no further productions, remains a mystery, especially in light of *Musical America*'s report that there was "no lack of enthusiasm" on the part of the audience, which "seemed to enjoy the silliness of the old piece hugely."

A new medium was explored when, on 15 November 1915, Arral began a week's vaudeville engagement at New Orleans's Orpheum Theater, sharing the bill with, among others, the Rigoletto Brothers ("feats of skill, dexterity, and strength" but probably no Verdi) and one Aileen Stanley (1893–1982), who a decade down the road would be crowned Victor's official "Victrola Girl" on the strength of her more than two hundred best-selling records of such songs as "My Little Bimbo Down on the Bamboo Isle" and "You May Be Fast, but Mamma's Gonna Slow You Down." Oh! to have two hundred records by Arral, whose rather more sedate "act" consisted on this occasion of an aria from *Mignon*, an unidentified "English lullaby," and the inescapable "Bird Waltz," this last sung to her own piano accompaniment. The day before the opening, a *Times-Picayune* puff identified the soprano as "a member of the Metropolitan Opera Company in New York where she is regarded as one of the greatest artists of that famous organization"—news, no doubt, to general manager Giulio Gatti-Casazza.

Apart from an entertainment "conducted under the direction of Mme Blanche Arral" at New York's Théâtre Français, 26 March 1916, no further activities have been traced prior to what is believed to have been her final public appearance, at City College (later Lewisohn) Stadium on 28 July 1918. One in a series of low-budgeted summer concerts—soloists were confined to such "B" list artists as Forrest Lamont, Margaret Romaine, and Regina Vicarino—organized and conducted by Arnold Volpe with whom she had made her New York debut nine years before, the evening also featured contralto Alma Beck (of whom nothing can be learned), the Metropolitan Opera chorus under director Giulio Setti, and the ad hoc Stadium Orchestra. As no review has been found, we have only an advertisement—in which the soprano's name is misspelled "Arrall"—to assure us that the program promised "numbers from *Rigoletto*, *Mignon*, *Carmen*, *Pagliacci*, and *Prince Igor*."

Thus, as far as is known, ended the colorful if decidedly erratic career begun thirty-five years before at the Opéra-Comique, leaving us to ponder why its final phase was so disappointing in almost every way. Why were major concert tours repeatedly planned and then apparently abandoned? Why was she not engaged by one or another of the opera companies then active in New York, Boston, Chicago, New Orleans, and Montreal? It's true she would have been limited largely to the French repertory, but that should not have been a handicap at a time when its varied riches were far more in evidence than they are today. And yet, in the decade 1908–18, Arral seems to have secured only a handful of sporadic engagements, almost all second-rate affairs with second-rank colleagues, and almost all confined to the New York area. On the evidence of those ecstatic initial reviews and her handful of splendid recordings, it must remain the ultimate "little harmless mystery" why a more important American career did not evolve.

Throughout the 1920s Blanche Arral presumably remained (to use her own word) buried in suburban New Jersey, relieving the tedium of her day-to-day existence with a little teaching. When she finally reemerged, it was into a world vastly different from that of 1918. Radio had grown from occasional experimental squawks to a popular new source of home entertainment, silent films had found a voice, and record companies had replaced acoustic horns with electric microphones. In the wake of that last historic upheaval, a new hobby was born as a handful of enthusiasts, mostly young and mostly male (today, alas, mostly old and still mostly male), set out to collect the now technologically obsolete records preserving the voices of great singers of the past. As we have read in his introduction, Ira Glackens's eager pursuit of such fast-vanishing treasures eventually led him from a five-and-ten-cent store on New York's Fourteenth Street to a "most unassuming house" at 224 Lawton Avenue, Cliffside Park, and his seminal meeting with Blanche Arral. (Mr. Glackens is almost as vague regarding dates as the lady herself, but, as he tells us she was "about sixty-seven" at the time, the year would appear to have been 1932).

At precisely the same moment, in Bridgeport, Connecticut, a like-minded one-time ballet dancer named William H. Seltsam (1897–1968) took matters a step farther by founding his International Record Collectors' Club, which offered subscribers the opportunity to purchase new limited-edition pressings of choice rarities by "golden age" singers, some even featuring labels individually autographed by the artist (who received no payment for his or her cooperation other than the satisfaction of being remembered by old fans and discovered by new). In April 1933 Blanche Arral joined this select list, which already boasted such fabled names as Farrar, Melba, Sembrich, Patti, Maurel, and Scotti, when Seltsam reissued her Victor recordings from *Jérusalem* and *Faust* as IRCC 19, with labels personally signed by her. Over the next fifteen years almost a dozen of her old disks and cylinders would gain a new lease on life under the distinguished IRCC banner. During this period, too, the aging singer had the occasional joy of being sought out and fussed over by various admirers, most probably previously unaware that she was still alive and living in the United States.

We do not know the genesis of Arral's short-lived radio series, but on 6 April 1935 she was heard in the first of at least seven fifteen-minute programs produced by the Bamberger Broadcasting System for station WOR in Newark, New Jersey. Titled "The Sketchbook of a Great Singer," the broadcasts were aired at three o'clock on occasional Saturday afternoons through at least 22 June. Each installment offered the delightfully spirited seventy-year-old recalling highlights of her career in conversation with one "Monsieur Mack" (or Mac—unfortunately, this amiable interlocutor has eluded definite identification) and singing three numbers with piano accompaniments by Corinne Wolersen. At least four of these fascinating aural documents, each preserving one or two selections otherwise unrecorded by her, survive and received limited circulation on a long-play record released in 1969.

In 1936 Ira Glackens published an article about his friend in *Hobbies* magazine; in 1937 they finished their work on her memoir, which she called *Bravura Passage*; and in 1939 she was interviewed by yet another "old record" enthusiast, Stephen Fassett, as part of his popular radio series for New York's WQXR. Six years later, on 3 March 1945, eighty-year-old Blanche Arral died at Maple Lodge Sanitarium in Palisades Park, New Jersey, her passing barely noted by a world once more at war. She was buried in the Wheeler family plot at Elmwood Cemetery, Middle Granville, New York, just across the Vermont border from Lake Bomoseen. Those seeking to visit the singer's grave, however, face one last "little harmless mystery" unless forewarned that, in a final variation on her lifelong penchant for changing names, the lady was interred, not as Blanche Arral, but as Clara L. Wheeler.

Blanche Arral and Jack London

by Jim McPherson

RRAL MET FAMED American writer Jack London (1876–1916) in Fiji in May or June 1908 while he and his wife were in Suva attending to repairs on his boat *Snark*. She must have made quite an impression, because although he never wrote the story of her life, which she claimed he wanted to do, he did introduce her, thinly disguised, into his 1912 novel *Smoke Bellew*: "The man did not exist in Dawson who would not have been flattered by the notice of Lucille Arral, the singing soubrette of the tiny stock company that performed nightly at the Palace Opera House." Unfortunately, Lucille Arral appears only in chapter 10 ("A Flutter in Eggs") and even there is used essentially merely as a plot device, the instigator of an amusing but ultimately disastrous scheme to corner the egg market in Dawson City.

Set in the Yukon Territory in 1897, London's eleven-chapter book chronicles the adventures of young gold-seeker Christopher "Kit" Bellew, his friends Jack "Shorty" Short and Joy Gastell, his enemies Thomas Stanley Sprague and Doctor Adolph Stine, and such peripheral characters as Big Olaf, Sitka Charley, Harvey Moran, Baron Von Schroeder, Colonel Bowie, and Captain Consadine of the Northwest Mounted Police.

Although such London classics as *Call of the Wild* (1903), *The Sea Wolf* (1904), and *White Fang* (1906) have been filmed many times, *Smoke Bellew* appears to have reached the screen only once, in the form of an obscure low-budget feature made by an outfit called Big 4 Productions, directed by one Scott Dunlap and released in January 1929 with fifty-year-old stage-and-screen veteran Conway Tearle as Smoke (he's twenty-seven in the novel). Based on the only available cast list (which may be incomplete), Lucille Arral does not seem to have been included in this minor curiosity, which the trade paper *Variety* reviewed unfavorably ("Ran around sixty minutes and seemed a month") on 6 February 1929. It cannot have helped that the film was silent at a time when most people were eagerly embracing the burgeoning new "talking pictures."

In 1995 the Canadian company Cinévidéo Plus (in association with Ellipse Programme, Gaumont Television, and France 3) released four ninety-minute television films under the "umbrella title" *The Adventures of Smoke Belliou* (filmed in both English and French versions, the latter aired in 1996 as *Chercheurs d'Or*). The series, officially a Canada-France coproduction, was filmed in the scenic Gaspé area of Quebec with a cast of French, French-Canadian, and English-Canadian actors. Produced by Justine Héroux and Robert Rea, the films were written by Denis Héroux and Nicole Ricard and directed by Marc Simenon with original music by Jean-Claude Deblais and José Souc. The principal cast in all four episodes —*Stake Your Claim, Gambling on Paradise, The Golden Egg, The Motherlode of the Yukon*—includes Wadeck Stanczak (Smoke), Michael Lamport (Shorty), Michèle-Barbara Pelletier (Joy), Jean-Guy Bouchard (Big Olaf), Serge Houde (Sprague), and Lorne Brass (Stine).

Lucille Arral (played by Céline Pallas) appears prominently in all but the first film. Although proudly introduced to Dawson City by "protector" Big Olaf as an opera singer and "the belle of Paree," her subsequent performances at Elkhorn Tavern—which Big Olaf renames the Opera House in her honor—consists exclusively of rather feebly sung "boulevard" songs, plus, in the last film, a few bars of Martini's "Plaisir d'amour."

(The Huntington Library in Pasadena, California, has an extensive collection of Jack London material. The only reference to Blanche Arral they could find was a telegram from Blanche offering condolences to Charmian London following her husband's death in 1916.)

Chronology

With a few "best guess" exceptions, the following list is confined to those activities for which confirmation has been found.

1864

10 Oct.   Born Claire Lardinois in Liège, Belgium, seventeenth child of Count Jean Gregoire Lardinois and the former Caroline Frédéric.

c 1877–80 Studies harmony and solfeggio with Auguste Dupont and Mademoiselle Tordeus at the Brussels Conservatory and sings privately with Alfred Cabel.

1881

Fall   Studies briefly at the Paris Conservatory.

1882

Winter   Begins studies with Mathilde Marchesi.

Paris (Opéra-Comique)

8 Dec.   Debut as Israelite girl in Méhul's *Joseph*.

1883

Paris (Opéra-Comique)

13 March   One of the ladies in Mozart's *La flute enchantée* (*Die Zauberflöte*).
18 June   Anita in premiere of Lajarte's *Le portrait*.

1884

Paris (Opéra-Comique)

19 Jan.   Maidservant in premiere of Massenet's *Manon*.

1884–90   Stars in numerous operettas at various Paris theaters including the
          Théâtre de la Gaîté, Théâtre des Nouveautés, Théâtre des Menus-
          Plaisirs, Théâtre de la Renaissance, Théâtre des Bouffes-Parisiens, and
          Casino de Paris. Highlights of this period include:

23 April 1884   (Gaîté): Lucinette in Vasseur's *Le droit du seigneur*
4 April 1885   (Nouveautés): Victoire in Planquette's *La cantinière*
31 Dec. 1885   (Menus-Plaisirs): year-end revue *Pêle-Mêle Gazette*
1 May 1886   (Menus-Plaisirs): Azur in Lagoanère's *Il était une fois*
                (world premiere)
11 Dec. 1886   (Menus-Plaisirs): year-end revue *Volapuk*
8 Nov. 1887   (Menus-Plaisirs): Rose in Audran's *La fiancée des
                verts-poteaux* (world premiere)
11 Feb. 1888   (Nouveautés): Angela in Lecocq's *La volière* (world
                premiere)
15 March 1888   (Nouveautés): Églantine in Audran's *Le puits qui parle*
                (world premiere)
2 April 1888   (Menus-Plaisirs): Graziella in Lecocq's *La petite mariée*
18 Jan. 1889   (Menus-Plaisirs): Laura in Millöcker's *L'étudiant
                pauvre* (*The Beggar Student*) (Paris premiere)
4 March 1889   (Renaissance): Giroflé in Lecocq's *Giroflé-Girofla*
24 Oct. 1889   (Menus-Plaisirs): Fortunato in Offenbach's *Madame
                l'archiduc*
14 May 1890   (Bouffes-Parisiens): Jeanne in Lacôme's *Jeanne,
                Jeannette et Jeanneton*
31 Dec. 1890   (Casino de Paris): revue *Cocher, au Casino!*

1887
Brussels (Théâtre de la Bourse)
5 Jan.   Irma in Audran's *Le grand mogol.*

1890
Brussels (Théâtre de l'Alhambra)
Jan.–May   Operetta season.

Antwerp (Théâtre Scala)
Oct.   *Giroflé-Girofla.*

1891
Brussels (Théâtre des Galeries St. Hubert)
10 March   Suzette in Vasseur's *Le voyage de Suzette.*

St. Petersburg (Théâtre Arcadia)

June–July   Raoul Gunsbourg season, including title role in Audran's *Miss Helyett.*

Spa, Belgium

August   Operetta season.

Sept.–Nov.   Operetta tour to Nantes, Bordeaux, Monte Carlo, and Marseilles.

1891–94   Claims to have sung in both opera and operetta at St. Petersburg's Maly, Mariinsky, and Mikhailovsky Theaters.

1892
St. Petersburg

9 May   Marries Prince Sergei Nikolaevich Peshkov.

1892–93   Said to have sung in St. Petersburg, Egypt, and Middle East.

1893
Moscow (Hermitage Theater)

Fall   Claims to have sung two-week guest engagement in opera.

Brussels (Théâtre de l'Alhambra)

10 Oct.   *Giroflé-Girofla* with own company.
25 Oct.   *Le grand mogol* with own company.

1894   Said to have toured Eastern Europe.

1894–95
Dec.–Feb.   In Turkey, investigating Peshkov's death.

1895
Brussels (Théâtre Royal de l'Alcazar)

March   *La petite mariée*; Denise in Hervé's *Mam'zelle Nitouche.*
May   Title role in Boullard's *Niniche.*
Oct.–Nov.   Stella in Offenbach's *La fille du tambour-major; Mam'zelle Nitouche.*

c 1895–96   Claims to have sung with a touring opera company in Munich, Dresden, Leipzig, Berlin, Hamburg, Stockholm, Copenhagen, and Aix-la-Chapelle.

1896–97
Antwerp (Théâtre Royal Français)

15 Nov.   *La fille du tambour-major.*
1 Dec.   *Le grand mogol.*

1897
San José, Costa Rica (Teatro Nacional)
21 Oct.   As Blanche Arral, inaugurates the theater in Gounod's *Faust*.

1898
New Orleans
Jan.   Private concerts.

New York
Summer   Probable time of her Bettini recordings.

1898–99   May have visited India, Siam, China, Java, Australia, and New
                 Zealand.

1901
Cairo (Ezbekiya Gardens)
12 April   As "Ada Nelson," heads her own company until spring 1902.

1903–06   Travels in the Orient visiting Hanoi, Saigon, Haiphong, Hong
                 Kong, Shanghai, Hankow, Singapore (25 February 1904: concert
                 at Teutonia Club), Batavia, Rangoon, Bombay, Madras, and
                 Delhi. Claims to have met Hamilton Dwight Bassett, an insur-
                 ance agent from Cincinnati, while both were guests at Raffles
                 Hotel, Singapore, in early 1904.

1906–08   Tours Australia and New Zealand, presenting her "cameo operas"
                 in Perth, Adelaide, Albany, Melbourne, Sydney, Ballart, Bendigo,
                 Dunedin, Christchurch, Wellington, Auckland, Nelson, Napier,
                 Hobart, Launceston, and so forth, with return visits to the larger
                 centers. Confirmed dates include:

                 22 June 1906   Perth (Queen's Hall)
                 18 Aug. 1906   Melbourne (Princess Theater)
                 29 Sept. 1906 Sydney (Town Hall)
                 25 Dec. 1907   Melbourne

1908
May   Departs Australia. En route to the United States, meets Jack and
                 Charmian London in Suva, Fiji; gives concerts there and in
                 Honolulu.

San Francisco (Van Ness Theater)
25 Oct.–1 Nov.   Concerts with Steindorff's Grand Orchestra.

Sacramento

4 Nov.   Saturday Club concert.

San Francisco (Christian Science Hall)

19 Nov.   Concert with Steindorff's Grand Orchestra.

1909
New York

29 Jan.   Makes a test record for the Columbia Phonograph Company.

West Orange, New Jersey

3 Feb.   Makes four cylinders for the Edison Phonograph Company.

St. Louis, Missouri (Odeon)

9 Feb.   Apollo Club concert.

Camden, New Jersey

18–19 March   Makes eight Red Seal records for the Victor Talking Machine
                 Company.

Liège

April?   Homecoming concert.

London (Steinway Hall)

24 May–4 June   Concerts (unconfirmed).

New York (Carnegie Hall)

24 Oct.–5 Dec.   Concerts with the Volpe Symphony Orchestra.

West Orange, New Jersey

27–30 Dec.   Makes six more cylinders for the Edison Phonograph Company.

1911
Brussels (Town Hall)

10 May   Concert in honor of French president Armand Fallières.

1912
New York

July   Sings at two private functions in New York area.

New York (Aeolian Hall)

4 Nov.   Recital with Maurice Lafarge at the piano.

1913
New York (Aeolian Hall)
25 Jan.   Recital with Maurice Lafarge at the piano.

New York (Hotel Plaza)
8 May   New Assembly musicale.

New York (Casino Theater)
18 Nov.   Professional Women's League benefit.

New York (William A. Brady's Playhouse)
14 Dec.   *New York American-Evening Journal* Christmas fund benefit.

1915
Mount Vernon, New York
7 March   Italian earthquake sufferers benefit.

New York (Century Lyceum)
26 April   As Clara Lardinois, stars in performance of *Mam'zelle Nitouche*.

New Orleans (Orpheum Theater)
15–20 Nov. Plays a vaudeville engagement.

1916
New York (Théâtre Français)
26 March   Concert "conducted under the direction of Madame Blanche Arral."

1918
New York (City College Stadium)
28 July   Concert with Stadium Orchestra.

1933–38   William H. Seltsam of the International Record Collectors' Club reissues nine of her recordings with labels individually autographed by her.

1935
Newark, New Jersey (WOR studios)
April–June Stars in a weekly series of fifteen-minute radio broadcasts.

1935–37   She and Ira Glackens collaborate on her memoir, which she called *Bravura Passage*.

1945
Palisades Park, New Jersey (Maple Lodge Sanitarium)
3 March   Dies at eighty. Interred Elmwood Cemetery, Middle Granville, New York.

Blanche Arral and the Phonograph

WORK BEGAN on the preparation of this discography more than sixty years ago. Many hands have had a part in it through the years. My thanks to Jim McPherson, who has compiled the present version for publication here. While the listing of titles recorded by Madame Arral is probably now complete, it is unfortunate that copies of more than half of the titles listed have never been found. The singer had the misfortune to begin her recording career at a time when the art of the preservation of sound was in its infancy. Recordings were made on soft wax cylinders, and while the quality was surprisingly good, there was no way to duplicate the original cylinders except by playing them into another recording machine. This meant that the further a copy got from the original, the more extraneous noises were introduced, including the normal surface scratch introduced with each playing. Soon this became a roar, eventually completely obscuring the original sound, and the process had to begin over with a fresh new "master record." Edison became busy with his electric light, and the field was left open to others for the improvement of his phonograph. One who stepped in was an entrepreneurial Italian living in New York, Gianni Bettini, who was fascinated by the idea of recording great singers, many of whom he knew personally. To this end, he set up a recording studio where he was active for a few years in building an impressive list of recordings by great singers. He offered a great many of these for sale at what today seem very inflated prices for his fragile wax cylinders. The result was that sales were limited, and those records which have survived today are few indeed. A few copies of the Bettini catalogs have turned up, and three of these (for the years

1898, 1900, and 1901) have been reproduced by photo offset and are offered for sale by the Stanford University Archive of Recorded Sound.

For those interested in reading more about Bettini's activities and inventions, an excellent contemporary account can be found in Ray Stannard Baker's *The Boy's Book of Inventions: Stories of the Wonders of Modern Science* (New York: Doubleday & McClure, 1899), pp. 249–280, while a more current review of publications about Bettini and those he recorded can be found in *The Record Collector* 16: 7–8 (September 1965).

WILLIAM R. MORAN

The Recordings of Blanche Arral

Bettini cylinders
New York, 1898
(as Clara Lardinois)
(presumably all sung in French, with piano)

1. FAUST: Il était un roi de Thulé (Chanson du roi de Thulé) (Act 3) (Gounod)

2. FAUST: Ah! je ris de me voir (Air des bijoux) (Act 3) (Gounod)

3. FAUST: Faites-lui mes aveux (Air de Siébel) (Act 3) (Gounod)

4. LES VÊPRES SICILIENNES: Merci, jeunes amies (Sicilienne) (Act 5) (Verdi)

5.* L'AFRICAINE: Sur mes genoux (Air du sommeil) (Act 2) (Meyerbeer)

6. MIGNON: Connais-tu le pays? (Act 1) (Thomas)

7. MIGNON: Je suis Titania, la blonde! (Polonaise) (Act 2) (Thomas)

8. ROMÉO ET JULIETTE: Ah! Je veux vivre dans ce rêve (Valse) (Act 1) (Gounod)

---

* See Notes to discography

9. JOCELYN: Cachés dans cet asile (Berceuse) (Act 2) (Godard)

10. CARMEN: L'amour est un oiseau rebelle (Habanera) (Act 1) (Bizet)

11. CARMEN: Près des remparts de Séville (Séguedille) (Act 1) (Bizet)

12. CARMEN: Les tringles des sistres tintaient (Chanson bohémienne) (Act 2) (Bizet)

13. Villanelle (Eva Dell'Acqua)

14.* Grande Valse (Luigi Venzano)

15. Berceuse bleue (Montaya)

16. La fille à ma tante (Louis Varney)

17. Le reveil (Tyrolienne) (Jean-Baptiste-Théodore Weckerlin)

18.* Si vous croyez que je vais dire (La chanson de Fortunio) (Offenbach)

19. LA GRANDE-DUCHESSE DE GÉROLSTEIN: Dites-lui qu'on l'a remarqué distingué (Déclaration) (Act 2) (Offenbach)

20. LA FILLE DU TAMBOUR-MAJOR: Prenez les grappes empourprées (Chanson du fruit défendu) (Act 1) (Offenbach)

21.* LA CIGALE ET LA FOURMI: Un jour Margot allant à l'eau (Couplets de Margot) (Act 1) (Audran)

22. LA PÉRICHOLE: O mon cher amant, je te jure (La lettre) (Act 1) (Offenbach)

23. LA PETITE MARIÉE: Le jour, vois-tu bien, ma chère âme (Couplets du jour et de la nuit) (Act 2) (Lecocq)

24. LA PETITE MARIÉE: Pour vous sauver on se dévoue (Couplets des reproches) (Act 3) (Lecocq)

25. LES NOCES DE JEANNETTE: Voix légère, chanson passagère (Air du rossignol) (Massé)

26. LA FEMME À PAPA: Tambour, clairon, musique en tête (Chanson du Colonel) (Hervé)

27. LE PETIT DUC: Je t'aime (Act 1) (Lecocq)

---

* See Notes to discography

28. INDIGO UND DIE VIERZIG RÄUBER: Valse-Brindisi (Johann Strauss Jr.)

29.* DER OBERSTEIGER: Sei nicht bös' (Sois pas fâché) (The Obersteiger Waltz) (Act 2) (Zeller)

30. LE COEUR ET LA MAIN: Un soir, José le Capitaine (Boléro) (Act 2) (Lecocq)

31. LE GRAND MOGOL: Allons, petit serpent (Valse des serpents) (Act 1) (Audran)

32.* L'AMOUR MOUILLÉ: P'tit fi! p'tit mignon! gentil compagnon! (Valse) (Act 2) (Varney)

33. MAM'ZELLE NITOUCHE: À minuit après le fête (Couplets Babet et Cadet) (Act 2) (Hervé)

34. MAM'ZELLE NITOUCHE: Alleluia (Gloria in Excelsis) (Act 1) (Hervé)

35. GIROFLÉ-GIROFLA: Père adoré (Act 1) (Lecocq)

36. GIROFLÉ-GIROFLA: Le punch scintille (Brindisi) (Act 2) (Lecocq)

37.* LES CLOCHES DE CORNEVILLE: Couplets (Planquette)

38. LES CLOCHES DE CORNEVILLE: Vous qui voulez des servantes (Couplets des servantes) (Act 1) (Planquette)

39. LES CLOCHES DE CORNEVILLE: Nous avons, hélas! perdu d'excellents maîtres (La légende des cloches) (Act 1) (Planquette)

40. LES CLOCHES DE CORNEVILLE: La pomme est un fruit plein de sève (Chanson du cidre) (Act 3) (Planquette)

41. LA FILLE DE MADAME ANGOT: Tournez, tournez (Valse) (Act 2) (Lecocq)

42. LA FILLE DE MADAME ANGOT: Marchande de marée (La légende de la mère Angot) (Act 1) (Lecocq)

43. LA FILLE DE MADAME ANGOT: De la mère Angot, j'suis la fille (Act 3) (Lecocq)

44. LA FILLE DE MADAME ANGOT: Jadis les rois, race proscrit (Act 1) (Lecocq)

---

* See Notes to discography

45. LA MASCOTTE: J'aime bien mes dindons (Couplets des dindons) (Act 1) (Audran)

46. LA MASCOTTE: Le capitaine et les brigands (Chanson du capitaine) (Act 2) (Audran)

47. LE PETIT FAUST: Barcarolle (Hervé)

48. MADAME FAVART: Ma mère aux vignes m'envoyait (Couplets des vignes) (Act 1) (Offenbach)

Columbia
New York, 29 January 1909

49. Test recording, title unknown (file card marked "Rejected March 24 1909") 14646-1

Edison four-minute cylinders
Orange, New Jersey, 3 February 1909
(sung in French; with orchestra)

NUMBER	LATER NO.	OTHER NO.	78 RPM RR	LP/CD

50. MIGNON: Oui! Pour ce soir je suis reine des fées! . . . Je suis Titania, la blonde! (Polonaise) (Act 2) (Thomas)

35000	B-166	BA 28125	IRCC 160	Celebrity CEL 2
				Odyssey 32 16 0207
				Rubini SJG 204
				Symposium 1243

51. CARMEN: C'est des contrebandiers le refuge ordinaire . . . Je dis, que rien ne m'épouvante (Micaëla's air) (Act 3) (Bizet)

35001	B-167	——	IRCC 135	Club 99-69

52. LA PERLE DU BRÉSIL: Charmant oiseau (Air du Mysoli) (Act 3) (David)

35002	B-168	——	IRCC 112	Club 99-69

53. FAUST: Ah! je ris de me voir (Air des bijoux) (Act 3) (Gounod)

35003	B-169	——	——	——

Victor Red Seal

Camden, New Jersey, 18, 19 March 1909
(sung in French except 61 which is sung in Spanish; with orchestra)

MATRIX NO.	DATE	CAT. NO.	OTHER NO.	78 REISSUE	LP/CD

54. LA TRAVIATA: Ah! fors' è lui . . . Sempre libera (Act 1) (Verdi)

C-6903-1	18 Mar	——	——	——	——
-2,3	19 Mar	74132	——	——	Club 99-69

55. ROMÉO ET JULIETTE: Ah! je veux vivre dans ce rêve (Valse) (Act 1) (Gounod)

C-6904-1	18 Mar	74147	2-033079	——	Club 99-69

56.* DER BETTELSTUDENT: Doch wenn's im Lied hinaus dann klinget (Act 1) (Millöcker)

B-6905-1	18 Mar	64098	——	——	Club 99-69

57. JÉRUSALEM: Il respire ô transport . . . Quelle ivresse bonheur suprême (Polonaise) (Act 4) (Verdi)

C-6906-1	18 Mar	74146	15-1016	IRCC 19	Club 99-69
					Scala 865

58. FAUST: Ah! je ris de me voir (Air des bijoux) (Act 3) (Gounod)

C-6907-1	18 Mar	74147	15-1016	IRCC 19	Club 99-69

59.* LES NOCES DE JEANNETTE: Sa voix . . . Au bord du chemin . . . Voix légère, chanson passagère (Air du rossignol) (Massé)

C-6911-1	19 Mar	74142	——	AGSB 14	Club 99-69
					Symposium 1188

60.* L'AMOUR MOUILLÉ: P'tit fi! P'tit mignon! (Valse) (Act 2) (Varney)

B-6912-1,2	19 Mar	64099	901	——	Club 99-69
			7-33035	——	EMI RLS 724
					Pearl GEM 0067

61.* El bolero grande (probably Jules Vasseur)

B-6913-1,2	19 Mar	64107	——	IRCC 46	Club 99-69

---

* See Notes to discography

Edison four-minute cylinders
Orange, New Jersey, 27, 28, 30 December 1909
(sung in French; with orchestra)

NUMBER	LATER NO.	OTHER NO.	78 RPM RR	LP/CD

62. ROMÉO ET JULIETTE: Ah! je veux vivre dans ce rêve (Valse) (Act 1)
(Gounod)

35004	B-185	——	——	——

63. LE COEUR ET LA MAIN: Un soir, José le Capitaine (Boléro) (Act 2)
(Lecocq)

35005	B-190	——	IRCC 135	IRCC L-7028
				Club 99-69

64. La véritable Manola (Théophile Gautier; Èmile Bourgeois)

35006	——	——	IRCC 100	Club 99-69

65. LE GRAND MOGOL: Allons, petit serpent (Valse des serpents) (Act 1)
(Audran)

35015	——	——	IRCC 112	Club 99-69

66. GIROFLÉ-GIROFLA: Le punch scintille (Brindisi) (Act 2) (Lecocq)

35019	——	——	IRCC 160	Club 99-69

67. (a) MANON: Suis-je gentille ainsi? . . . Je marche sur tous les chemins
("Cours-la-reine" air) (Act 3) (Massenet); (b) MANON: Ce bruit de l'or . . .
A nous les amours et les roses! (Hôtel de Transylvanie air) (Act 4) (Massenet)

——	——	——	IRCC 100	IRCC L-7014
				Club 99-69
				TAP T-317

Radio transcriptions, WOR
Newark, New Jersey, April–June 1935
(sung in French except as noted; with piano by Corinne Wolersen)

68. INDIGO UND DIE VIERZIG RÄUBER: Ja, so singt man in der Stadt,
wo ich geboren (Waltz) (Act 1) (Johann Strauss Jr.)

69. MIGNON: Connais-tu le pays? (Act 1) (Thomas)

70. La véritable Manola (Théophile Gautier; Émile Bourgeois)

71. Pourquoi ne pas m'aimer? (Valse bleue) (Berger)

72. Parlez-moi d'amour (fragments) (words and music Jean Lenoir)

73. Valse bleue (composer not known)

74. Wake up! (H. Simpson; Montague Fawcett Phillips, No. 1 of *A Calendar of Song*) (sung in English)

75.* LA CIGALE ET LA FOURMI: Un jour Margot allant à l'eau (Couplets de Margot) (Act 1) (Audran)

76.* DER BETTELSTUDENT: Doch wenn's im Lied hinaus dann klinget (Act 1) (Millöcker)

77.* El bolero grande (probably Jules Vasseur) (sung in Spanish)

78. Regina coeli (Amurel) (sung in Latin)

79.* LE TIMBRE D'ARGENT: De Naples à Florence et de Parme à Vérone (Chanson napolitaine) (Act 2, Scene 2) (Saint-Saëns)

80.* L'AMOUR MOUILLÉ: P'tit fi! P'tit mignon! gentil compagnon! (Valse) (Act 2) (Varney)

Private acetates, Baldwin Recording Studios
New York, 1939
(sung in French; with piano)

81. MIGNON: Elle est là, près de lui (Act 2, Scene 2) (Thomas)

82.* MIGNON: Légères hirondelles, oiseaux bénis de Dieu (Act 1) (Thomas)

LP reissues

Celebrity CEL 2 *Cylinders of Stars from Metropolitan and Hammerstein Opera Companies (1900–1910)* contains 50

Club 99 CL 99-69 *Blanche Arral* contains 51, 52, 54, 55, 56, 57, 58, 59, 60, 61, 63, 64, 65, 66, 67

EMI RLS 724 *The Record of Singing, Volume One* contains 60

---

* See Notes to discography

The Golden Age of Opera EJS 466 *Blanche Arral* contains the four 1935 radio broadcasts preserving numbers 68–80 above

IRCC L-7014 *Souvenirs of Opera (Fourth Series)* contains 67

IRCC L-7028 *Souvenirs of the Cylinder Era* contains 63

Odyssey 32 16 0207 *The Fabulous Edison Cylinder* contains 50

Rubini SJG 204 *Edison Cylinders, Volume One* contains 50

Scala 865 *Coloratura Gems* contains 57

TAP T-317 *Twenty Great French Singers of the Twentieth Century* contains 67

CD reissues

Pearl GEM 0067 *The Marchesi School* contains 60

Symposium 1188 *The Harold Wayne Collection, Volume 25: The Marchesi School* contains 59

Symposium 1243 *The Four-Minute Cylinder, Part 2* contains 50

Notes to discography

5. The April 1900 Bettini catalog lists this selection simply as "Cavatina—2d Act," leaving little room for doubt that it is, in fact, Sélika's famous "Slumber Song."

14. The Bettini catalogs list this selection as "Valse Venzano" by L. Venzano. Presumably it is the same piece as the "Grande Valse" (Luigi Venzano, Opus 10) recorded in Italian by Luisa Tetrazzini and also known (according to *Baker's Biographical Dictionary of Musicians*) as "Valzer cantabile."

18. Offenbach originally wrote the song known as "La chanson de Fortunio" as an incidental piece to be interpolated into the second act of Alfred de Musset's play *Le chandelier* (Comédie Française, 1850). Unfortunately, the actor playing the character of Fortunio couldn't sing, so he simply recited the words over

the orchestra. Ten years later the composer revised the song and inserted it into his one-act *opéra bouffe* entitled *La chanson de Fortunio* (Bouffes-Parisiens, 5 January 1861) in which it was sung by the hero, Valentin, a travesty role. As the Bettini catalogs list it simply as "Chanson du [sic] Fortunio," it is assumed that Arral sang the original, not the revised, version. The opening words of both are "Si vous croyez que je vais dire . . ."

21, 75. Although known as the "Couplets de Margot," this selection—which tells the story of an unfortunate young woman named Margot, who falls into a well and is rescued by some passing youths only after they have extracted a promise of a kiss as their reward—is in fact sung by the character of Thérèse. There are four verses in all, of which, on her radio broadcast, Arral sings the first and third.

29. This piece was composed for famed Vienna operetta star Alexander Girardi, who introduced it in the premiere of *Der Obersteiger* (Theater an der Wien, 6 January 1894). Such was its success that, as the "Obersteiger Waltz," it soon became a favorite concert piece with sopranos. In England, George Edwardes "borrowed" it, had Adrian Ross write English lyrics, and interpolated it into the second act of *An Artist's Model* (1895) as the duet "Don't be cross," sung by Marie Tempest and Hayden Coffin.

32, 60, 80. Arral was credited as the composer of this piece on the label of the first edition of her Victor recording (which was, by the way, by far her best-selling Victor title, and the only one in the series to achieve double-sided status; it was finally superceded in the catalog by Lucrezia Bori's 1924 recording of the same selection). Arral may indeed have "adapted" or "arranged" the version she sang, but the original was composed by Louis Varney and is found in the second act of *L'amour mouillé*, his 1887 *opéra comique*, where it is sung, in part as a duet, by Lauretta and Carlo, the principal characters in the story. Although also known as the "Valse d'oiseau" (the title under which it was always listed in the Victor catalogs) and the "Valse de colibri," it is in fact designated in the score as simply "Valse." The libretto of *L'amour mouillé* (and hence, presumably, the lyrics of this piece) was by Jules Prével, a Paris journalist and theater critic credited with having invented the theatrical gossip column in *Le Figaro* in 1865, and Armand Liorat.

37. As the Bettini catalogs list this selection simply as "Couplets," it is not possible to identify it further.

56, 76. This selection was always identified by Victor, both on the label and in the catalogs, as simply "Czardas" (and, indeed, Arral herself refers to it as such in the course of one of her radio broadcasts). But the czardas is, of course, a Hungarian dance, and the plot of *Der Bettelstudent* is set in eighteenth-century Poland (and quite devoid of any bogus Hungarians, à la Rosalinde in *Die Fledermaus*); nor is the piece written in the traditional czardas form. In fact, it's neither a czardas nor identified as such in the score. It's simply a brilliant solo passage (marked *Allegretto*) for Laura near the end of act one. It is, by the way, the nearest thing we have to an Arral "creator's record"—she sang the role of Laura when Millöcker's operetta was introduced to Paris, as *L'étudiant pauvre*, 18 January 1889.

59. Reverse of AGSB 14 is Claudia Muzio's 1911 Milan HMV recording (matrix 298aj) of *Bohème*: Mi chiamano Mimì.

60. Reverse of Victor 901 is Maria Michailova's 1906 St. Petersburg G. & T. recording (matrix 1152r) of *La traviata*: Addio del passato, sung in Russian. See also 32.

61, 77. Although Arral identifies "El bolero grande" as simply a Spanish song taught to her by Elena Sanz, her Victor recordings of the piece always gave the composer as Vasseur. This was probably not Paris-based Léon Vasseur (1844–1917), in several of whose popular operettas Clara Lardinois performed, but the much less celebrated Jules Vasseur (dates not found), whose forgotten catalog includes a song called "El caballero," subtitled "Boléro espagnol," published in Paris in 1876 with French lyrics by C. Barthélemy. It seems a strong possibility that Sanz, then at the height of her career, added this number to her repertory in Spanish translation and later passed it along to Arral.

75. See 21.

76. See 56.

77. See 61.

79. Although Arral describes this selection in her radio broadcast as the song of a "troubadour," it is in fact sung in Saint-Saëns's opera by the baritone villain of the piece, Spiridion, a role created at the 23 February 1877 premiere by the celebrated Léon-Pierre Melchissédec.

80. See 32.

82. This is, of course, the famous Swallow Duet, sung in the opera by Mignon (mezzo-soprano) and Lothario (bass) but "arranged" here as a soprano solo.

Index